THE GOLDEN GAZETTE

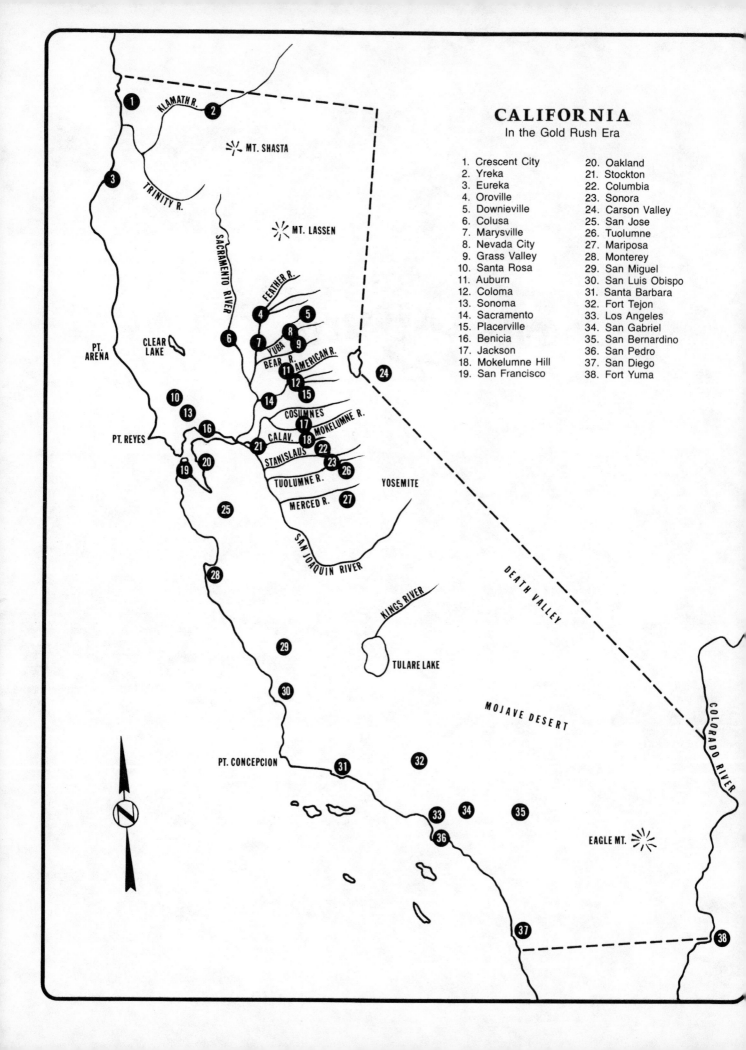

CALIFORNIA
In the Gold Rush Era

1. Crescent City
2. Yreka
3. Eureka
4. Oroville
5. Downieville
6. Colusa
7. Marysville
8. Nevada City
9. Grass Valley
10. Santa Rosa
11. Auburn
12. Coloma
13. Sonoma
14. Sacramento
15. Placerville
16. Benicia
17. Jackson
18. Mokelumne Hill
19. San Francisco

20. Oakland
21. Stockton
22. Columbia
23. Sonora
24. Carson Valley
25. San Jose
26. Tuolumne
27. Mariposa
28. Monterey
29. San Miguel
30. San Luis Obispo
31. Santa Barbara
32. Fort Tejon
33. Los Angeles
34. San Gabriel
35. San Bernardino
36. San Pedro
37. San Diego
38. Fort Yuma

THE GOLDEN GAZETTE

News from the newspapers of 1848–1857. Hundreds
of events reported from the exciting years following
the great California discovery of gold.

Edited by Dudley T. Ross

Design by Jack Galliano

Fresno 1978

To California's
pioneer newspapermen

Foreword

When I took over the editorship of *Westward* magazine I soon found that the "Golden Gazette" was the most popular feature in the publication. This was in 1960, and the news items were then chronicling the silver stampede at Virginia City.

Readers were forever writing in and asking whether this item or that was genuine—and it was my pleasure to assure them that it was. At first I used to check with Dudley Ross to satisfy myself that his research was thorough. Later I used to check *other* writing in *Westward* against the "Golden Gazette" to be sure our narrative material did not conflict with newspaper accounts of the day. If they did, we explained it to the reader.

So in a sense, the "Golden Gazette" helped assure the authenticity and accuracy of the rest of the magazine. It is with great pleasure that I have re-read these fascinating pages. They tell a story that bears endless repeating for afficionados of western history and a wonderful first experience for the newcomer to our coterie.

The pages of this book make California's golden history come alive in a unique way.

Gene Drossel
Editor, *Westward* Magazine
'60–'62

Introduction

The Golden Gazette reports events of the exciting decade that opened with the gold discovery at Sutter's Sawmill in 1848. The common link between the hundreds of happenings is that they attracted the attention not only of residents of California and other Pacific areas, but also of eastern Americans and foreigners. The Gold Rush and California were of international significance and attracted immigrants from many lands. California's cosmopolitan character was rapidly established.

Although some events are included largely because of their historical significance, no effort has been made to report all that can be so classified. It would be impossible, for example, as well as tedious, to try to cover the ramifications of early California politics.

The prime criterion for the selection of events has been that they be interesting in themselves. The range is broad, from such as the widespread impact of the gold discovery and California's statehood to a boy's wild ride in a runaway balloon, a "flying man" hoax and the killing of two grizzly bears with a single shot.

Although *The Golden Gazette* is far from being formal history, care has been taken to make its reports as accurate as possible. The primary sources have been newspapers of the time, and great credit is due to California's pioneering newspapermen. Their writing style, however, has been modified to make the accounts more readable today.

Editing this book has given me a vivid sense of the great difference between life than and life now. Although we are no strangers to violence today, the degree of violence in the golden decade was much greater in proportion to population. Men and women alike routinely accepted risks in daily living and travel of a nature now almost unthinkable.

The Golden Gazette originated with the concept of giving immediacy to the telling of events in order to provide some feeling of what it was like to live then. It was syndicated for a time to a number of California newspapers and was a monthly feature for several years in *Westward*, the magazine published by Kaiser Steel Corporation. I am thankful to the editors of *Westward* for their enthusiastic support, and especially grateful to the corporation for permission to reproduce from the columns of the magazine.

Practically all of the research was carried out in the extensive California newspaper collection at the Bancroft Library of the University of California at Berkeley, with some gaps filled in from other contemporary records. Bancroft staff members were always extremely helpful.

Dudley T. Ross

Gold Discovered At Sutter's Mill

SAN FRANCISCO, March 18, 1848 — Gold has been found on the American River, but no one in the town is inclined to place much importance on it.

The Californian, one of the two weekly newspapers, reported briefly today that gold had been discovered sometime ago "in considerable quantities" at the sawmill being erected by Capt. John A. Sutter, the illustrious pioneer of the Sacramento Valley. Only tangible production so far known here is that $30 in gold has been brought to Sutter's Fort.

A gold placer was discovered a few years ago near San Fernando Mission, but the deposit produced only a tiny quantity.

The Californian's editor has little faith in this new find, and his feeling is shared by most residents.

MORE GOLD FOUND

SAN FRANCISCO, April 22, 1848 — The California Star reported today that, on unquestionable authority, another still more extensive and valuable gold mine has been discovered near the head of the American Fork. The editor has seen several specimens totaling 8 to 10 ounces of pure virgin gold.

PROBE OF INDIAN HOSTILITY ORDERED

MONTEREY, May 25, 1848 — Col. Richard B. Mason, military commandant and ex-officio governor, issued orders today to Maj. James A. Hardie at San Francisco to investigate the reported hostile intentions of Indians north of Sonoma.

Maj. Hardie is authorized to organize two companies at Sonoma if a campaign appears necesasary.

Col. Mason wrote Gen. M.G. Vallejo, sub-Indian agent, "The Indians are right in pressing their wish that the whites should not intrude on their lands."

———o———

Counterfeit Coin

LOS ANGELES, April 10, 1848 — Col. Jonathan D. Stevenson, commander of the Southern Military Department here, today reported the arrest of C.C. Canfield, Ruel Barnes, Samuel Myers and others on a charge of passing counterfeit gold coin purporting to be coin of the United States.

It is expected that Alcalde Stephen C. Foster will hold a special trial court.

Gold Depopulating Towns Of California

SAN FRANCISCO, May 27, 1848 — Following the rapid spread of increasing evidence the gold regions are both rich and extensive, California towns are being depopulated as hundreds leave for the mines.

The last doubters were convinced when Sam Brannan came down from Sutter's Fort recently with a bottle of gold dust and crying out, "Gold! Gold! Gold from the American river!"

The whole country, even as far away as Los Angeles, is responding to the lure of gold. Stores have been shut down here as at least 150 men have left for the mines this month. Everything is neglected except the manufacture of shovels and pick-axes.

Several respectable residents of San Jose have returned from a visit to the gold regions and will leave with their families next week to take up mining. The town innkeeper plans to open an outdoors hotel in the gold areas at $3 a day for boarders.

The whole crew of Capt. Phelps' vessel proposed going to the mines. He made a bargain to go with them and continue paying them in return for receiving two-thirds of the gold found.

———o———

FIVE DROWN IN BAY

SAUSALITO, April 5, 1848 — Five men were drowned today when their small boat was swamped by the heavy seas at the mouth of San Francisco Bay. They were in the employ of Capt. William A. Richardson.

———o———

S.F. POPULATION 812

SAN FRANCISCO, March 18, 1848 — A census shows the white population of this town to be 575 males, 177 females and 60 children of school age.

CALIFORNIA GLORIES TOUTED BY NEWSPAPER

SAN FRANCISCO, April 1, 1848 — Samuel Brannan, prominent merchant and publisher of The California Star, wants people of the United States to learn of the glories of California.

His weekly newspaper, edited by Edward C. Kemble, today issued a special edition that will be carried to the East by an overland courier. It devoted much space to an article prepared by Dr. Victor J. Fourgeaud, San Francisco druggist, that details the many advantages of California.

Dr. Fourgeaud describes at length the beauties of the country, its ag-ricultural possibilities, commercial prospects and equitable climate.

Also discussed are the untapped mineral resources known to exist, including a mine of gold discovered some time ago on the south branch of the American Fork 30 miles from New Helvetia. A probable estimate of its magnitude cannot be derived from any information so far received.

It was stated that explorations 12 miles to the south and five to the north report continuance of the gold strata in equal abundance, and that a stream flows near the mine so that washing the gold will be comparatively easy.

Col. Mason Closes Visit To Gold Area

SUTTER'S FORT, July 11, 1848 — Col. Richard B. Mason, ex-officio governor of California, and his aides have left to return to Monterey, where he expects to prepare a comprehensive report to the U.S. Government on his inspection of the gold regions. He is convinced of their great wealth and collected samples of the gold being found.

During his tour of the mines Col. Mason visited Sutter's Sawmill at Coloma. He was guided by James W. Marshall, who made the gold discovery, along the north bank of the South Fork of the American River where a great deal of coarse gold has been found in the beds of small streams and ravines.

At Weber Creek he saw the gold washings of Sunol & Co. who employed 30 Indians, paying them in merchandise. Further up the creek many men were at work. A gutter, not more than 100 yards long, 4 feet wide and 2-3 feet deep, was shown him as the spot where William Daly and Perry McCoon had obtained $17,000 in gold in seven days.

Capt. Charles M. Weber is operating a store there in an arbor of bushes. He told the governor that two men had employed five whites and 100 Indians and, at the end of a week's work, paid off their party and left with $10,000 in gold.

Col. Mason is satisfied that gold exists in the beds of the Feather, Yuba and Bear Rivers, and in many streams between the latter and the American Fork, as well as in the Cosumnes to the south.

The principal store here, Brannan & Co., has taken in $36,000 in gold from May 1 to July 10. Flour is already bringing $36 a barrel.

The governor was surprised to learn that so far crime of any kind is infrequent and no thefts or robberies had occurred in the gold district.

---o---

Gold Messenger Sails for the U.S.

MONTEREY, Aug. 30, 1848 — Lt. Lucien Loeser, messenger carrying the official report of Col. R.B. Mason to the United States Government on the gold discoveries in California, sailed today on the chartered sailing vessel Lambayecana to Payta, Peru. He hopes to get from there to the Isthmus of Panama and thence to the United States.

NEW FINDS OF GOLD STEADILY ON INCREASE

SUTTER'S FORT, Aug. 30, 1848 — Practically every day come reports of new gold diggings being found. Gold seekers have fanned out to countless ravines and stream beds both north and south.

The greatest concentration of miners is along tributaries of the Sacramento and San Joaquin rivers. Furthest north is the strike made by Pierson B. Reading on the Trinity river, which he has worked with his Indians. Camps are growing fast to the south along the Mokelumne, Cosumnes, Calaveras and Stanislaus rivers.

It is calculated that there are 5000 or more men now in the diggings, with an average return in many cases running to $20 or more a day. Some immigrants have already arrived from the Sandwich Islands, Oregon Territory and Mexico.

Among reports of great success is that of John Sinclair on the North Fork of the American River. With the labor of 50 Indians, he washed out $16,000 in a few weeks. At Rich Dry Diggings on the North Fork several men are said to have collected $800 to $1500 in a single day.

---o---

Mormon Diggings Busy

MORMON DIGGINGS, July 7, 1848 — Even in the heat of mid-day, 200 men are hard at work here washing for gold at this camp some 25 miles above Sutter's Fort.

Some men are using tin pans and some, close-woven Indian baskets. Gaining popularity is a rude machine known as a cradle, which generally is operated by a crew of four. One such party has been averaging $100 a day.

The hillsides are thickly strewn with canvas tents and brush arbors. A store and several boarding shanties have been put in operation.

---o---

News Received of Peace Treaty

MONTEREY, Aug. 7, 1848 — Official announcement was made today of the ratification of the peace treaty with the Mexican Republic by which Upper California is ceded to the United States. Under its conditions all those who reside in the territory will be admitted to American citizenship.

LARKIN'S REPORT DECLARES GOLD REAL
FORECASTS BIG RUSH

MONTEREY, June 28, 1848 — Thomas O. Larkin, U.S. consul to California and naval agent, today completed a report to Secretary of State James Buchanan declaring that there are vast amounts of gold in California.

On a visit to the gold regions, Larkin wrote the secretary, he found their wealth all he had heard and "much more." He is certain gold will be found on many branches of the Sacramento and San Joaquin rivers. Larkin found miners already scattered over 100 miles and believes that on the American Fork, Feather and Yuba rivers there are presently some 2000 of them. The majority working there began in May.

In 1849, as news of the gold spreads, Larkin calculates the immigration should be many thousands strong and still more in 1850. A complete revolution in the ordinary state of affairs is taking place in California, Larkin wrote the secretary.

His report, with a gold sample, is being turned over to the commander of the U.S.S. Southampton to forward to the United States by the first opportunity via Mexico.

---o---

GOLD FEVER RAGING IN SANDWICH ISLANDS

HONOLULU, July 8, 1848 — California gold fever is running high here, and many are preparing to emigrate to that land in hopes of making a fortune. The ministry of foreign affairs is busy issuing passports, except to absconding debtors.

First solid news of the gold finds was brought here by the Hawaiian schooner Louise, along with two pounds of the metal as tangible proof, when it arrived June 17 after sailing from San Francisco May 31. Today at least half a dozen vessels are making ready to sail for California.

The editor of The Polynesian in an article congratulated the merchants of this place on the prospect of speedy payment of debts due from Californians, "probably not less than $150,000."

Oregon Party Seeks Gold In California

OREGON CITY, Ore. Ter., Sept. 8, 1848 — Spurred by the reports of rich gold finds, 150 hardy pioneers are leaving by ox team for the Sacramento Valley in California.

The dense forests and mountains to the south have never yet been crossed by wagons. One of the men is even taking his wife and children.

Peter H. Burnett, territorial chief justice, is captain, and Thomas McKay, who has taken pack animals to California several times, will be the scout.

Judge Burnett organized the group in a week's time when he became convinced of the truth of the reports of gold. Hundreds of other Oregonians have left by sea or pack train in recent weeks after hearing the first wild rumors.

News of the gold finds reached here in July: by ship from San Francisco to Honolulu, then back across the ocean. The judge said he did not believe in California gold until he saw a letter from L.W. Boggs, former Missouri governor, at Sonoma, California, telling of the gold riches.

The Oregon company will follow the Applegate Trail to Klamath Lake and then turn southward to break a new road.

———o———

MINERS SUFFERING FROM SICKLY SEASON

SUTTER'S FORT, Sept. 27, 1848 — Many miners are abandoning their activities at least temporarily as a result of the "sickly season" that has been occurring in the heat of recent weeks.

Numbers have been prostrated with fevers, and numerous deaths have resulted from the debilitating effects.

It is back-breaking work to dig and wash the rich dirt. In most cases it is necessary to pick and shovel the earth and then wash it.

———o———

SAILORS DESERTING

MONTEREY, Sept. 15, 1848 — Desertion of sailors is becoming a problem here as well as in San Francisco. Capt. Christopher Allyn of the ship Isaac Walton said today all of his hands but two have left, and they will go as soon as cargo is landed and ballast put aboard.

OFFICIAL GOLD REPORTS REACH NATION'S CAPITAL

WASHINGTON, D.C., Sept. 20, 1848 — News of the discovery of prodigious gold regions in California is spreading today throughout the United States.

Extracts of official dispatches to the Secretaries of State and the Navy were published yesterday in the Washington Union, and copied today by the Baltimore Sun and the New York Herald. The dispatches

Gold Dust Priced At $16 Per Ounce

SAN FRANCISCO, Sept. 10, 1848 — California's ever-increasing pile of gold dust is raising a monetary and price problem.

Because of the scarcity of coin and the amount of dust from the mines being offered in payment of goods and debts, the largest public meeting ever held in the town last night voted unanimously that gold dust shall circulate here at a value of $16 an ounce. The meeting also voted a committee to draw up a petition to the U.S. government to establish a branch mint to relieve the coin shortage.

Some speakers declared lack of available coinage is stagnating trade and expressed fears of the depreciation of the price of gold, which has sold very cheaply in the mining district, as low as $4 and often at $8-10 an ounce.

———o———

FIRST WHARF OPENS IN SAN FRANCISCO

SAN FRANCISCO, Sept. 22, 1848 — Although not entirely completed, the first wharf here opened today with the docking of the brig Belfast. This ship thus became the first of any size to land without the aid of a lighter.

The wharf, built by William S. Clark, juts out 150 feet into the bay at Clark's Point at the foot of Broadway.

Arrival of the Belfast, 163 days out from New York with a varied cargo, demonstrated the wharf's value. The price of goods immediately fell by 25 percent while nearby real estae rose 50 to 100 per cent. A lot at Montgomery and Washington streets, which had no buyers at $5000, drew a ready bid of $10,000.

Merchants predict San Francisco is about to enter on a new era as the chief port of California.

were brought here by Passed Midshipman Edward F. Beale of the Navy in the fastest journey yet known to have been made from the Pacific to Washington.

"The most extraordinary intelligence which Mr. Beale brings," the Union reported, "is about the real El Dorado, the gold region in California. His accounts of the extraordinary richness of the gold surface, and the excitement it has produced among all classes of people, are confirmed by letters from Commodore Jones and Thomas O. Larkin, the United States naval agent at Monterey, California."

In a letter dated July 1, Larkin writes, "I do not think I am exaggerating in estimating the amount of gold obtained in the rivers I have mentioned at ten thousand dollars a day for the last few days. There is every reason to believe the amount will not this season be any less. Many who have seen the 'Placer' think it will last thirty or forty years." The Union reported it has seen specimens of the California gold.

Beale's journey was made at urgent speed against many hazards. He left La Paz, Baja California, August 1, crossing the Gulf of California to Mazatlan, Mexico. Then came a stormy voyage in a small boat to San Blas. From there he left for Mexico City by horseback, and en route was held up by three highwaymen, but held them off. Later on, he sailed from Vera Cruz on the sloop-of-war Germantown to Mobile, Alabama, and thence to Washington.

———o———

MINES BOOM TULEBERG

TULEBERG, Sept. 29, 1848 — This place at the head of summer navigation on the San Joaquin River now is assuming importance as a depot for the southern gold regions.

It consists mainly of the store of Capt. Charles M. Weber, who has been highly successful with his mining and trading company, and Joseph Russell's tavern, the only wooden building so far.

From Weber's company, named for Commodore Stockton, Tuleberg is also becoming known as Stockton. It is destined to grow quickly as new gold finds are being steadily made along the Cosumnes, Mokelumne, Tuolumne and Stanislaus rivers.

Sutter's Property Signed Over To Son

SUTTER'S FORT, Oct. 15, 1848 — Amid all the gold being taken from the enormously rich placers on and around his huge land grant, Capt. John A. Sutter is in difficulties from the lack of it.

Thus this most prominent resident of California today signed over all his properties to the name of his son, John August, Jr., who recently arrived from Switzerland. The step was taken in an effort to avoid loss of his holdings under the pressure of claims by creditors for old debts.

Despite the business done at his fort and the rentals from it and in spite of the fact he had had groups of Indians digging for gold, Sutter, the man who has been overlord of great valley region and the benefactor of hundreds of immigrants, is in such serious financial straits that the existence of his empire is threatened.

His troubles originated in his pledge of his New Helvetia grant of eleven square leagues as guarantee of $30,000 to pay for the purchase of Ross and Bodega when the Russians were abandoning their California colony in 1841.

Cash Offered For Navy Deserters

MONTEREY, Oct. 18, 1848 — The U.S. Navy, as well as the army and cargo vessels, suffers from desertions. A sailor's life and pay hold no attraction for any bitten by the gold bug.

Commodore Thomas Ap Catesby Jones of the Pacific Squadron today publicly advertised rewards totaling $40,000 for the return of deserters. He plans to pay in silver dollars on delivery of a deserter: $500 each for the first four and $200 apiece for each subsequent deserter caught.

Ships Tied Up In Bay

SAN FRANCISCO, Oct. 1, 1848 — A score of ships lie in the bay today without full crews, but some captains are hopeful they will soon be able to depart.

Fourteen vessels arrived during September, and only four departed.

1st Steamer Leaves For Pacific Mail Run

NEW YORK, Oct. 6, 1848 — The steamer California sailed today on the long journey around Cape Horn to become the first ship in the Pacific Coast link of mail and passenger service to the far western lands by way of the Isthmus of Panama.

A festive party, including nearly 100 guests of William H. Aspinwall, president of the Pacific Mail Steamship Co., sailed as far as Sandy Hook. All aboard marveled at the ship's comfort and speed as she made 12 miles an hour. There are no through passengers for California, only four courtesy passengers for South American ports.

---o---

MINING SEASON ENDING

SUTTER'S FORT, Oct. 29, 1848 — With the beginning of the rainy season at hand, digging in the gold placer regions is nearly over for 1848.

Every launch leaving the Sacramento river Embarcadero here for San Francisco carries many miners who have abandoned operations for the winter. Nights have turned extremely cold in the mines. Rain and snow will make transportation difficult.

Digging for gold itself, however, continues as good as ever, if not better. Great quantities have been recently discovered in the region of the North Fork.

---o---

OREGONIANS ARRIVE

LASSEN'S RANCH, Oct. 27, 1848 — The first wagon train to cross from Oregon Territory to California has successfully arrived in the Sacramento Valley.

Party members, led by Peter H. Burnett, are resting today on the ranch of Peter Lassen before proceeding on to the gold fields.

---o---

RIVER FLEET EXPANDS

SAN FRANCISCO, Oct. 11, 1848 — The schooner Ann, just arrived from Astoria, Oregon Ter., with a load of produce, is being added by C.L. Ross, San Francisco merchant, to his line of packets running from here up the Sacramento river to New Helvetia.

FIRST MURDER IN GOLD MINING AREA

COLOMA, Oct. 2, 1848 — The scene of the first gold discovery last January has become the scene of the first recorded murder in the gold mining region.

This sad event occurred last night in Sutter's Sawmill in a violent outburst arising out of a drunken spree. Peter Raymond, a former member of the New York Volunteer Regiment, fatally stabbed John R. Von Phister, an American recently arrived from the Sandwich Islands to hunt for gold.

Von Phister and other men were sleeping in the sawmill when Raymond, obviously drunk, came in and demanded more liquor. He called out for Von Phister, whom he knew. The latter got up and apparently quieted Raymond. But when they shook hands Raymond grabbed a knife and struck.

Although unable to stop the crime, three men ran after Raymond and forcibly seized him. The killer was later taken to Sutter's Fort for confinement and trial.

---o---

KILLER ESCAPES

SUTTER' FORT, Oct. 23, 1848 — Peter Raymond, who committed murder at Sutter's Sawmill some three weeks ago in a drunken outburst, has fled from custody here. It is apparent that he had help from the outside.

Col. Richard B. Mason, acting governor of California, through Lieut. William T. Sherman, today offered a reward for Raymond's capture. This is in addition to a reward of $5000 for Raymond alive or dead that has been put forward by the San Francisco alcalde, Thaddeus M. Leavenworth.

Visiting here on a tour of the gold regions, Col. Mason minimized reports of lawlessness in the diggings.

---o---

Governor Has Store

COLOMA, Oct. 27, 1848 — Because of the difficulty of living on army pay Col. Richard B. Mason and three associates have established a store here to serve miners in the area. N.S. Bestor, former army clerk, is direct charge.

Mexicans Flock To Rich Diggings

SONORIAN CAMP, Nov. 19, 1848 — This camp, one of the richest in the new El Dorado, takes its name from the great number of miners from Sonora here. There are hundreds of them, including many women and children.

The name of this camp marks it from the nearby American camps of Jamestown and Wood Creek. Indications are that here is one of the biggest reservoirs of gold in the territory.

Migration of gold-seekers from Sonora and other northern provinces of Mexico has largely concentrated here. By virtue of their experience in mining, Sonorans are among the most successful miners. The largest lump of gold so far recorded, weighing 23 pounds, was found here.

Mexicans are not the only foreigners flocking to California for the gold. Since the first news reached the Sandwich Islands, nearly 30 vessels have left Honolulu with some 300 Europeans, plus many natives, bound for the mines.

Several days ago two vessels arrived at San Francisco with the first gold-seekers from Chile. The largest group was aboard the Chilean ship Virginia, with 60 passengers, who said there were hundreds of others awaiting a chance to sail for California. This is a prophecy of things to come.

———o———

Navy Transports Gold

SAN FRANCISCO, Nov. 28, 1848 — At least half a million dollars in gold was secured in the hold of the U.S. Navy's ship Lexington when she left today for the United States.

The gold is owned by private persons taking advantage of the navy's offer to freight it safely at low rates. The storeship is bound for New York by way of Valparaiso and Rio de Janeiro.

———o———

Grapes Promising

SONOMA, Nov. 12, 1848 — When the glitter of gold is gone, the grape may take a more prominent place in this area. Grapes have been going in 1000-pound lots almost weekly from the vineyard of Jacob P. Leese. A vineyard of 1000 vines on three acres produces nearly $1000 a season.

AUTHORITIES FAVOR CIVIL GOVERNMENT

SAN FRANCISCO, Nov. 25, 1848 — The highest officers of the U.S. government in California now favor the organization of a provisional civil government by the citizens. There is only one proviso: that a move not be taken if word is received that Congress provided for a territorial government at its last session.

Results of the conference between Governor Mason and Commodore Jones were disclosed today. Both are impressed with the need for quick action, especially to preserve law and order. The two officers have been placed in an embarrassing position by lack of instructions from the national government.

They will support a movement for the election of delegates by the people to frame laws and make other arrangements for a provisional California government.

———o———

S.F. Newspapers Merge

SAN FRANCISCO, Nov. 18, 1848 — The California Star resumed publication here today as The California Star and Californian, absorbing the territory's first newspaper. Editor and proprietor is Edward C. Kemble.

Both newspapers ceased publication in the early rush to the gold fields. The Californian resumed more than two months ago, but now becomes a part of the revived Star.

———o———

DIKES USED IN MINING

ON THE YUBA RIVER, Nov. 29, 1848 — At new diggings on the Middle Fork, men of the Oregon immigration are getting from $5 to 5 ounces of gold a day by building dikes to turn a stream from its normal channel.

False Friends Kill, Rob Two Companions

SUTTER' FORT, Nov. 21, 1848 — The most deliberate, brutal murder yet to occur in the gold regions was disclosed today when a party of men found the bodies of the two victims.

Those slain were a Mr. Pomeroy, a recent immigrant from Oregon Ter., and a companion whose name is not known. They had had good success, and were carrying a large amount of gold dust.

With two acquaintances they left the fort two days ago to travel to San Jose. Shortly after leaving, the four men passed a wagon party. Early today the wagon arrived at their campground and found the two bodies. All evidence pointed to the fact the false friends, Joseph Lynch, formerly of the New York Volunteer Regiment, and a navy deserter, murdered them in the night and took their gold.

This crime, the killing of two miners by Indians and reports of other disturbances are causing concern as to the likelihood of further outbreaks.

So far as can fairly be learned there have been only two cases yet of trial, conviction and hanging by "popular tribunal" in the mining areas.

———o———

Sutter, Jr., Plans City Of Sacramento

SUTTER'S FORT, Nov. 1, 1848 — A new town, Sacramento City, will arise around this fort and the Sacramento river Embarcadero.

John A. Sutter, Jr., who has taken over his father's properties, plans to create the city as soon as a survey can be made. Young Sutter today revised his partnership with Samuel J. Hensley, Pierson B. Reading and Jacob R. Snyder to make way for his appropriation of lands "to the city of Sacramento for its own use and benefit."

Prospects for the city's future are bright because of its strategic location and the expansion of population in the gold regions. The only rival to Sacramento City is Sutterville, which was established by Captain Sutter on high ground three miles from the fort. But that place is off the main lines of transport.

President Confirms Gold In California

WASHINGTON, D.C., Dec. 5, 1848 — The President of the United States today officially confirmed the gold discoveries in California.

In his message to Congress at its opening session President Polk gave a long account of the large amount of gold being taken from the mines. The message includes a detailed report from Col. Richard B. Mason, ex-officio governor there, telling of the tremendous wealth being uncovered.

"The accounts of the abundance of gold in that territory," the President told Congress, "are of such an extraordinary character as would scarcely command belief were they not corroborated by the authentic reports of officers in the public service, who have visited the mineral district and derived the facts which they detail from personal observation.

"Reluctant to credit the reports ... of gold, the officer commanding our forces in California visited the mineral district in July last for ... accurate information. ... His report is herewith laid before Congress.

"When he visisted the country, there were about 4000 persons engaged in collecting gold. ... The explorations already made warrant the belief that the supply is very large and that gold is found at various places in an extensive district."

The discovery has "produced a surprising change ... in California," the President stated. "Nearly the whole male population of the country has gone to the gold districts."

President Polk recommended authorization of a branch mint there, action to establish a territorial government and measures to preserve the mineral areas for the use of the United States.

———o———

Mania For Gold Becomes Epidemic

WASHINGTON, D.C., Dec. 8, 1848 — Although it is only three days after President Polk put the authority of his office behind the almost unbelievable accounts of wealth of gold in California, groups of adventurers are forming in city after city throughout the East to get there as fast as they can.

Two ships are preparing at Philadelphia for almost immediate departure for California. The bark John Benson will sail in a couple of days from New York to connect with the Pacific Steamer at Panama, and have a full list of passengers. Similar preparations are being made at almost every port of consequence on the Atlantic Coast. The steamer Falcon had only 95 passengers when she sailed for Panama a week ago.

———o———

GOLD THE REAL STUFF

PHILADELPHIA, Dec. 12, 1848 — The director of the U.S. Mint here today reported that the gold brought from California averaged 892 to 897 thousandths fine compared to the mint standard of 900. The official gold samples weighed 216 ounces before melting and 211.47 afterward, for a value of $3910.10.

First private gold deposit was that of David Carter, whose dust weighed over 1804 ounces, worth $36,492. In gold bars the average value was $18.50 an ounce.

———o———

UNUSUAL COLD WEATHER

SAN FRANCISCO, Dec. 31, 1848 — With temperatures dropping to 37 degrees, the past week has been unusually cold in this area. Much rain has fallen, and hills in the Contra Costa area have been covered with snow for several days.

London Told Of Gold

LONDON, Dec. 22, 1848 — The august London Times gave much space today to the official confirmation of California gold by President Polk. It carried his presidential message in full.

In an editorial, The Times stated, "Experience is equally against the presumption that California, be its treasures great or small, will prove of real benefit to the United States."

———o———

THREE ROBBERS HANGED

SAN JOSE, Dec. 18, 1848 — Three men involved in a highway robbery near here were hanged before a large public gathering in the plaza here today.

ROBBERS MURDER TEN AT SAN MIGUEL

MISSION SAN MIGUEL, Dec. 9, 1848 — The massacre of all the residents of this mission, ten in number, was discovered today by a government courier, who gave the alarm to the neighborhood.

It seems certain that the killings were committed by a band of five men known to have stopped at the mission a few days ago. The band is believed led by Joseph Lynch, already hunted for two slayings on the road from Sutter's Fort to Stockton.

The victims included William Reed, a grantee of the mission rancho, his wife and young son. Seven bodies, all slain with axes, were in a heap in one room. Reed had recently returned from the mines with a considerable quantity of gold from sale of a flock of sheep.

A pursuit has been organized to follow the killers south.

———o———

KILLERS EXECUTED AT SANTA BARBARA

SANTA BARBARA, Dec. 29, 1848 — The three surviving members of the band that murdered ten persons at San Miguel Mission were executed today.

Joseph Lynch, Peter Raymond or Remer, also wanted for the murder of Von Phister at Sutter's Fort, and Peter Quin were shot near the corner of De La Guerra and Chapala streets after they were tried, convicted and sentenced.

The other two members of the gang were killed in battle with a posse at the ocean edge south of here two weeks ago. One posse member was killed and several wounded.

Col. Richard B. Mason, governor of California, had approved execution if the killers were properly found guilty.

———o———

A CHRISTMAS WEDDING

PARK'S BAR, Dec. 25, 1848 — Charles Covillaud, who has been operating a store here, was married this Christmas Day to Miss Mary Murphy, a survivor of the Donner party disaster of two years ago. Covillaud bought a half-interest a few months ago in the New Mecklenburg rancho of Theodoro Cordua.

THE GOLDEN GAZETTE 1849

JANUARY 1849

FIRST STEAMER

SOUTH AMERICAN SHIPS
CROWD S. F. HARBOR

SAN FRANCISCO, Jan. 31, 1849—The knowing ones here say the first steamer of Pacific Coast service may be daily expected to arrive in the bay. When she comes, the citizens ought to show their joy, for she means speedier transportation to the East by Panama. The California, first of the Pacific Mail Steamship Co. fleet, left New York last October to travel around Cape Horn.

Nine ships arrived this month from South America, three from Mexico and four from other Pacific ports. Each had full loads of gold-seeking passengers as well as cargo. It is reported several thousand Latin Americans are preparing to come to California for the dust. One of the ships brought iron flasks for the New Almaden quicksilver mines.

Little Aid At Hand To Combat Indians

MONTEREY, Jan. 21, 1849— The military governor of California today offered what little aid is available to the citizens of San Juan Bautista to guard against the depredations of Indians against their ranchos.

They petitioned Colonel Mason for powder and lead, and asked for the election of a district alcalde. Lieut. Henry W. Halleck, secretary of state, approved such an election and said he would issue to the alcalde named a quantity of powder and lead. "The governor regrets he has not at present a disposable military force to send in pursuit of the Indians," he informed the community.

SEVERE WINTER SLOWS MINING

SACRAMENTO CITY, Jan. 23, 1849—Unusually severe weather has been experienced in the past few weeks. This is said to be the coldest winter since that of 1823-24.

In much of the gold regions snow is four feet deep. At Sutter's Fort ice has been observed three inches thick. As a result, all mining activity has practically ceased, though hundreds are wintering in cabins at Dry Diggings and on the Yuba River. Most are foreigners or immigrants, as Californians have largely retired to ranchos and towns.

At San Francisco streets have been repeatedly whitened with snow and hail in the past two weeks, and the hills across the bay have been capped with snow.

FIRST S. F. BANK

SAN FRANCISCO, Jan. 9, 1849 —The first regular banking house in town was established today with the opening of an "Exchange and Deposit Office" by Naglee and Sinton in the Parker House on Kearny st. fronting Portsmouth Square. Members of the firm are Henry M. Naglee, former captain in the Stevenson New York Regiment, and Richard H. Sinton, ex-paymaster of the U.S.S. Ohio.

SACRAMENTO LOTS SELL FAST

SACRAMENTO CITY, Jan. 15, 1849—First auction of lots in this new town were held this week, and sales have been brisk. The proprietor is John A. Sutter, Jr., son of the famous captain. First sales were near the Fort, but many are now being made near the Embarcadero. Sam Brannan, a leading merchant, is planning to move his store from the Fort to the river front.

THREE MEN HUNG AT DRY DIGGINGS
NOW IT'S HANGTOWN

DRY DIGGINGS, Jan. 25, 1849 —Dry Diggings is Hangtown today.

Three men, by name Pepi, Tchal and Antoine, were hung by the citizens of this mining camp after it was learned they had been connected with murders in the gold region.

Together with a fourth man, Montreuil, they were first arrested by an armed party for having robbed the proprietors of a gambling and drinking house of $600. The citizens then assembled, selected three judges and 12 jurors, who returned a verdict of guilty.

The sentence of banishment after the receipt of 39 lashes each was duly executed on Sunday. When the men's earlier murderous career became known subsequently, the citizens resolved to find them again and hang them. The three named above were strung up with expedition when recaught.

HO! FOR CALIFORNIA GOLD RUSH BEGINS

NEW YORK, Jan. 29, 1849—A great gold rush for California is on now that the reports of the immense wealth of her mines is fully confirmed.

A summary today shows that 5,719 people have sailed for that territory so far in 99 ships—80 vessels via Cape Horn, 14 for Chagres to connect with Pacific steamers, etc., at Panama across the Isthmus and five with men planning to cross Mexico or Texas. Thousands more are planning to sail, with nearly 150 more ships advertised at practically every eastern port.

7

WHIPPING POPULAR
LASHING EFFECTIVE SUBSTITUTE FOR JAILS

MONTEREY, Feb. 20, 1849—Lashing of offenders on the bared back "with the end of a reata well laid on" is now one of the most customary punishments by the courts of California towns.

Several such punishments have been meted out in the past two weeks. It is used because there are no jails for safe custody of a criminal, and many believe the whippings are an effective deterrent to crime.

Lugardo Rios was sentenced here to 15 lashes and pay $13.50 damages for stealing a horse. At Santa Cruz Jose Romero was given six lashes, fined $50 and costs and banished forever from the community on being found guilty of forging the papers of the land on which he and his family were living. In the same town William Stephens was sentenced to 50 lashes and banishment.

Where a large number of lashes are ordered, the practice is to divide them over several days.

EUROPEAN GOLD FEVER

PARIS, Feb. 1, 1849—The craze for California gold is spreading all over Europe. In both France and England several ships are preparing to proceed thither, and similar moves are reported from the principal ports of the continent in Spain, Holland and Germany.

In the wave of popular excitement speculators are forming companies for mining and trading. One such here, "Expedition Francaise pour les Mines D'Or de Sacramento," has been organized by three sea captains and a jeweler to be capitalized at a million francs, in 100,000 shares to be subdivided into fourths of 25 francs each.

GOAT ISLAND SOLD

SAN FRANCISCO, Feb. 15, 1849—Nathan Spear, well known resident of the town, has sold his interest in Yerba Buena Island in the middle of the bay to Edward A. King, San Francisco harbor master, for a consideration reported to be 100 cents.

With William H. Davis, Mr. Spear has kept a herd of goats on the island for several years. Last

CREW DESERTS FIRST STEAMER

SAN FRANCISCO, Feb. 28, 1849—The first steamship is here! The California, first of the ships of the Pacific Mail Steamship Co., arrived today with more than 350 passengers.

The California is a beautiful new side-wheel steamer of 1050 tons, 200 feet long and 34 feet in beam, built especially for this service. Her voyage from New York, which began last October 6, was an epic cruise around Cape Horn. She met up with the gold craze at Callao, Peru.

On her arrival at Panama January 17, 1500 persons, many with through tickets to San Francisco, demanded passage. They had gathered at the Isthmus after trips by steamer and sailing ships from Atlantic ports after President Polk had officially confirmed to the country the news of California's gold.

The crew of the steamer is also stricken with the gold fever, and sailors started deserting almost the very minute she came to anchor.

fall they had trouble from men who would row over to the island and shoot the goats, either for sport or for their meat.

PLANS TO BRING WOMEN TO CALIF.

NEW YORK, Feb. 1, 1849—Mrs. Eliza Farnham, former resident of California and the respected widow of Thomas W. Farnham, attorney who died in San Francisco last fall, proposed today a novel plan to bring a number of young women to California.

She feels that the absence of virtuous women will have a bad effect on the men planning to join the Gold Rush. Her plan received favorable comment from Editors Horace Greeley and William Cullen Bryant, and the well known preacher, Henry Ward Beecher.

"Among the many privations and deteriorating influences to which the thousands who are flocking thither will be subjected," she said in her announcement, "one of the greatest is the absence of woman, with all her kindly cares and powers, so peculiarly conservative to men under such circumstances.

"It would exceed the limits of this circular to hint at the benefits that would flow to the growing population of that wonderful region, from the introduction among them of intelligent, virtuous and efficient women. Of such only it is proposed to make up this company."

Her plan is to take only women under 25, who have from a clergyman or other authority satisfactory testimonials of education, character, capacity, etc., and can contribute $250 for the voyage and accommodation in California until they can enter some gainful occupation.

WARRING COUNCILS OUSTED IN S. F.

SAN FRANCISCO, Feb. 21, 1849—Fifteen members of a district legislative assembly were elected today to succeed the two town councils who have been rivals for full authority in the town.

It is hoped that this, along with the selection of three justices of the peace, will end the disputes between political partisans who have been warring over the past two months.

SUTTER AND SON WAR OVER TOWNS

SACRAMENTO CITY, Mar. .15, 1849 — A battle for supremacy is under way between this town and neighboring Suttersville.

Its bitterness is intensified by the opposition between the famous Captain Sutter and his son, August. To prevent foreclosure of his extensive property for debts, the captain last fall transferred it to his son's name and then went to Coloma for the winter.

August laid out Sacramento City and has been realizing large sums from the sale of lots. Angered by his son's move, Capt. Sutter has associated himself with George McDougal and Lansford W. Hastings to promote Suttersville, an older town site three miles distant.

McDougal's trading firm today announced the opening of a hotel at Suttersville and the storeship Thili for receiving goods. The brigantine Hope will make regular trips to San Francisco, and steamship service is advertised for the summer.

Whether this competition will harm Sacramento City remains to be seen. The population here is now over 1000.

———o———

METALSMITH BUSY

SACRAMENTO CITY, Mar. 18, 1849—Ephraim Wadleigh is on his way to making a fortune here as a metalsmith and tinsmith. In his shop at Sutter's Fort he has been working day and night making pans suitable for miners, which he sells at $16 each, with a small discount for wholesale purchases by traders. The smallest job on a gun or pistol costs $16 by the gunsmith at the fort, and shoeing a horse or mule is $16 per shoe.

———o———

COLTON HALL COMPLETED

MONTEREY, Mar. 8, 1849—The town hall, named in his honor by the citizens, was reported completed today by the Rev. Walter Colton, former alcalde. Colton Hall has been built through the sales of town lots, the labor of convicts, taxes on liquor shops and fines against gamblers.

LOCATION OF S. F. POOR, SAYS GENERAL

$18,000 Rental Charge for House Angers Army Head

SAN FRANCISCO, Mar. 15, 1849 —Gen. Persifer F. Smith, new commander of the Army's Pacific Department, today forwarded to his superiors at Washington an adverse report on San Francisco.

"The harbor at Yerba Buena is a very inconvenient one," he declared, "the sea too rough three days out of seven to load or unload vessels; and the town of San Francisco is situated at the extremity of a long point cut off from the interior by an arm of the bay more than 30 miles long, having no good water and few supplies of food."

It is possible that the general's pessimistic view of this place is prompted by his experiences since his arrival on the steamer two weeks ago. Because of the crowded condition of the town, it was only within the past few days that he could get quarters on shore. Besides, he received a rude shock when an ex-soldier of the New York Volunteers Regiment who has struck it rich offered to rent him a house for $18,000 a year—a sum much greater than the general's pay and allowances combined—and gave him one day to take or leave the offer.

———o———

IMPATIENT MINERS WARNED

SACRAMENTO CITY, Mar. 20, 1849 — Already a note of preparation is sounded for the gold mining season of '49. Hundreds have started on their summer tour in search of the yellow dust, and thousands are preparing.

Fine weather a few weeks ago seemed to indicate the winter's end, but recent rains and snows are a danger and affect the traveling. Men will be well advised not to go to the mines too early, as the ground will be wet and cold for some time. Those there will expose themselves to disease and death.

———o———

17,000 GO WEST

NEW YORK, Mar. 23, 1849 — A total of 17,341 persons have sailed from the Atlantic Coast for California since the truth of the great gold discoveries was established.

Large numbers of people are reported to be assembling at Independence and St. Joseph, Mo., to start across the plains and Rocky Mountains to California as soon as the spring grass grows sufficiently to subsist their animals.

———o———

SHIP STRIKES SHOAL

SAN FRANCISCO, Mar. 22, 1849 —The Chilean ship Julia was aground today by the Presidio Shoal. She struck while coming into port. The ship was uninjured and will be taken off at high water.

STATEHOOD HINTED

SAN FRANCISCO, Mar. 22, 1849 —Twelve prominent men from various parts of the territory today urged that the convention to form a provisional civil government be postponed until August 1 and be held at Monterey, instead of San Jose. One of the reasons cited is that it is possible by that date the number of inhabitants of California will be great enough to require the immediate formation of a state constitution.

———o———

POST OFFICE ESTABLISHED

SAN FRANCISCO, Mar. 13, 1849 —A postoffice is finally established here. William Van Voorhies, the postal agent who brought the mail on the first steamer, has completed arrangements to deliver letters at the store of Ross, Benton and Co., with Charles L. Ross acting as postmaster. Our citizens will now have a place to call for letters and the privilege of mailing them.

———o———

LAND TITLES INDEFINITE

MONTEREY, Mar. 1, 1849 — A lengthy report on the vital question of land titles in California was issued today by Capt. Henry W. Halleck, secretary of state in the provisional government. He concluded that large numbers of titles were very indefinite and that many grants from Mexican governors existed which had antedated.

WHITES, INDIANS CLASH IN KILLINGS
TROOPS CALLED

SACRAMENTO CITY, April 28, 1849 — Such serious trouble has broken out between white men and Indians in the gold mining regions along the American and Cosumnes rivers that Capt. John A. Sutter, who is Indian agent, has appealed to the military for troops.

About a week ago miners accused some Indians of robbery and rounded up a group of the savages. Some of the Indians were shot and killed as they faced trial. A few days ago two white men were killed in apparent retaliation.

A report was received here today that a large party of white men had attacked Indians living on the ranch of William Daylor, killed 27 of them, carried off 34 women and children and left 22 men missing.

In appealing to the military government for aid, Capt. Sutter declared that in most cases the whites are the aggressors and he fears a wave of assassinations on the one hand and massacres on the other.

Bands of whites are raiding and attacking any Indians they meet, innocent or guilty, peaceful or turbulent, according to Sutter, and the Indians are greatly alarmed. Capt. Sutter asserts that the whites responsible are mainly immigrants who cry, "Let's exterminate the Indians."

SAN FRANCISCO, April 17, 1849 —Stock lists in a company formed to construct Central Wharf out into the bay from Montgomery street, were opened today, and $120,000 was subscribed almost at once.

CAPTAIN FOILS CREW

SAN FRANCISCO, April 12, 1849 —The steamer Oregon, second of the Pacific Mail's fleet, sailed late today for Panama and intermediate ports with 19 passengers and $160,000 worth of gold dust.

Vigilance of Capt. R. H. Pearson on the Oregon's arrival here April 1 prevented loss of all his crew like the first steamer, California. When he sailed into the bay, he tied up alongside the U.S.S. Ohio, put them aboard the naval vessel and had them kept under close watch until shortly before the ship's departure.

OVERLAND TREK FOR GOLD ON

INDEPENDENCE, Mo., April 25, 1849 — The great overland emigration of '49 to California's gold fields is well underway.

Several thousand people have gathered here and at St. Joseph to start on the long hard journey across plains, mountains and desert to the Pacific Coast. Companies leave each day, but early starters have been frequently stopped by creeks or rivers difficult to ford. They have had to empty their wagons to make crossings, and one party lost all its outfit. The early plains grass has also been too short and too new for oxen and mules.

Cholera has made its dread appearance and is striking the emigrants in large numbers. Of one party of 13 from New York, 12 have died.

At St. Joseph between 4000 and 5000 are in camp, as many as the existing ferry can take across the Missouri river from now to July 1. There is but one flatboat, which can make two trips a day.

MISSION TILES TAKEN

MONTEREY, April 2, 1849—Don Mariano Soberanez, owner of the Rancho of the Ojito, was strictly forbidden today from removing any more tile buildings of the San Antonio Mission. The order was issued by Capt. Henry W. Halleck, secretary of state of the territorial government, on information Don Mariano was taking tile from good mission houses to roof a new building of his own.

DIVING BELL BUILT

SACRAMENTO CITY, April 16, 1849—One of the novelties of the season is a diving bell being constructed for use in gold gathering. The builder believes the ponderous machine will help him reach the immense wealth supposed to exist in river beds deep under water.

SAN FRANCISCO, April 24, 1849 —Several iron warehouses are soon expected here. Among the number is one 120 feet long for the enterprising firm of Starkey, Janion and Co., due on the ship Antelope from Liverpool, Eng.

L. A. ACCUSED OF BEING BACKWARD

LOS ANGELES, April 16, 1849—Unwillingness of the residents of the district of Los Angeles to take any initiative regarding local government was reported today by Stephen C. Foster, American-appointed alcalde, to territorial officials.

The Mexican population is "too unenterprising" to do anything about local government, and the foreign residents are too few and too Mexicanized, according to Mr. Foster, who believes it can be solved only by an order from the supreme government.

A town election last December failed when not a single vote was cast. By Mexican law Los Angeles is entitled to have a council of seven, but it has had none since 1847 and no grants or sales of town lands have been made since then, he reported.

In the Los Angeles district are about 5000 inhabitants of Hispano-American origin, 6000 Indians and 40 to 50 foreign residents, mostly Americans. The property, mostly in cattle and vineyards, must amount at a low valuation to $1,500,000, Mr. Foster estimates.

Only other authorities besides Alcalde Foster in an area of some 600 square miles are two local alcaldes at points of little importance.

7,000 IN FIELDS

SACRAMENTO CITY, April 15, 1849—Movement to the gold mines for the season is well started, with the snow fast melting and the placers generally clear. One shrewd observer who has just made a survey of the placer area estimates the 7,000 gold hunters already in California and the thousands on their way will take out $30,000,000 in gold dust this year.

LARGE NUGGET FOUND

SAN FRANCISCO, April 9, 1849 —A large piece of gold, weighing 6½ pounds troy, has been brought here from Stockton by Capt. Charles M. Weber. At $16 an ounce it is worth $1248. The piece is about 6 inches long, 2½ wide and ¼ to ⅝ of an inch thick.

CRIME WAVE OF INDIAN ENDS IN NOOSE

LOS ANGELES, May 10, 1849 — Juan Antonio, former Indian neophyte of San Gabriel Mission who has been a terror to this district for 15 years, was hung from a scaffold here this afternoon.

Juan was charged with many murders, burglary, theft and aiding horse thieves of the Tulares regions. He had been captured several times before but always managed to make good his escape.

After his recent recapture, he was tried in the alcalde's court before a jury of six, convicted and sentenced to death. The sentence was carried out speedily to prevent another escape. Religious consolation was given him before the noose was put around his neck.

———o———

INDIAN CHIEF SHOT BUT WILL RECOVER

STOCKTON, May 24, 1849 — Jose Jesus, celebrated Indian chief who is a great friend of Charles M. Weber, founder of this thriving town, has been wounded by an American ex-soldier named Huddart in a quarrel. Jose was shot through the breast but will recover. Both men were reported to have been intoxicated at the time. Huddard was tried by a jury of 12 and sentenced to three years in irons.

———o———

S. F. POLITICS FLARE

SAN FRANCISCO, May 31, 1849 —San Francisco's political turmoil led today to the forcible occupation of the office of Alcalde Thaddeus M. Leavenworth and the seizure of his records and papers by Sheriff John C. Pulis.

———o———

GOLD COIN MADE

BENICIA, May 31, 1849 — Five-dollar gold coins have been struck here under the private stamp of the firm of Norris, Greig and Norris. The coin, which bears a San Francisco imprint, resembles U. S. coin in general appearance.

SHIP FROM EAST IN RECORD 113 DAY TRIP

SAN FRANCISCO, May 18, 1849 — With a list of 34 gold - seeking passengers, the American ship Grey Eagle arrived today after a record voyage from the East via Cape Horn.

The vessel, skippered by Capt. Power, took 117 days to reach this port from the Delaware capes, including a four-day stopover at Valparaiso, Chile. Her running time of 113 days is the quickest passage any sailing craft has yet made from the Atlantic Coast. The Grey Eagle cleared the capes January 21 and has beaten more than a score of other ships which set out earlier.

WEST TOO WILD?

Californians will be grieved to learn Mrs. Eliza Farnham, who planned to bring more than 100 young women to California, has been able to induce only three to sail with her from New York on the ship Angelique.

California to Have "New York" of Own

SAN FRANCISCO, May 23, 1849 —Creation of a new California town, with the grandiose name of New York-by-the-Pacific, was announced today by its promoter, Col. Jonathan D. Stevenson, former commander of the famous New York Volunteers Regiment in California during the Mexican War.

A town site has been laid out on Suisun Bay at its junction with the Sacramento and San Joaquin rivers. As yet there is not a house at the spot. Its center street is 100 feet in width, and the others 75.

———o———

HIGH WATERS SLOW MINER'S GOLD HAUL

SACRAMENTO, May 30, 1849 — High waters in mountain and foothill streams through the gold mining regions have been a great impediment this month to the activities of diggers.

There is lots of gold dust being mined and frequent reports of sensational individual hauls. But it is calculated the daily average of the thousands now in the area does not exceed from half an ounce to an ounce of the real stuff per day.

Many of the new arrivals who rushed to the mines as soon as they reached this land of gold are bitterly discouraged. Some are facing outright hardships. Others have quickly concluded there is more wealth in trading, freighting, gambling, wood-cutting and the like than in frantically probing the earth for the yellow dust.

Greatest extension of new discoveries is in the southern district, with prospecting miners finding luck as far south as the Mariposa river. Sonoranian Camp, which takes its name from the many Sonora Mexicans there, is becoming known as one of the richest camps in all California.

———o———

Oregon Territory Split

OREGON CITY, May 13, 1849— Gov. Lane today published a proclamation dividing Oregon Territory into three judicial districts. The first includes Vancouver and several counties south of the Columbia river: the second, the remaining counties of the Willamette valley; the third, Lewis county, all territory north of the Columbia, including the Puget Sound territory. A census of the territory showed a total of 8903 souls, present and absent. There are 2509 voters, but many are now absent in the California mines.

———o———

DESERTERS FACE RETURN TO EAST

MONTEREY, May 18, 1849—Gen. Bennet Riley, California's governor and military commander, wants to have army deserters returned to the East because he believes such punishment, if carried out quickly, will help prevent soldiers skipping to the gold mines.

He asked Commodore Jones of the Navy today for an early opportunity to send between 25 and 30 recently captured and convicted deserters back on a ship-of-war. Lieut. William Tecumseh Sherman was instrumental in rounding up the deserting soldiers.

MINERS FEUD
RICH GOLD STRIKE

SACRAMENTO CITY, June 25, 1849 — Gold hunting is looking up for the thousands in the mining camps along the streams and ravines of the Sierra Nevada foothills. On the North and Middle Forks of the American the daily average runs 1-1½ ounces. Near Mormon Island three men took out $4,848 in three days by operating two machines. Sullivan's Camp is one of the richest diggings, with the average $75 a day. Some have been making $200 to $300 with relative ease.

American hostility to foreign miners is rising in some districts. Chileans on the American River have been threatened, and as a result are abandoning their workings there. The same feeling is rife on the San Joaquin and its tributaries to the south, which are overrun with gold-seekers. There the bitterness is against immigrants from Mexico. At Sonoranian Camp there are not less than 2,000 of these people, and many more, some of them well armed, are arriving daily.

———o———

SHIP DESTROYED IN BAY FIRE

SAN FRANCISCO, June 28, 1849 — The ship Philadelphia was completely destroyed by a spectacular early morning fire in the bay today. Breaking out in the forecastle about 5 a.m., the flames spread so rapidly that it was only a few minutes before the entire forward part of the ship was ablaze.

Crews from ships anchored nearby fought vainly to stem the fire. When the ship had burned to the water's edge, her cables were cut and the hulk drifted away with the tide. The personal effects of Capt. Samuel Weare, owner and master, and his wife were barely saved. With the ship's boats they were the only salvage. The Philadelphia, a vessel of 543 tons, was under charter to sail to Manila. She was insured for $15,000.

———o———

OREGON ELECTION

OREGON CITY, June 15, 1849 — Samuel R. Thurston was elected delegate to Congress from Oregon Territory today by a majority of 70 votes. Mr. Thurston emigrated from the state of Maine.

Convention Called

MONTEREY, June 20, 1849 — A convention will meet here September 1 to draft a constitution for a state or territorial government for California. Gen. Bennett Riley, the provisional governor, issued a proclamation for the convention early this month because of chaotic conditions in this golden land after he received official news by naval ship from Mazatlan that Congress had adjourned without providing for a government for California. Delegates will be elected August 1.

Riley provided for 37 delegates from ten districts: San Diego, two; Los Angeles, four; Santa Barbara, two; San Luis Obispo, two; Monterey, five; San Jose, five; San Francisco, five; Sonoma, Sacramento and San Joaquin, four each Because of the rapidly rising population, districts are permitted to elect supernumerary delegates if they think they are entitled to greater representation.

———o———

BILL PROTESTED

SAN FRANCISCO, June 21, 1849 — Alcalde Thaddeus M. Leavenworth today submitted a bill for $600 for the cost of an express from here to Monterey, a distance of some 150 miles. Major Edward H. Fitzgerald, government quartermaster, thinks the service could have been performed for no more than $200 and is asking the governor to set what he considers a fair amount to reimburse the alcalde.

———o———

Stockton Lots Jump

STOCKTON, June 14, 1849 — The site of Captain Weber's store and a couple of other ramshackle structures and generally called by the name of Tuleberg, today claims 1,000 residents. Stockton now has 200 houses and tents. Prosperity can be measured by the fact some water lots, bought for $300, recently sold for $5,000.

✝✝✝✝✝✝✝✝✝✝✝✝✝✝✝✝✝✝✝✝✝

SOBER MAN WANTED

An industrious, sober man, acquainted with the care of horses and cows is required. To a capable person high wages will be paid. Apply to this newspaper office.

❀❀❀❀❀❀❀❀❀❀❀❀❀❀❀❀❀❀❀❀❀

NEW TOWN SITES BOOM IN CALIF.

SACRAMENTO CITY, June 20, 1849 — The success and immense growth of this new city and of Stockton is spurring promoters to establish other town sites to take advantage of the tens of thousands of people coming in the rush for gold. At least eight new towns have been established in recent weeks. Each claims great advantages for its location and commercial possibilities, but most exist only on paper.

The newest are Fremont, laid out by Jonas Spect on the west bank of the Sacramento River opposite the mouth of the Feather; its rival, Vernon, on the Feather's east bank at the junction with the Sacramento; Boston, a few miles above Sacramento City; Webster, four miles below this place; Suisun, half way to San Francisco, which has already reserved several large squares for a university; Tuolumne City, at the head of navigation on that river; Stanislaus, established by Sam Brannan & Co. on that stream's north bank; and the ambitiously-titled New York-on-the-Pacific, where the Sacramento and San Joaquin rivers join the bay of San Francisco.

———o———

SUTTER REGAINS TITLE TO LAND

SACRAMENTO CITY, June 25, 1849 — The famous Capt. John A. Sutter was back in control of his Rancho New Helvetia property today with its reconveyal to him by his son, August. Under heavy pressure by creditors in the months following the discovery of gold at his sawmill at Coloma, the captain last winter put all his property in his son's name.

Through the sale of lots in this city since, the junior Sutter, aided by his agent, Peter H. Burnett, has cleared most of his father's old debts. Even Sutter's contract with the Russian-American Fur Co. to buy Ross and Bodega several years ago was cleared with a final payment of $14,448 recently.

———o———

LOS ANGELES, June 2, 1849 — Because there is no proper plot of the streets and lands of this Pueblo, the town council today asked Gen. Bennett Riley, California governor, to send down from Monterey an officer qualified to make a survey.

NEW GOLD DEPOSITS BEING UNCOVERED

SACRAMENTO, July 25, 1849 — New, rich deposits have lately been found in both the northern and southern districts of the gold region.

A particularly good find has been made on the North Fork of the American River, where many are having good fortune. One Baltimorean took out $6000 in one week. Other new finds have been made on the Yuba and Feather rivers, while to the south it is rumored much gold has been uncovered on the Mariposa grant owned by the famous Colonel Fremont.

The Mormon Island Mining Association, which has been hard at work building dams, has nearly completed its object of diverting the stream from previously covered gold beds. Shares in it are now selling for $5000.

——o——

MILL STONES IN DISPUTE

SAN LUIS OBISPO, July 19, 1849 — A dispute over the ownership of a pair of mill stones is proving such a problem to Miguel Avila, first alcalde of the district, that today he asked the government of the whole territory of California to make a decision.

One Vincente Feliz has possession of the stones, given to him, by John Price, former alcalde, but Padre Gomez of Mission San Luis Obispo claims them. Alcalde Avila thinks the stones ought to go back to the priest, but he would like the governor to tell him what to do.

——o——

Market Glutted

SAN FRANCISCO, July 25, 1849 — The continued arrivals of many ships from the Atlantic Coast has resulted in the market being overstocked in many kinds of merchandise. Some of the prices quoted by auction merchants currently are: flour, $12-13 bbl.; Oregon corn, $1½-2 bu.; pork old prime, $5-8 cwt.; pork new prime, $18-22 cwt.; brandy. $1-2 gal.; good whiskey, $1-1½ gal.; common whiskey, 60-85c gal.; four-wheeled wagons, $500 700; white pine and scantlings, $300-350 per thousand; house frames, $1200-2500.

'HOUNDS' TROUBLES COME TO A CLIMAX

SAN FRANCISCO, July 23, 1849 — The "Hounds," an organization of young men who have terrorized the community for some time, was broken up today when eight of its members were convicted and sentenced by a people's court for conspiracy, riot, robbery and assault with intent to kill.

This group, largely made up of ex-soldiers, had been wont to parade about town in fantastic dress and had headquarters in a tent on Montgomery street named "Tammany Hall." Lately they have committed various outrages.

On Sunday night, the 15th, an armed group attacked tents in the Chilean district, tore down and shot some of their occupants after an afternoon of parading with fife, drum and banner. The next day Sam Brannan called for action at a mass meeting in the Plaza. By sundown 17 ringleaders were arrested and put aboard the U.S.S. Warren, and the chief leader, Sam Roberts, was caught on a schooner bound for Stockton.

A grand jury of 24 indicted the group on the 17th. In the following days the "Hounds" were tried before Alcalde Leavenworth, with William M. Gwin and James C. Ward as associate judges. Roberts and Theodore R. Saunders were sentenced to ten years in prison, and five others were given lesser sentences.

It is hoped this will help end rowdyism in San Francisco.

——o——

Argonauts Pour In Via Panama, Cape Horn

SAN FRANCISCO, July 31, 1849 — The great rush to California by the sea routes, via Panama and around Cape Horn, brought 3614 persons to California this month, according to a report by Edward A. King, the harbor master. Of these 3000 were American, and only 49 women.

In one 24-hour period there were 17 ship arrivals, with 889 passengers: from New York, 6 ships with 400 immigrants; Boston, two with 55; New London, one with 56; Nantucket, one with 20; Beverly, Mass., one with seven; Sandwich Islands, one with 21; Chili, three with 163; Mexico, one with 134; Sydney, Australia, one with 23.

$3000 Fee Paid For Survey of L. A.

LOS ANGELES, July 18, 1849 — The town council of the Pueblo of Los Angeles will pay Lieut. E. O. C. Ord $3000 to make a survey plat of the town.

Lieut. Ord, sent down by Gov. Riley to map Los Angeles after he found that there was none in existence, submitted two propositions to the ayuntamiento. He offered to map the municipal lands and boundaries for $1500 in coin, ten lots and vacant lots totaling 1000 varas (Spanish yards) to be selected in sections of 200 varas each at his choice, or for $3000 in coin.

The latter offer was taken after the president of the council remarked that the time might come when the land which the officer would receive under the alternative plan would be worth $3000 by itself.

Money for the survey is being borrowed from Juan Temple at an interest rate of 1 per cent a month.

——o——

SEVERAL SHIPS STRIKE ON COLUMBIA RIVER BAR

ASTORIA, Ore. Ter., July 11, 1849 — Several ships have struck on the sands while trying to cross the bar at the mouth of the Columbia River.

The French bark Morning Star hit on North Breaker. After pounding for two hours, she was able to force herself into the channel. Other craft assisted her, and after 20 hours of hard work got her into Baker's Bay with four feet of water in her hold.

At almost the same time the brig Belfast grounded, but not over the bar without damage. On the first, the ship Walpole hit the middle sands and lost her false keel, while a Hudson's Bay Co. bark which struck on the same time escaped without damage.

——o——

Gold Seeker A Suicide

SAN FRANCISCO, July 21, 1849 — A man by the name of Walker, who came to California by ship from Baltimore, committed suicide today on the outskirts of town. He put a pistol to his head and fired. No reason for his act is known.

Gold Quartz Vein On Fremont Grant

MARIPOSA, Calif., Aug. 15, 1849 —The first gold quartz vein to be found in California has been discovered on the grant of Col. John Charles Fremont.

Bearing 2 ounces of gold to every 25 pounds of quartz, the vein was 2 feet thick where it was found at the surface and gradually widened as it descended and showed larger particles of gold.

This find is likely to be of extreme importance, because all previous workings of gold have been in placer washings. There is every reason to believe that this vein may be traced many leagues in extent and be found to be of uninterrupted richness. The gold MINES of California are now in reality discovered.

——o——

IDLE SHIPS PILE UP IN HARBOR AT S.F.

SAN FRANCISCO, Aug. 31, 1849 — In the bay of San Francisco at the present time are 61,585 tons of shipping, mostly idle and abandoned by crews who have deserted for the gold mines. This figure is exclusive of some 60 river craft of various kinds and sizes.

Arriving by sea during August were 3806 men and 87 women, of whom 81 were unmarried. While the tide of Forty-Niner immigration rises steadily, there is also a smaller reverse trend. Outbound passengers during the past week totaled 755, to Valparaiso, Mazatlan and Callao.

At the Embarcadero at Sacramento City are tied up 36 square-rigged vessels, many of them serving as stores and warehouses.

——o——

New Alcalde Chosen By Large Majority

SAN FRANCISCO, Aug. 1, 1849— John W. Geary, a colonel in the Mexican War from Pennsylvania who arrived here a few months ago to be postmaster, was almost unanimously chosen alcalde in spirited voting here today.

Geary received 1516 votes out of 1519 ballots cast in the election.

ALL IN READINESS FOR CALIFORNIA CONVENTION

MONTEREY, Calif., Aug. 31, 1849 —Though only a few of the delegates have arrived here, arrangements are completed for the opening of the convention here tomorrow to organize a state, or a territorial, government for California.

Brig. Gen. Bennett Riley, ex-officio governor, has had the second-story chamber of Colton Hall prepared for the sessions. The school ordinarily held there was dismissed so that carpenters could install a railing across the room to divide convention members from spectators. Long tables have been placed for the delegates, and a rostrum built for the convention president.

Elections were successfully held throughout the country on August 1 to choose delegates. Those from the southern regions are likely to be delayed in arriving. The U. S. steam propeller Edith was sent south to transport them here, but the Edith ran aground in the fog on Pt. Concepcion on the down trip, and was wrecked. The brig Col. Fremont is carrying many of the northern delegates from San Francisco, but she has not yet arrived.

This sleepy town of some 1200 is hard put to house the visitors. Native Californians may lodge with friends or relatives, but the only hotel is one "extemporized" for the occasion.

——o——

Firm Asks Permit to Issue Gold Coin

MONTEREY, Calif., Aug. 7, 1849 —Wright and Co. of San Francisco has asked Governor Riley for permission to issue gold coins in $10 and $5 denominations.

The firm offers to give bonds for any amount that its coin will be equal, if not superior, in value to the coin of the United States mint, and asks that it be received in the payment of customs duties.

——o——

SACRAMENTO CITY, Aug. 31, 1849 — Two small steamboats are now plying on the Sacramento river. They were brought in knock-down form on vessels from the Atlantic Coast.

HEAT DRIVES MANY FROM GOLD MINES

SACRAMENTO CITY, Aug. 20, 1849—The extreme August heat has driven many from the gold placer mines, and there has been much sickness. New arrivals, however, take the places of those leaving as more wagon trains arrive by the overland routes day by day.

The most southerly stream now being worked for gold is the Mariposa, about 20 miles southeast of the Merced.

Companies that have turned the river on the North Fork of the American are reported to be taking out from $3000 to $5000 a day. At Beal's Bar the North Fork Dam and Mining Association completed a lateral canal, and in three days made $15,000 in gold. A party is operating on the Middle Fork with a "submarine armor."

At Mormon Island a company is employing quicksilver in extracting the metal from ground that had previously been worked over. With a new type of machine they are averaging $200 a day.

Despite these gains the general average for miners is probably less than an ounce a day. Many are finding gold digging hard and discouraging work.

——o——

Mail Schedules Set For Weekly Service

SAN FRANCISCO, Aug. 23, 1849 —Returning from a tour of the interior of California, R. T. P. Allen, federal postal agent, announced he had made arrangements for weekly mail service to several cities and towns.

The schedules are: Benicia, by water, Charles W. Hayden, postmaster; Sacramento City, by water, Henry E. Robinson, p.m.; Stockton, by water, William Hipkins, p.m.; San Jose, by water, Jacob D. Hoppe, p.m.; Vernon, by water from Sacramento, Gilbert A. Grant, p.m.; Coloma, by horseback from Sacramento, Jacob P. Little, p.m.; Sonoma, by horseback from San Francisco, L. W. Boggs, p.m.

In a recent mail from the East there were 18,000 letters, but Mr. Allen declares that there seems to be little care taken of mails on the steamships, especially on the Atlantic run to Panama.

HUGE SUMS WAGERED IN GAMBLING HOUSES

SAN FRANCISCO, Sept. 15, 1849 —Thousands of dollars in gold dust change hands each day in this boom city's multitudinous gambling houses. Everyone from miner to merchant, laborer to lawyer, appears to spend his evenings at cards.

Faro is the big favorite, and at one table recently $16,000 was wagered in a single bet, with the loser paying cheerfully. A majority of the buildings around Portsmouth Square house gambling games. Some have ten or a dozen tables.

Biggest and most exclusive game of all is at the Parker House. Gamblers who occupy its entire second floor are said to pay an annual rental of $60,000. The whole building nets its owners $125,000 a year in rents. Even a modest, rudely built store building requires $3000 rent a month, paid in advance, in this city of shacks and tents.

————o————

Los Angeles Seeking Help Against Thieves

PUEBLO OF LOS ANGELES, Sept. 29, 1849—Arms to combat "Indian horse thieves and other evil disposed persons" were asked from Gen. Bennett Riley, California governor, by Prefect Stephen C. Foster today.

Foster declared the Los Angeles district is exposed to the depredations of these individuals, "and at present the inhabitants are badly armed, and powder cannot be procured at any price."

For the defense of lives and property of the citizens, Foster asked to have placed at his disposal 100 flintlock muskets, 10,000 musket ball and buckshot cartridges and 500 musket flints.

————o————

New Signal Station For Ship Arrivals

SAN FRANCISCO, Sept. 10, 1849 —An improved station for the signalling of ship arrivals by telegraph is being erected. It will be a two-story house, measuring 25 by 18 feet.

California Writing State Constitution

MONTEREY, Calif., Sept. 30, 1849 —The 48 delegates to the convention here for forming a civil gov-

Glitter of Gold Sometimes False

SACRAMENTO CITY, Sept. 20, 1849 — The thousands of men who have rushed to California's gold regions are finding that there is plenty of gold, but that the hoped-for wealth and rewards are hard to obtain. Unused to the hard labor and the unfamiliar climate, many have been stricken with severe illness during the hot weather. The haul in good yellow dust varies so widely that many find that the costs of food are greater than the gold they can dig.

As a result, many are deserting the diggings in the hope of finding more stable and gainful occupations, and an increasing number is seeking to return to the Atlantic Coast. Their places in the diggings, however, are taken by the ever-flowing horde of immigrants with fresh enthusiasm.

————o————

OFFICER ON SURVEY KILLED BY INDIANS

GOOSE LAKE, Sept. 27, 1849 — Capt. William H. Warner, well known officer of the army's topographical corps, and two other members of his survey party were killed today when they were ambushed by a party of Indians. Captain Warner was struck down by nine arrows.

The party was under orders to explore the Sierra Nevada to ascertain if the mountains might be passable for a railroad.

————o————

CHURCHES ORGANIZED

SAN FRANCISCO, Sept. 4, 1849 —In the midst of the frenzy for gold, religion is not being overlooked by some of the newcomers to California. Several churches have been organized here in the past several weeks. Most recently dedicated church is that of the Baptists. Episcopalians, Presbyterians, Congregationalists and Methodists have also organized, and the Catholics have their church.

ernment for California are nearing the end of their labors.

It will be a constitution to organize California as the 31st state of the United States, if the document is approved by the territory's voters and accepted by Congress. Gen. Bennett Riley, acting governor, has made it known that he will turn over his powers to the new government as soon as it is regularly voted by Californians.

At the very outset it was decided that a state, not a territorial, government would be formed and that slavery would be banned in California. One of the most troublesome issues has been the boundaries of the proposed state. Some suggestions have been made that the eastern line should be located far east of the Sierra Nevada, while the majority appears to believe that these lofty mountains provide a natural boundary.

Most common quality of the delegates is youth. More than half are less than 35, with nine still in their twenties. Some have been Mexican citizens, like Gen. Mariano G. Vallejo and Pablo de la Guerra. One of the delegates is Captain Sutter, at whose sawmill gold was first discovered last year.

It is anticipated that the draft of the constitution will be concluded within the next two weeks, with submission to the people of California to follow in November.

————o————

160 Argonaut Ships Have Come from East

SAN FRANCISCO, Sept. 30, 1849 —Sixty-six ships bringing fortune-seekers from the United States sailed into San Francisco Bay this month, the greatest total since the first Argonaut ships began arriving in June.

In all, 160 ships have come with freight and passengers in the past four months in the great rush for California which began in the East when news of the great gold finds was confirmed there last winter. In addition, it is calculated that there have been 200 or more ships from South American and other foreign ports.

Delegates Approve State Constitution

MONTEREY, Oct. 13, 1849 — A constitution for the State of California was finally approved and signed by the convention delegates today. If the citizens approve it at an election next month, a government will be established under it immediately without waiting for the United States Congress to admit the new state formally.

As the signatures were affixed, the American flag was run up on a flagstaff by the government buildings, and ten guns began booming a salute. First Captain Sutter and then other delegates burst into cheers. At the 31st shot in the salute, there was a shout of "That's for California," which will be the 31st state.

On completion of the signing the delegates proceeded in a body to the house of General Riley, who has been acting as California governor. Captain Sutter spoke in tribute to him.

In reply, the doughty old warrior said: "Gentlemen, I never made a speech in my life. I am a soldier — but I can feel; and I do feel deeply the honor you have this day conferred on me . . . I am satisfied now that the people have done right in selecting delegates to frame a constitution . . . you have framed a constitution worthy of California. And I have no fear for California while her people choose their representatives so wisely."

Under the constitution slavery is absolutely prohibited in California. One of the most ardently disputed questions was the state boundary. Some delegates wanted to set the eastern line beyond the Salt Lake, but it was finally agreed that it should follow generally the line of the Sierra Nevada.

———o———

Delegates Approve Convention Costs

MONTEREY, Oct. 12, 1849 — Expenses of the constitutional convention here have run high. The 48 delegates voted themselves $16 a day and $16 a mile traveling expenses, with $25 for the convention president, Dr. Robert Semple.

Salaries of the secretary and interpreter were $28 a day each, and other officials were paid on a similar scale.

CALIFORNIA MOTTO

MONTEREY, Oct. 13, 1849 — The Greek motto "Eureka" (I have found) has been chosen for the seal of the new state of California. It applies either to the principle involved in the admission of the state or to the success of the miner at work.

Shown on the seal are the goddess Minerva, with a bear by her side; a miner at work, and a Sacramento river scene with the Sierra Nevada in the background.

———o———

BALL CELEBRATES CONVENTION CLOSE

MONTEREY, Oct. 14, 1849 — A gala ball last night celebrated the close of the convention which wrote a constitution for California.

The affair was given by the delegates for the citizens of Monterey who have entertained them so hospitably during the past six weeks. The members raised $1100 by contributions of $25 each.

Colton Hall, scene of the convention, was cleared of tables and decorated with pine boughs. More than 60 ladies were present in their finest attire. But the dress of the men was considerably varied because of the scarcity of gentlemen's proper attire. One man paid as much as $50 for a pair of patent-leather boots for the occasion.

General Riley, California's governor, and his officers, however, were in full-dress uniform. Don Pablo de la Guerra, one of the native California delegates, was floor manager.

Music for the waltzes, contradances and quadrilles was supplied by a band of two violins and two guitars. Supper was served to the guests at midnight. Though some left the dance at 2 a.m., it was still going strong an hour later.

———o———

Oregon Prices

OREGON CITY, Ore., Oct. 15, 1849—Current prices quoted in Oregon are: beef on hoof, 6-8c per lb.; beef in the market, 10-12c; pork, 16-20c; butter, 62c; cheese, 50c; flour, $14 bbl.; wheat, $1.50-$2 per bushel; oats, same; potatoes, $2.50 a bushel; apples, $10 a bushel.

MINING SEASON IS NEARLY OVER

SACRAMENTO, Oct. 30, 1849 — With California's annual rainy season approaching and likely to break almost any day, good gold mining for 1849 is nearly over.

Wise miners are starting to flock toward the towns rather than spend the winter in isolated camps. But there are thousands who intend to keep at thir work as long as possible, especially the most recent arrivals in the year's great Gold Rush from the Atlantic states and foreign countries.

Fears are felt for the safety of those wagon trains from the East which still have the Sierra Nevada to cross. Late comers report oxen and mules are suffering from the lack of grass along the trail. Because of memories of the tragedy that resulted in '46 when the Donner party was trapped by Sierra snow, plans are being discussed for sending relief parties to aid unfortunate travelers who may be similarly caught.

———o———

THEATER COMES TO CALIFORNIA

SAN FRANCISCO, Oct. 29, 1849— Professional theatrical entertainment is now available to California residents with plenty of gold dust in their pockets.

Rowe's Olympic Circus opened here today with the Ethiopian Serenaders, the first public dramatic spectacle in the city. It was greeted enthusiastically by a capacity audience.

Less than two weeks ago the first professional dramatic performance in Sacramento was given in a tent.

———o———

Chinese Ladies Here

SAN FRANCISCO, Oct. 29, 1849— Three Chinese ladies of rank arrived here today on the English bark Helen Stewart.

———o———

SAN FRANCISCO, Oct. 21, 1849— Nathan Spear, 47, well known merchant who has lived in California for many years, died today of heart disease.

California Votes State Constitution

MONTEREY, Nov. 13, 1849—Citizens of California, the Gold Rush land, today went to improvised polls in boom towns and mining camps and ratified a constitution that will make California the 31st state of the United States provided the nation's Congress approves.

The constitution was adopted by a sizable majority, 12,061 votes for and 8111 against. At the same time, Peter H. Burnett was chosen first governor and John McDougal, lieutenant governor. G. W. Wright and Edward Gilbert, the noted editor, were elected to be California's first representatives to Congress.

It was considered an excellent turnout of voters in view of the fact that the rainy season has started in earnest, and made all communication difficult.

Vote totals were: For governor—Burnett, 6783; W. S. Sherwood, 3220; Capt. John A. Sutter, 2201. For lieutenant governor — McDougal, 7374; Richard Roman, 2368.

———o———

Honolulu Ship Fire

HONOLULU, Nov. 9, 1849 — The whaling bark Mercury burned to the water's edge in the harbor here today. The Mercury had been out for 16 months, and had aboard 1200 barrels of oil. Capt. G. Pendleton could not say what caused the fire.

NOTICE

As several persons have been found in the act of stealing and killing my cattle on my rancho, known by the name of Temescal, or San Antonio, opposite the city of San Francisco, I hereby forbid all and every person whatsoever from trespassing on my rancho, either to kill my cattle, or cut wood, or such, will be prosecuted to the fullest extent of the law. Any person having business with me is requested to call at my house, about a mile from the Embarcadero.

—Vicente Peralta.

MINERS GO INTO WINTER QUARTERS

SACRAMENTO CITY, Nov. 29, 1849—Miners in the placer regions have gone into winter quarters, although they are taking advantage of the rising waters in the streams to wash for more gold whenever the weather permits.

Travel to the mining areas has been pretty much cut off by rain and the bad roads. As a result, provisions are rising in price at the mines. On the Feather River flour has been selling at $1.75 a pound.

Much success has been reported on the South Fork of the Feather above Bidwell's Bar. on the American's South Fork the Georgetown diggins are the most famous at the present time. Gold pieces up to 10 and 12 pounds have been found, and the average haul for day laborers is three ounces.

———o———

CARPENTERS ASK FOR HIGHER WAGE

SAN FRANCISCO, Nov. 19, 1849—The journeymen carpenters and master builders are at odds over wages. The carpenters demand an increase in their daily wage from $12, the going scale here for several months, to $16. At first, the master builders resolved not to pay more than $12 "unless as a mere matter of preference," but today offered $13 a day up until December 7, and $14 thereafter.

———o———

Merchants' Exchange

SAN FRANCISCO, Nov. 29, 1849—E. E. Dunbar has opened a Merchants' Exchange and Reading Room on Washington street. The latest shipping and commercial intelligence will be available to subscribers.

———o———

RIVER RUN IS MADE ALL BY DAYLIGHT

SAN FRANCISCO, Nov. 7, 1849—On her first return trip from Sacramento City, the new steamer Senator left that place at 8 a.m. today, and arrived here at 6 p.m., 9 hours' sailing time. It was the first trip ever made between the cities "through by daylight."

Rainy Season Opens Violently

SAN FRANCISCO, Nov. 15, 1849—California's winter rainy season has opened with some of the wildest storms remembered by old residents. In one week more rain has fallen than in November and December of last year.

The rains began November 2. At Sacramento City it was a tremendous storm, accompanied by wind and followed by a flood. The river there has risen nine feet. In San Francisco it rained nearly every day for more than a week, with a fall of more than 12 inches, in level places, on the night of the 6th.

The Sierra Nevada are already covered with snow. The American River near Mormon Island carried away a miners' dam, and caused much damage.

As a result of the rains, San Francisco's streets are in a terrible, muddy condition. The editors of the Alta California demanded that the town council do something about them. They described the streets as a "fathomless sea of mud," with "soundings difficult to obtain."

———o———

Ships Wrecked

SAN FRANCISCO, Nov. 20, 1849—Two ships went aground in San Francisco Bay today.

The American ship Tonquin struck on the sand bar off Washwoman's Bay and was a total loss, although most of her cargo of lumber, stoves and bricks will be saved. Going out the bay, the Hanovarian ship Crown Princess hit on Pt. Diablo. She was pulled off by boats from the U.S.S. Savannah and then towed onto the flats by the steamer Senator.

On the 8th the American bark Rochelle, Capt. John Paty, struck on a ledge of rocks southeast of Pt. Pinos in Monterey harbor. She was a complete wreck.

———o———

CENSUS IN HAWAII

HONOLULU, Nov. 10, 1849 — A census just completed shows that the population of the Hawaiian Islands totals 80,641. Of these 78,854 are natives. There are nine English schools, six high schools and 505 common schools with 18,022 pupils.

IMMIGRANTS SAVED FROM WINTER SNOW

SACRAMENTO CITY, Dec. 12, 1849 — All the immigrants coming to California on the long overland journey across the Rockies are safely over the Sierra Nevada, the last mountain barrier before passes closed for the winter.

To avert a tragedy similar to that which trapped the Donner party three years ago, Maj. Gen. Persifer F. Smith, the army's western commander, has given $100,000 and ordered Major Rucker to purchase animals, provisions, etc., and send out search parties along all known routes.

Rescuers found many immigrants in bad condition as they desperately tried to complete the last stages of the long and difficult journey. John H. Peoples, in charge of one rescue group, saved 19 women in one stranded party and brought them safely to Lassen's Ranch. At one time he had a brush with the Digger Indians.

---o---

WOMEN'S SMILES ADD TO HOLIDAY SCENE

SAN FRANCISCO, Dec. 20, 1849 — The San Francisco scene was considerably brightened for Christmas and the New Year today when no less than 25 females arrived on different vessels. Some are married, but others are still in their spinsterhood.

"Our hopes and anticipations," remarked The Alta California, "are beginning to be realized, and the smiles of lovely women are fast losing their similitude to angels' visits by being few and far between."

---o---

SACRAMENTO'S FIRST ELABORATE WEDDING

SACRAMENTO CITY, Dec. 10, 1849 — In the first truly elaborate and splendid wedding held here, E.J.C. Kewen was married to Miss Fannie White, daughter of Dr. T.J. White, by the Rev. Burcham today.

Rude costumes are usually the mode, even at social gatherings, but this time the men wore dress coats, white vests and kid gloves. There were 20 women dressed with fashionable taste. After the ceremony a band played music for dancing.

FIRST CALIFORNIA SENATORS NAMED

SAN JOSE, Dec. 22, 1849 — This golden land today has a functioning state government, without waiting for the U.S. Congress to approve admission of California to statehood.

Meeting in accordance with the state constitution voted by citizens last month, the legislature selected Col. John C. Fremont, the noted pathfinder of the West, and Dr. William M. Gwin to be United States senators. They will leave soon for Washington, D.C. to press for admission of California to the Union and take their seats in the senate.

Gov. Peter H. Burnett, elected as first governor of the new state, took office today and delivered his message to the legislature.

---o---

SLIM RATIONS IN MINING CAMPS

SACRAMENTO CITY, Dec. 25, 1849 — It was a rather grim Christmas in many of the mining camps because of the bad weather which has been prevailing for the past several weeks.

This has meant shortages of both food and liquor, the latter especially necessary for the miners' celebration, because transportation has been blocked.

There are about 15,000 in the American river mining section. Winter weather has been a barrier to much activity, but a few lucky strikes are still reported. One young man recently made $6000 in 13 days, and bought a store. Being a merchant is easier and more steadily profitable than digging for gold.

---o---

Anti-Foreign Feeling Brings Fatal Attack

STOCKTON, Dec. 26, 1849 — The bitter feeling of American miners toward foreign gold diggers lay behind an affray on the Calaveras today in which two Americans were killed and three wounded.

American miners had ordered the Chilenos to leave the diggings. A writ against this action was issued by the Stockton prefect and turned over to some Chilenos. As a result a party of armed Chilenos attacked an American camp, and a bloody fight resulted.

PRE-CHRISTMAS FIRE RAVAGES CITY OF S.F.

SAN FRANCISCO, Dec. 24, 1849 — A damper was put on San Francisco's celebration of Christmas by the huge fire which today ravaged a large part of the heart of the city. Damage is estimated at over $1,000,000.

The blaze broke out early in the morning in Dennison's Exchange. The flames reached up to the painted cotton ceiling and then ignited the roof.

Although the morning was still, the fire spread rapidly to the famous Parker House next door, and to the United States Restaurant. The crowd which gathered to witness the fire stampeded when a false alarm was spread that powder was stored in the Parker House.

Buildings along Portsmouth Plaza were ordered blown up to halt the fire. Before the flames burned out, they destroyed a great section along Washington street between Kearny and Montgomery.

Despite the disaster, merchants are determined to rebuild. Lumber has risen to $325 per thousand superficial feet because of the sudden demand.

One result of the fire is a plan to organize an independent unpaid axe company, to be supplied by the city with axes, hooks, ladders, rope and a wagon to be prepared to fight future blazes. The great fire hazard lies in use of wood, or wood and canvas for most buildings. If there had been a high wind today, the whole city might have burned to the ground.

---o---

Express Lines Busy

SAN FRANCISCO, Dec. 30, 1849 — Express companies are now active in the carrying of mail and goods to inland cities. Hawley and Co. and Angel, Young and Co. operate to Sacramento, and Todd and Bryan to Stockton. G.R. Bryan has announced plans to establish a triweekly mail to San Jose.

---o---

Steamers Ply Rivers

SAN FRANCISCO, Dec. 1, 1849 — Six steamers are now in service on the Sacramento and San Joaquin rivers. Largest is the Senator, 750 tons, which takes from 100 to 200 passengers between this city and Sacramento on each trip at a fare of $30 each.

THE GOLDEN GAZETTE
1850

LAW ASKED AGAINST BULL, PRIZE FIGHTS

SAN JOSE, Jan. 23, 1850 — The legislature of the new "state" of California has adopted a resolution asking its judiciary committee to bring in a bill to suppress prize fights and bull fights, and all other brutal exhibitions, on the Sabbath, and also consider suppressing bull fights on any occasion.

The cause was the holding of some Sunday bull fights here, and a prize fight for $500 a side in which eyes were gouged out, etc.

A bill was passed today to divide California into 25 counties, San Diego, Los Angeles, Santa Barbara, San Luis Obispo, Monterey, Branciforte, San Francisco, Santa Clara, Mount Diablo, Marin, Sonoma, Solano, Yolo, Mendocino, Sacramento, Coloma, Sutter, Yuba, Butte, Colusa, Shasta, Trinity, Calaveras, Tuolumne and Mariposa.

COAL DISCOVERY REPORTED IN SOUTH

RANCHO DEL CHINO, Near Los Angeles, Jan. 24, 1850—Great quantities of bituminous coal are believed to exist in the hills near here, according to A. S. Welch.

Mr. Welch reports finding vast amounts of bituminous tar, or naphtha, on the surface, changed to a dark-colored substance which mineralogists call petroleum. He thinks there is little doubt that this portends deposits of coal.

RAILROAD URGED

SAN FRANCISCO, Jan. 31, 1850 —A group of San Francisco and Sacramento businessmen meeting here today voted resolutions to take immediate measures toward constructing a railroad from Sacramento to a central point in the mining districts.

EMIGRANT PARTIES SUFFER HARDSHIPS

LOS ANGELES, Jan. 15, 1850— Reports drifted into this pueblo that several parties of overland immigrants have run into serious troubles and hardships in a desert valley northeast of here.

Too late to cross the Sierra Nevada before the winter snows, these groups turned south from Salt Lake to come here by the old Spanish trail. Efforts to follow a reported short-cut brought near-starvation and other difficulties, not the least being Indians. It is hoped that this will not turn out to be "Death Valley" for many of them.

CITY REBUILDING

SAN FRANCISCO, Jan. 31, 1850 —New buildings are fast rising in the area burned over by the great Christmas Eve fire.

The most striking is a three-story building on Washington street near Montgomery which will have the new Theatre Nacionale on its second story. Burgoyne & Co. are completing a pretty brick building, with stuccoed front, on the Washington-Montgomery corner, and another is also going up close by. There also are many new iron buildings and warehouses.

Dennison's Exchange, destroyed in the fire, was reopened in a new building, much superior to the old, in less than two weeks.

Sacramento City Hit By Disastrous Flood

SACRAMENTO CITY, Jan. 14, 1850 — This city has just gone through several days of dire disaster from the overflowing river. Several lives have been lost—how many is not known—and great damage done.

On the night of the 8th there was a great gale, accompanied by heavy rain. The next day the Sacramento River began to overflow. By the 10th the water had spread over a great part of the city. People and animals tried to reach higher ground.

Tents, sheds and buildings were swept away as the streets became rapid rivers, rising as high as the second stories of buildings. A new brick building at J and Third streets collapsed.

Hundreds of boats plied the streets, and they rented for as high as $30 an hour to frantic residents. Two men drowned in the streets when they fell out of boats. Many persons are homeless and completely destitute.

On an average the water rose six feet in the city, while the river was up 25 to 30 feet. Lumber is now selling for $220 to $225 a thousand feet for rebuilding.

S. F. Water Lots Sold

SAN FRANCISCO, Jan. 3, 1850— A total of 434 water lots were sold by the municipal authorities in a brisk auction today. The lots brought $635,130, all to be paid up in nine months.

CHINESE RESTAURANT

SAN FRANCISCO, Jan. 4, 1850— A Chinese restaurant is operated on Jackson street by Jon-Ling, a Chinese. The celestial sent retainers around to the newspaper offices with a fancy-decorated cake. And very good, too.

Congress Fight Likely Over California Plea

WASHINGTON, D. C., Feb. 28, 1850—A bitter congressional fight is in prospect between the northern and southern states over California's application to be admitted as the Thirty-first State of the United States.

Action on the constitution approved by the residents of California last November was delayed again today, and it appeared likely there would be many sharp debates before the matter is put to a vote. Heart of the question is that the citizens of the golden land of the Pacific Coast provided for the exclusion of slavery. Her admission would upset the balance in Congress between the slave and free states. This arouses the fears of most southern representatives.

This issue looms as one of the most delicate and important problems facing the present session. A few weeks ago Henry Clay introduced a compromise resolution that California ought to be made a state without any restriction on the slave question, but Southerners were opposed.

On the 13th of this month President Taylor officially forwarded to Congress copies of the California constitution given to him by William M. Gwin, who has been chosen one of the senators-elect of that land should it be made a state. The constitution specifically includes the slavery ban.

Today Congressman Bell of Tennessee urged in resolutions that California be admitted immediately as a state. Though a Southerner and not in accord with the exclusion of slavery, he said this point should be conceded. He met with no support from his colleagues.

---o---

Theatre Opening Draws Full House

SAN FRANCISCO, Feb. 4, 1850—With a capacity audience in attendance the Olympic Amphitheatre opened tonight for a dramatic campaign here.

Many of the city's most respectable families were present to see Mr. Carleton portray Othello. The farce "Bachelor's Buttons" was also presented on the program.

---o---

NEW TOWN PROSPERS

MARYSVILLE, Feb. 15, 1850—This town at the junction of the Feather and Yuba rivers is prospering. It now has 500 inhabitants, with a floating population of perhaps 1,000, and lots are selling fast.

Stephen J. Field, recently named alcalde, has taken prompt steps to suppress cattle stealing.

Formerly known as Yubaville, this town is acquiring a new name in honor of the wife of the founder, Charles Covillaud. She is the former Mary Murphy, a member of the party that met with disaster in trying to cross the Sierra four years ago. It is expected that soon there will be regular communication with Sacramento by steamer and other boats.

---o---

SAN FRANCISCO, Feb. 17, 1850—Twenty-six square-rigged vessels arrived in port today. Sixteen of these were from the United States.

Huge Gold Nugget Found at Diggings

STOCKTON, Feb. 15, 1850—A 23-pound lump of gold is causing a sensation here. It was found near Wood's Dry Diggings between the Stanislaus and Tuolumne rivers. As if that were not enough, reports are heard of the existence of a 93-pound lump.

---o---

RIVER LEVEES PLANNED

SACRAMENTO, Feb. 2, 1850—A total fund of $200,000 is pledged for the construction of river levees to guard Sacramento City from such floods as that which caused great devastation and loss here last month. Both citizens and the authorities are cooperating in flood protection plans.

---o---

WOOLLY KEARNEY WINS

SAN FRANCISCO, Feb. 16, 1850—A prize fight was held on Goat Island this afternoon before 200 spectators. The match was for $100 a side.

The battle was between Woolly Kearney of New York and a "Slasher" from Sydney. It lasted for 25 rounds, with Kearney, although 30 pounds lighter, adjudged the victor.

New Packet Line Headed by Larkin

SAN FRANCISCO, Feb. 21, 1850—With $700,000 in capital subscribed in two weeks, the California Steam Packet Company has been organized here as an independent steamship line to compete with the Pacific Mail steamers.

Thomas O. Larkin, formerly the American consul to California during the Mexican regime, has been named president of the company. He will soon go to the United States to buy or build four steamers of about 2,000 tons each.

---o---

Squatters Evicted From Rincon Hill

SAN FRANCISCO, Feb. 28, 1850—In a wild melee in which the force of United States soldiery was used, squatters were thrown off Rincon Hill today.

Most of the hill lies within a government land reserve, and was leased to Theodore Shillaber. The land, however, had been thickly occupied by squatters from Sydney, Australia.

As a result, a company of 20 soldiers was marched to the hill and evicted the squatters. All the tents and shanties erected on the government land were demolished as well.

Squatterism is a problem in California now.

---o---

MORMONS ASK ABOUT JOINING CALIFORNIA

SAN JOSE, Feb. 20, 1850—The Mormons who have established a residence in the region of the Great Salt Lake indicate they might like to join the state of California.

Gov. Peter Burnett has presented to the California legislature, in session here, an address from the citizens of Deseret asking that California hold a new constitutional convention to allow the people of this state to vote on the proposition to unite Deseret and California.

The petition was presented to the governor by John Wilson and Amasa Lyman.

Indians are Attacked By White Horsemen

SONOMA, March 4, 1850—A campaign of extermination against Indians in the Napa Valley is causing much excitement here.

The trouble has arisen since the killing of Andrew Kelsey by Indians near Clear Lake. A party of more than two score horsemen, led by a kinsman, Samuel Kelsey, organized to wipe out the Indians from the valley.

First, the group proceeded to Yount's Rancho and chased 100 Indians into the mountains. Then the men went to Fowler's ranch and shot 15 Indians. From there they went on to Santa Rosa and a Sonoma ranch where two Indian servants were killed.

Peaceful citizens of the valley are much alarmed, and the Indians themselves are terrified. It is feared the Indians who have fled to the mountains will in return kill every white man they can reach.

MANY GOLD CAMPS FOUNDED IN WINTER

SACRAMENTO CITY, March 15, 1850—Many new settlements have sprung up in the Sacramento gold mining district during the winter.

Among the prominent communities are Spanish Bar, Georgetown, Hangtown (now Placerville), Kelsey's Diggings, Weberville, Auburn and Greenwood Valley. Road communication is bad, but the population has increased greatly. Most of the miners are satisfied with their winter's haul.

Stockton Has Newspaper

STOCKTON, March 16, 1850—The first newspaper to be issued in the San Joaquin Valley became a reality today with the publication of the first copy of the Stockton Times, which is to be a weekly.

This town is stirring with miners going to the southern gold mines. Captain Charles M. Weber, founder of the town, has built a bridge over the slough.

On display here, the famous Sonorian lump of gold, weighing 22 pounds, 6 ounces, has been creating a sensation. It was found at Sonora by three Mexicans, who have squandered all they gained in riotous living.

Gold at Los Angeles

LOS ANGELES, March 1, 1850—There seems to be every prospect that gold has been found near here. Texans here are fitting out teams, and 13 groups have already started for the reported scene.

A piece of gold and quartz weighnig 8 pounds, 4 ounces, was shown at the American Hotel kept by Captain Robert Haley.

Panama Steamer Sails with Huge Gold Cargo

SAN FRANCISCO, March 1, 1850 — The steamer Oregon, Captain Patterson commanding, sailed for Panama today with 250 passengers and $1,117,836.27 in gold dust. The size of the gold cargo was surprising, as the money market has been tight for several weeks. It makes matters look bright for business this year.

Fast Time Made On Business With East

SAN FRANCISCO, March 1, 1850 — Business transactions with the United States are being completed at unusually rapid intervals these days.

A commission house of San Francisco and New York received on the Oregon, February 21, goods shipped from New York January 17. These goods have been sold at good profit, and the returns were sent back by the same steamer and will be in New York by April 10.

For merchandise to travel 6000 miles to market and the returns, in gold, to be back in 80 days requires just the energies which men of business have here.

SONORA IS BOOMING AS MINING CENTER

SONORA, March 30, 1850—Almost like magic a town has sprung up here. Sonora today is the depot for all the mining region lying between the Tuolumne and Stanislaus rivers.

Saloons and gambling halls are flourishing in the wake of the rich business with miners, and have brought attendant excitement. Only last Sunday night a man named Miles O'Connor drew a pistol to shoot some persons he thought had insulted him. But he missed his aim, and killed two passersby. Miles then fled, and so far has not been apprehended.

The gold mine riches are the real thing. At Mariposa over $10,000 has been reported taken out of a single hole only eight by sixteen feet.

GRAND BALL HELD at HALL OF GUARDS

SAN FRANCISCO, March 13, 1850—The most elaborate social event in the history of this town was held tonight in the hall of the First California Guards. The ball was a grand event. The Board of Managers sent invitations to the most distinguished citizens of this and the state's other principal cities. Despite the rain, about 50 members of the fair sex were present, and a sumptuous feast was served.

MISSION POPULAR AS SUNDAY RESORT

SAN FRANCISCO, March 4, 1850—The Mission Dolores district a few miles from the center of town is proving to be quite a place of resort lately, and is much frequented by parties of pleasure, especially on Sundays.

A line of omnibuses has been established, and sail and row boats ply between this town and the mission for those wishing to exchange the noise of the city for the quietude and green shades of the mission.

Over 36 inches of rain fell in Sacramento during the just-ended rainy season.

CONGRESS STUDIES CALIFORNIA PLEA

WASHINGTON, D. C., April 18, 1850 — After weeks of intermittent wrangling, the Senate today finally voted for a definite study of the request of California for admission to the United States as the 31st state of the union.

A committee of 13 headed by the famous Henry Clay was named to investigate and report. However, it seems probable that there is still a long and stormy road ahead for the California application because of the bitter political differences dividing Congress.

In general, members from the southern states oppose the admission of California under the free state constitution that it adopted last fall because it would upset the present balance in the Senate between free and slave states.

Opponents of admission have been presenting various arguments: such as, that the constitution was adopted illegally, that the proposed state takes in too large an area, that the proportion of foreigners in its population is too great, that California should be given a territorial government at the present time.

A leader in the fight against statehood is Senator Foote of Mississippi, while Senator Benton of Missouri, father-in-law of Col. John C. Fremont, senator-elect from California, is in the forefront of California's advocates. What to do about California is one of the major issues of the present session.

———o———

Vallejo Offers Sites for Capital

SAN JOSE, April 9, 1850 — Gen. Mariano G. Vallejo today lavishly offered to give the new state of California a capitol.

A native of this land and one of the greatest leaders and land-holders from Spanish and Mexican days, General Vallejo proposed to the state legislature to devote some of his lands on the Strait of Carquinez and the Napa river as a permanent location for the capital. He would lay out a city, and call it Eureka.

Included in Vallejo's generous offer are acreage for the capitol and the governor's house, state university, etc., and large sums for the necessary buildings, such as $125,000 for a capitol and $10,000 for its furnishings.

Machine Used for Gold Dredging

SACRAMENTO, April 15, 1850 — American ingenuity, plus the universal desire to get more gold faster, is bringing about the introduction of a new "machine" for washing gold in the placer mining areas.

It is the "Long Tom," a box about 10 or 12 feet long and open at the top and ends. Across the bottom are placed bars, called riffles. A stream of water is passed through the box, and dust-bearing dirt is shoveled into it. The heavier gold particles sink to the bottom, and are caught by the riffles.

More of the finer bits of gold are lost by this process, but it offers the great advantage over the popular cradle of permitting the speedy washing of larger quantities of earth continuously by a group of miners working together. As a result, it is being popularly adopted in the gold region although the miner's pan and the cradle are still the standbys of prospectors and diggers who prefer to work alone.

———o———

SEVEN MEN DROWN

MARE ISLAND, April 5, 1850 — Seven men from the ship Argonaut of Boston, en route to the gold mines, drowned today in Suisun Bay.

The group was sailing in the ship's yawl. When it was opposite Mare Island, the wind capsized the boat, and all were drowned. The men had only recently arrived in California.

———o———

BATHING FACILITIES MADE AVAILABLE

SAN FRANCISCO, April 11, 1850 — At last this city has a place where the luxury of a bath can be enjoyed to perfection.

Messrs. Mygatt, Bryant & Co. have opened up a neat, convenient and comfortable bathing house in Maiden Lane, a few doors from Washington st.

———o———

Cities Incorporated

SAN JOSE, April 5, 1850 — The legislature today finally passed an act for incorporating the city of San Francisco. Other cities of California, including Sacramento, have already been incorporated.

STEAMER BRINGS RECORD NUMBER

SAN FRANCISCO, April 15, 1850 — The new steamer Tennessee yesterday brought from Panama the largest number of immigrants ever to arrive at this port in one vessel. She carried 551 passengers. When she left Panama, there were about 800 more persons awaiting transportation to California.

In the year ending today California's Gold Rush has brought through the port of San Francisco a total of 60,744 men and 1979 women by 695 American and 418 foreign ships. Now operating out of here are 57 river craft, the largest of nearly 700 tons and the smallest 6 tons.

———o———

S. F. TOWN HALL IS BOUGHT FOR $150,000

SAN FRANCISCO, April 1, 1850 — The town council today voted to buy the Graham House at Pacific and Kearny streets for a town hall for the sum of $150,000.

The building measures 100 by 64 feet and is four stories high with a metallic roof. The sellers will take the present town hall in for $50,000 of the price. Object of the move is to get all the town offices and courts under one roof and to save rent. Room for the county court alone would cost $500 a month.

———o———

CHINESE ARRIVE

SAN FRANCISCO, April 19, 1850 — Between 20 and 30 Chinese arrived in California today by the British brig Warlock from Hong Kong.

They were objects of much interest as they proceeded in double file through Montgomery street in their singular costums, broad-leafed hats and antique umbrellas.

———o———

SAN FRANCISCO, April 1, 1850 — The muddy condition of the streets has modified female costumes. Some wear heavy boots, and bona fide pantaloons have been detected peeping out from under flowing skirts.

Industry Flourishes

SAN FRANCISCO, May 3, 1850—The hills and sand dunes in the Happy Valley Section are being removed rapidly as grading and house building is extended even to the extreme end of Rincon Point. Machine shops, blacksmiths, wheelwrights, boiler makers and ship builders flourish in the area.

Now building and on the stocks are eight sailing vessels ranging from 30 to 100 tons. Constructed in little more than two weeks for the Sacramento river trade, a steamer 120 feet long is near launching. The keel of another steamer for the Stockton trade is being laid, and an iron steamer of 100 tons is under way. At anchor and receiving their finishing touches are four other steamers.

Seek State Capitol

SACRAMENTO, May 3, 1850 — Sacramento citizens today launched a move to secure the California state capitol for this city. They will take collections and donations of real estate to make an offer of a site.

Gold in Oregon!

ST. HELEN'S, Ore., May 29 — Reports of a gold discovery near the Wallah - Wallah are causing great excitement. Many Portland merchants left for that region after a parcel of sand brought in by Indians showed 50 per cent gold. There are reports also of abundant gold on the Rogue's River.

SUTTER'S MILL, May 29, 1850—Receipts from tolls average $250 a day for the new bridge erected across the South Fork above here by J. T. Little. The bridge cost him $20,000.

FOREIGN MINERS PROTEST TAX

SONORA, May 25, 1850—A critical situation has developed here between foreigners and Americans as a result of the special tax levied against foreign gold miners.

The Mexican, French and Chilean population of the town bitterly protested the tax, and it was feared that the situation would develop into a fight with Americans. In retaliation, several hundred armed Americans came into town for a time. Fortunately, there was no general affray. Only one man was killed, a Mexican who made an attempt on the life of Sheriff Work.

5,000 SEEK GOLD

COLUMBIA, May 15, 1850—This new town about five miles above Sonora already has 5000 people as a result of the rich gold placer located here. The placer has been dug to a depth of 62 feet, and is believed to be not less than three miles square.

There are glowing accounts of prospects all through the Southern mines, and much movement into placers on the Calaveras. The great undertakings in damming the Tuolumne are beginning to pay off.

Three men are reported to have taken $30,000 out of one hole in the diggings near here in three weeks. One lump weighed five pounds.

Many thousands of Mexicans are reported on the road toward the gold mines.

San Francisco Fire

SAN FRANCISCO, May 4, 1850—A spectacular early morning fire today burned over a large portion of the city's main section and caused losses estimated at between three and five million dollars.

It is suspected that incendiarism was the cause of the fire, and a reward of $10,000 has been posted.

Big Gold Shipment

SAN FRANCISCO, May 1, 1850—The Panama sails today with $1,500,156 in gold dust and 150 passengers. Over 3½ millions of gold have been shipped in the last three steamers from this port. The British steamship Driver carried $200,000 to Valparaiso.

INDIAN TROUBLE
MANY ARE SLAIN

SONOMA, May 28, 1850 — Word was received here today of the killing of a large body of Clear Lake Indians by an expedition from the United States garrisons at Sonoma and Benicia.

The Indians had been driven to the mountains, and subsequently made raids from them. As a result of complaints, 75 soldiers were dispatched. They came upon a body of 200 to 300 Indians at the lake. The soldiers surrounded the aborigines and fired on them—men, women and children—as they attempted to escape.

A treaty has been made in an attempt to end Indian troubles in the gold regions. Maj. Gen. Thomas J. Green of the California militia and the Indian chiefs Weema, Buckler and Poollei signed the treaty at Kearney, Yuba County, to keep the peace, ensure justice to the Indians and prevent depredations on both sides.

This follows several clashes between Indians and miners in the gold area. Recently near Kelly's Bar on the North Fork a search group killed seven Indians after the latter robbed a wagon party. At Barnes' Bar the Indians killed one miner in his tent at night and wounded another.

At least two other whites have been killed by Indian robbers, and others wounded. Near Auburn 25 Indians bodies were found, among them a woman and child. An Auburn party returned with several scalps.

It has been believed that some renegade white men have been among the Indians and inciting them.

Congress Committee Favors Statehood

WASHINGTON, D.C., May 8, 1850—The special senatorial committee headed by Henry Clay today submitted a majority report favoring the admissin of California to the Union as a state.

Some question was raised as to the great size of the proposed state of California as provided in the constitution its people adopted by vote last fall, but the committee favored accepting the boundaries laid down.

Greatest Fire Yet In San Francisco

SAN FRANCISCO, June 14, 1850 —This city was swept again today by the third great fire in six months, and this was the most serious yet, with damage mounting to $5,000,000. High winds fanned the flames.

Starting at 8 o'clock this morning in the Sacramento Bakery from a defect in the chimney, it quickly burned the Merchants' Hotel and spread along Sacramento, Clay and California streets to the water's edge. Much valuable property between Montgomery street and the bay front was dstroyed. Sam Brannan lost $50,000 or more, and Mellus, Howard & Co., prominent mercantile firm, suffered a $100,000 loss.

In the Sacramento Building a liquor cask, in which had been placed the body of a man awaiting shipment East for burial, burned, leaving the corpse exposed to view.

The ravaging fires which this city has experienced make it obvious that preventive steps must be taken. San Francisco needs an efficient fire department, and it is hoped that one of the first items of business for the board of aldermen will be the construction of reservoirs. Buildings of a more substantial nature are required. An ordinance is proposed to permit no wooden structures more than 15 feet high.

Gold Quartz Is Used For Washington Monument

SAN FRANCISCO, June 1, 1850 —California's gift to the Washington Monument to be erected in the nation's capital, a block of gold-bearing quartz weighing 125 pounds, was shipped today on the steamer Oregon.

The rock, taken from Mariposa Diggins near Fremont's mines, will be delivered to the Washington Monument Society for placement in the structure when it is commenced.

John Bidwell and H. A. Schoolcraft were appointed by Gov. Peter H. Burnett to accompany the block to Washington and make the presentation.

———o———

OREGON CITY, June 15, 1850—Governor Lane of Oregon Territory has resigned his office. He plans a trip to the Umpqua river in search of gold.

GOLD FIND HOAX

MARYSVILLE, June 10, 1850 — Great excitement was caused in all the towns along the Sacramento river by the reports of terrific gold finds at Gold Lake, which was variously reported to be 100 to 200 miles distant in the mountains.

Hundreds of men took up the journey there, and the prices of provisions and mules took a terrific jump, with supplies scarce. The story of the great discovery was told by two or three men who said they had been to Gold Lake. Everybody believed it for a time, but it was found to be complete humbug.

———o———

PEDDLER ATTACKED BY TWO MEXICANS

MONTEREY, June 2, 1850 — An elderly Englishman, who has been peddling jewelry in this neighborhood, is near death after he was attacked on the Salinas plains.

The assault was perpetrated by two Mexicans, who lassoed the Englishman, dragged him for several hundred yards, shot him three times and stabbed him in several places. After he was discovered unconscious and bleeding by travelers, he was taken to the ranch of Senor Thomas Blanco.

———o———

GRIZZLY BEAR CAUGHT

SAN FRANCISCO, June 22, 1850 —A grizzly bear was caught by lasso today near the Mission Dolores. The bear weighed 500 pounds, and was young and tender. It was bought by the proprietor of Fulton Market, the meat finding a ready sale at 50 cents a pound.

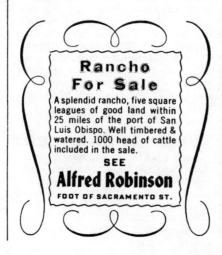

Rancho For Sale

A splendid rancho, five square leagues of good land within 25 miles of the port of San Luis Obispo. Well timbered & watered. 1000 head of cattle included in the sale.

SEE

Alfred Robinson

FOOT OF SACRAMENTO ST.

SQUATTERS EVICTED AT SACRAMENTO CITY

SACRAMENTO CITY, June 24, 1850—Drastic action was taken today aganist some of the squatters who have been locating on property here under the claim that the original title to the land held by Captain Sutter was not valid.

Twenty citizens went to the levee and helped Sam Brannan remove a building that had been erected on his lot, and also a canvas tenement built by "settlers." A large crowd gathered, but there was no serious outbreak of trouble although feeling ran high.

———o———

The First Overland Emigrants Arrive

WEAVERVILLE, June 8, 1850— A party of 40, the first overland emigrants of 1850, arrived here today from Missouri by the Carson route.

They left Independence, Mo., on April 1, and traveled by pack mules. Soon after their start they passed some 600 teams, bound for California, which had begun the journey before them. In the mountains they found the snow to be from 15 to 30 feet deep.

———o———

BANDITS ACTIVE

STOCKTON, June 17, 1850 — Highway robberies are becoming frequent on the roads between here and the mining district.

A Frenchman had his horse shot under him and he was beaten and robbed of $2800. Mr. Dent of Knight's Ferry and another man found a dying miner who had been robbed of a large amount of gold.

———o———

487 STEAMER PASSENGERS

SAN FRANCISCO, June 20, 1850 —A total of 487 passengers, including 26 ladies, was brought here today by the steamer Tennessee from Panama. More than 2000 persons were waiting for passage at the Isthmus when she left.

———o———

River Steamers Collide

BENICIA, June 11, 1850 — The river steamer McKim sank today after a collision with the steamer Gold Hunter three miles below the Straits of Carquinez near here.

JULY 4 CELEBRATED IN GRAND STYLE

SAN FRANCISCO, July 4, 1850—Independence Day was celebrated with a will in California.

Here, the ship Carolina brought down from Oregon as a present to San Francisco a timber 111 feet long, a foot in diameter at the base and 3 inches at the top, to serve as a Liberty Pole. Protection Fire Company No. 2, first of the new companies to make a public demonstration in uniform, had the honor of putting up the pole in the Plaza. They wore red shirts, glazed caps and uniform pantaloons.

Firing of cannons began last night in celebration. Two fire companies were out testing their machines, and there was a free fight at Clark's Point between 40 and 50 men which lasted until broken up by police. Tonight the building of the California Guards and other structures were brightly illuminated. During the day the Rev. William Taylor delivered the July 4 oration, and salutes were fired.

At San Jose a parade honored the day, with 500 people participating. In the line of march were 13 young ladies, clad in blue spensers and white skirts and mounted on horses, who represented the 13 original states.

New Steam Press

SAN FRANCISCO, July 4, 1850— The Daily Alta California today opened a new era in California journalism by printing its papers on a new steam press, brought from the States and just installed.

CAPT. SUTTER DEEDS AWAY HIS LANDS

SACRAMENTO, July 20, 1850 — The famous Capt. John A. Sutter today published a deed transferring all his lands, which embraced many thousands of acres including this city, with the exception of his present home at Hock Farm, to Messrs. Robinson, Fowler, Eugene Gillespie and John McDougal.

The action was taken by Captain Sutter to rid himself of the trouble of defending his titles against squatters, etc. He is to be paid a sixth of the net proceeds of all properties, and $6000 cash down.

His son, John A. Sutter, Jr., has also sold his interests to Messrs. Brannan, Bruce, Graham and Wetzlar for $125,000 and left the country.

Two Finders Exhibit Huge Gold Nugget

SACRAMENTO, July 15, 1850—A 30-pound lump of quartz containing 23 pounds of pure gold, believed to be the largest yet found in California, is being displayed here.

It was dug from a ravine at Jim Crow Diggings near the Yuba River by William H. Julius of New York City and John Grives of New Orleans. Julius had been a year in the diggings and had not averaged over $10 a day previously. The find was made in a deserted hole the two men had taken over.

Julius and Grives refused an offer of $10,000 for it at Marysville. Now they are showing it at Mc-Knight's Sutter Hotel for 50 cents a head. They plan to take it to the States and make a fortune showing it there.

---o---

ICE $1 A POUND!

SACRAMENTO, July 14, 1850 — Another cargo of the inestimable luxury, ice, has just reached town. Mr. Pickett brought in 2000 pounds, and it was immediately purchased by Mr. Keith of The Empire for $2000. Creams, cobblers and juleps are the order of the day.

---o---

Many Ships on River

SACRAMENTO, July 15, 1850— Plying between Sacramento and San Francisco now are 50 schooners and sloops totaling 577 tons and 16 steamers of 2269 tonnage. There are 6628 tons of storeships here.

---o---

Will California Be Granted Admission?

SAN FRANCISCO, July 30, 1850 — Californians are beginning to despair of favorable action on this territory's application for admission to the Union as a state.

Each steamer that comes in brings only word of more debate in Congress. After several months no vote has been taken, and opponents of the move bring up new arguments. Are we ever going to get our just due?

Violence Reported In Gold Mining Regions
Many Murders, Robberies

STOCKTON, July 6, 1850 -- A great wave of violence, some of it stemming from the resentment of Americans against foreign miners, is reported throughout the southern gold mining district. Many murders and robberies have occurred recently.

A guerrilla party, headed by a famous Mexican robber, is rumored to have headquarters in the mountains. It is generally unsafe to travel, and every man is armed with revolver and knife.

Among known murders are the following. Two men were found naked, with their throats cut, at Chinese Diggings. Two Mexicans were shot at Jamestown. One man was killed with lances at Montezuma Tent and two others critically wounded. Two men were found dead and robbed near Sonora.

Near Knight's Ferry a Mr. Ford, of Massachusetts, was found killed in his tent by a hatchet. The missing partner of Mr. Morgan, who has a trading tent on the banks of the Mercedes, was found floating in the river and robbed of $2500. Another man was killed, and his partner badly wounded by three Mexicans. Three Chilenos murdered another American.

In addition, Indian trouble has arisen on the Tuolumne. Seizure of the squaw of an Indian chief by an American led to a bloody fight in which three Americans were shot.

---o---

Overland Parties Facing Hardships

SACRAMENTO, July 23, 1850 — Reports are received here that many immigrants traveling by the overland route to California are in much distress.

It is estimated that between 80,000 and 100,000 have started across the plains, and there are stories that 15 to 20 have died on the road from starvation, that their animals are weakened from the journey and lack of food and that grasses along the trail have given out. Flour is reported selling for $2 a pound at Carson River.

Public-spirited citizens are attempting to organize relief measures.

Final Vote Near On Calif. Statehood

WASHINGTON, D. C., Aug. 20, 1850—Favorably voted by the Senate over the opposition of southern senators, the bill to make California the 31st state of the Union is expected to get final action in the House within the next two weeks.

Although Senator Davis of Mississippi bitterly fought California statehood and declared the bill subversive to the Constitution, it passed in the Senate by a vote of 34 to 28.

Even after this action, however, the South continued its opposition. Ten senators submitted a signed protest to the admission bill on the basis that it excluded the slave-holding states from the territory to be made into a state. A good deal of excitement has arisen in Alabama and other southern states over the California bill, and it has even been said Georgia will secede if it passes the House.

Good Prices for Lots

SAN FRANCISCO, Aug. 1, 1850 —Sales of city lots are drawing fine prices. Six lots in the square bounded by Montgomery, Pacific, Jackson and Sansome streets brought a total of $39,400. Most of the lots measured 20 by 60 feet. Total sales today totaled $109,955.

Brig Lost on Reef

SAN FRANCISCO, Aug. 5, 1850— The brig Frolic of Boston has been lost on a reef about 60 miles above Fort Ross, according to word reaching here today. Six of her crew drowned. The vessel was on her way here from China with $150,000 in goods. She was adjudged to be about 50 miles from land when she hit the reef.

CHINESE GIVEN WELCOME

SAN FRANCISCO, Aug. 28, 1850 — Chinese residents of this city were welcomed today at a ceremony in Portsmouth Square at which Mayor John W. Geary and a committee presented them with tracts, papers and books printed in Chinese. The Chinese marched in procession clad in their native costume, and fine addresses were given on both sides.

Sacramento Torn By Squatter Riots

California Pioneers Organize Society

SAN FRANCISCO, Aug. 20, 1850 — The Society of California Pioneers has been organized by prominent men of the community who were early arrivals in this golden land.

Eligible as first-class members are all who lived in California prior to January 1, 1849; and as second-class members, citizens of the old states who arrived before January 1 of this year. William D. M. Howard, a leading merchant, is president; vice presidents are Sam Brannan, Jacob R. Snyder and G. Frank Lemon.

FAMOUS PUGILIST FINED

SAN FRANCISCO, Aug. 5, 1850 — Tom Hyer, the famous pugilist recently arrived here, was fined $50 today for drunk and disorderly conduct in one of the city's well-known resorts.

Sentence was passed despite Hyer's attorney's claim that "it was not unusual for gentlemen to drive their horses into bar rooms; everybody does so on first arriving in this city. For the first week or two they are all in a sort of mist. They want to see the elephant, and so they mount a horse and hunt him out."

One witness, however, reported, "Hyer was high and got higher and higher."

SACRAMENTO CITY, Aug. 17, 1850 — This city has just gone through a period of rioting, arising from the land title controversies, in which several men have been killed.

The trouble began after the courts had upheld the claims of those who hold titles from Capt. John A. Sutter. Eviction was resisted by the squatters, and on the 13th several were arrested for resisting the law. Two of those arrested were held on board the prison brig anchored at the river front.

On the next day, the 14th, armed squatters marched on the brig to release their friends and firing broke out. In the melee City Assessor Woodland and Mahloney, leader of the squatters, were killed, and Mayor Harden Bigelow and several others on both sides were wounded.

At Brighton, about six miles south, Sheriff Joseph McKinney and three squatters were killed in another outbreak. Several of the posse were also wounded in the fight, in which some prisoners were taken.

A plea for help in preserving the peace was hastily dispatched to Mayor Geary of San Francisco. The California Guard and Protection Fire Company No. 2, both well armed, quickly came up the river on the steamer Senator. By the time of their arrival, however, things had quieted down.

At the height of the trouble Lt. Gov. John McDougal went down on a steamer to Benicia to get a supply of arms from the army.

New Wharf in S. F.

SAN FRANCISCO, Aug. 1, 1850 —A new wharf at the foot of Battery street is opened for business.

CHOLERA RAVAGES SHIP'S PASSENGERS

PANAMA, Aug. 21, 1850 — The steamer Panama arrived here today from San Francisco with nearly 50 of her passengers and crew dead from cholera. The dread disease broke out on the 17th shortly after the ship had made a stopover at Acapulco. In one horrible night it claimed 12 victims.

When she left San Francisco, the Panama carried 240 passengers and $2,300,000 in gold.

GREAT TUNNEL DUG FOR GOLD

COLOMA, Sept. 15, 1850 — A great tunnel designed to lay bare the gold sands of a section of the South Fork of the American river is nearing completion.

The tunnel, which has caused great interest in all the mountain gold district, will turn the river from its present course if successful. It is being dug through solid granite six feet high and seven feet wide, and will be 700 feet long. Its greatest depth underground is some 60 feet.

About 40 workmen have been digging day and night since July. J.T. Little, prominent merchant, has been financing the undertaking with supplies and equipment and giving shares to the workers. It is reported that as high as $10,000 has been offered for a share, so sure are many of the tunnel's success. Total cost is estimated at $40,000.

The tunnel will dry up three-quarters of a mile of the river. The location is not far from the site of the 1848 gold discovery.

———o———

Financial Panic Brings Run on S. F. Banks

SAN FRANCISCO, Sept. 14, 1850 — The failure of two or three businesses at Sacramento has caused a run on several San Francisco banks that lasted for several days. But today the panic seems to have run its course, with only the bank of Henry M. Naglee closed.

The first run commenced on James King of William, but then moved to Burgoyne & Co. and Naglee. After one heavy day, Mr. Naglee's doors remained closed, but the other houses were able to open. For a time great crowds massed around the various banks seeking to withdraw their money.

———o———

Jail Break At L.A.

LOS ANGELES, Sept. 23, 1850 — Because of the insecurity of the building prisoners were able to break out of the jail here. Two murderers and three others made good their escape. The jail is in a structure built by United States troops during the Mexican War and used as a guard house.

CALIFORNIA FINALLY BECOMES 31st STATE

WASHINGTON, D.C., Sept. 9, 1850 — California is the 31st state of the United States!

The great golden territory of the Pacific Coast gained statehood today when President Millard Fillmore signed the bill of admission passed by Congress. Her victory came after months of bitter debate by the nation's legislators marked by division between the northern and southern states.

There was great excitement in Congress as final action approached. By last Friday, the 6th, it became apparent the California bill would pass the House. For three days half the senators had been attending House sessions and working on their friends.

Final passage came on Saturday, with California winning her place in the Union by a vote of 150 to 55. Representatives of the North were unanimous for statehood with 123 votes, but the South opposed with 55 votes against to 27 for. Only four southern states, Delaware, Maryland, Kentucky and Missouri, gave a majority for California. Eight southern states' delegations were unanimously against, and Virginia and North Carolina were nearly so.

At the same time the Texas boundary bill and the New Mexico and Utah territorial bills passed.

That night California statehood was celebrated here with a grand salute of 100 guns. A large crowd, accompanied by a band, serenaded several leaders in the fight, including Henry Clay, Daniel Webster and Stephen Douglas.

JUDGESHIPS FIXED FOR CALIFORNIA

WASHINGTON, D.C., Sept. 20, 1850 — In the first bill passed by Congress in connection with California's new status as a state, the United States judicial system was extended to that land. It provides for two federal judges at annual salaries of $5500 each.

Another bill for collectors of customs and ports of entry is causing discussion. As introduced by Senator Gwin it provided that San Francisco, Monterey, San Diego, Sacramento City and Benicia should be ports of entry.

Sacramento has been cut down to port of delivery only despite Gwin's plea that Sacramento has grown to a 20,000 population and that there are as many as 65 vessels lying in the river.

Both California senators moved to reduce the status of Benicia, but it was retained as a port of entry.

———o———

ANOTHER BIG FIRE

SAN FRANCISCO, Sept. 17, 1850 — This city was swept today by another great fire, the fourth such terrible conflagration to strike San Francisco.

Several squares along Jackson, Kearny, Pacific, Washington and Dupont streets were consumed. It is estimated that some 125 buildings were destroyed. The fact that most of them were one-story shanties kept the property loss from being as high as in previous fires. Probably $300,000 will cover all losses.

The fire started in the Philadelphia House. At first the air was calm, but the wind came up and spread the fire rapidly.

The Pacific News, one of the city's newspapers, lost its building and all its equipment. Among other heavy losses were the Bella Union gambling saloon, valued at $20,000, and the Rendezvous gambling saloon, whose loss was set at $12,000.

Californians Seated

WASHINGTON, D.C. Sept. 10, 1850 — With California formally admitted as a state, California's representatives and senators who were elected nearly a year ago took their seats in Congress for the first time today.

In the drawing for senatorial terms Col. John C. Fremont drew a ballot limiting his term to March 4, 1851, and Dr. William M. Gwin drew the term ending March 4, 1855. Senator Fremont gave notice he would soon introduce 18 bills relating to California.

———o———

17 Million In Gold

PHILADELPHIA, Sept. 1, 1850 — Gold deposits in the U.S. Mint here since January 1 have totaled $17,041,210. Receipts from California prior to that date amounted to $4,558,000.

★★★★★★★★★★★★
STATEHOOD AT LAST!
★★★★★★★★★★★★
CALIFORNIA CHEERS HER ADMISSION

SAN FRANCISCO, Oct. 18, 1850—The joyous, long-awaited news that California has been admitted to the Union as a state reached here today. The entire city burst into a spontaneous celebration, and the news has been dispatched post-haste to all parts of California.

At about half-past ten this morning, the booming of cannon was heard in the bay. Soon the beautiful steamship Oregon hove into sight, covered with flags with the starry flag of our country proudly waving over all. As she came up to the city, her heavy guns fired in quick succession, and they were answered by ships in the harbor, cannon on shore and the guns of warship at anchor at Sausalito.

Hills and housetops were soon covered with multitudes of cheering people as the Oregon proceeded to her anchorage at Rincon Point. In the afternoon salutes were fired in the Plaza before a great crowd. In the evening there were great bonfires, and celebrations featured by illumination of public buildings.

The Common Council of the city voted $5000 for the expenses of a Grand Celebration to be held commemorating the admission of California as the 31st State.

RAINS SLOW DOWN DIGGING FOR GOLD
Dams Washed Away

STOCKTON, Oct. 15, 1850—Early rains have slowed down the pace of gold diggings in this southern section of the gold region.

No less than 36 dams on the Tuolumne river, erected by gold-seekers, have been washed away. But so great is the faith of the diggers that the bed of the stream will pay off that most of the workers have been busy making repairs on the dams. The Tuolumne has been the stream which has proved anything nearly as rich as these workers have hoped, though there is great difficulty in working the channel to advantage.

Although the stream has been turned in many places, there is still water. The gold is so fine that there is difficulty in obtaining it. However, if the real rains hold off for a few weeks, a good deal should still be taken.

Many miners are now looking for winter quarters. Sonora will be crowded again; several thousand are expected at Chinese Diggings, and many plan staying at Carson's near the Stanislaus river.

———o———

57,000 Gold Miners In Northern Areas

SACRAMENTO, Oct. 26, 1850 — The best estimates are that there have been 57,000 miners at work this past season on the Feather, Yuba, Bear and American rivers, and that they have obtained $30,240,000 in gold in the past five months.

Average returns to the miners are about $120 a month, or $600 for the five-month period. A common return has been $5 a day on the American, and $4 on the Bear.

Indians on the upper Sacramento and Trinity are reported to be troublesome. Reports have reached here also of an engagement between a party of whites at the mouth of the Salmon, on the Klamath. In the battle 24 Indians were killed and several white men severely wounded.

Ship Blast Mars Big Celebration

SAN FRANCISCO, Oct. 29, 1850—The explosion of the steamer Sagamore, with between 30 and 40 killed, added tragedy today to the city's grand official celebration of California's statehood.

The Sagamore was casting off from Central Wharf with a large list of passengers for Stockton when the boiler burst. The boiler was nearly new, and it is thought that she may have been lacking water because her pumps had given trouble. The Sagamore was built here only five months ago.

A grand parade, fire arms and salutes featured the formal San Francisco celebration. All shipping in the bay was decked with flags. In the evening there were bonfires and fireworks from Telegraph Hill, Rincon Point and the islands in the bay. Five hundred men and 300 ladies attended the biggest ball ever held in San Francisco.

———o———

Prisoner is Elected To the Assembly

SACRAMENTO, Oct. 6, 1850—Dr. Charles Robinson, a prisoner held in the brig and awaiting trial for his part in squatter difficulties here, was elected to the state assembly in the election yesterday.

———o———

MORMON GULCH, Oct. 12, 1850 —Two men committed the atrocious murder of two Indians here, while robbing them of no less than 29 pounds of gold. The suspected villains are now the object of a vigorous pursuit.

———o———

VALLEJO PICKED AS CAPITAL CITY

SAN FRANCISCO, Oct. 8, 1850—The city of Vallejo has ben chosen as the seat of government for California, according to returns from the general California election yesterday. First returns showed Vallejo 4765; San Jose, 324.

CHOLERA CAUSES HIGH DEATH TOLL

SACRAMENTO, Nov. 18, 1850—This city, center of the epidemic of cholera which has ravaged California in the past month, is beginning to revive from the scourge.

About 1500 victims of the disease lie buried in two graveyards, and it is believed that the total mortality is probably 2000.

This city suffered the worst effects, but at the height of the epidemic, 48 cases were reported in one day in San Francisco, with 26 fatalities. At times men who were apparently in the best of health were so suddenly stricken that they died in public places, and bodies of victims were frequently found in the streets.

———o———

Iron Warehouse Built For Gov't.

SAN FRANCISCO, Nov. 14, 1850—A fine, English iron warehouse has been erected at the corner of Battery and Pacific streets for the United States government.

It has four stories and measures 25 by 100 feet. Weight of the material is 270 tons. The iron pillars supporting the building weigh one and a half tons each. The roof is of heavy scalloped iron. Cost of the building, when completed, will be about $60,000.

LANDS OF VALLEY RICH FOR FARMING

STOCKTON, Nov. 2, 1850—Outside of South Carolina there are no such rice lands as in the San Joaquin Valley. This area indeed has a great agricultural future.

The land will produce every class of vegetables and almost any kind of fruits. Its agricultural products in the future will supply a greater shipping tonnage, in proportion to the territory embraced, than is employed on the Ohio or Mississippi.

In this town itself now are many large and handsome buildings. It has a great trade to the southern gold mine towns.

———o———

Gambling Condemned By S. F. Grand Jury

SAN FRANCISCO, Nov. 29, 1850—In a report to the court today the San Francisco Grand Jury declared gambling in the city to be "a crying evil."

The jury also urged enforcement of the law against carrying deadly weapons and of the law against fast driving; recommended that something be done about the numerous houses of ill repute; condemned prize-fighting; urged appointment of an officer to inspect meats and produce on sale; and reported that the City Hospital is a nuisance and the city jail insecure and inadequate.

———o———

Paintings of California

SAN FRANCISCO, Nov. 1, 1850—William Cogswell, who has been sketching in all parts of California, has on display a series of paintings. He plans to take these to the eastern states to show graphically and truly California scenes, men and women.

———o———

INDIAN SKIRMISH

SACRAMENTO, Nov. 11, 1850—Several persons were killed in a skirmish with Indians at Johnson's Ranch, among them Lt. Col. L. H. McKinney. Capt. Francisco de Allison, Fremont's guide, was wounded.

SACRAMENTO HAS 9500 POPULATION
Many Businesses

SACRAMENTO CITY, Nov. 18, 1850—A total population of 9500 is estimated for Sacramento by William N. Johnson, deputy to his brother, J. Neely Johnson, United States census agent.

Johnson reported his count as 6000 inhabitants, including 460 women; about 1500 missed because of the cholera which has been raging here, plus a floating population of 2000.

Other figures are: 323 stores, 80 clothing stores, 65 blacksmith shops, 3 steam mills, 8 cabinet shops, 2 soda manufacturies, 3 lemon syrup manufacturies, 2 breweries, 8 livery stables, 90 physicians, 70 lawyers, 7 churches and over 100 establishments such as the flour and corn meal mill of Merritt and Co., which has annual proceeds of $92,250.

It is also estimated that a total of 87,000 people, largely in the northern gold mines, are dependent on Sacramento, divided between counties as follows: Butte, 10,000; Sutter, 10,000; Yuba, 25,000; El Dorado, 20,000; Sacramento, 12,000; a portion of Trinity and Shasta, 5000; one-half of Calaveras, 5000.

———o———

Challenger Beaten By Stockton Horse

STOCKTON, Nov. 9, 1850—Capt. Sparrow of Stockton has two fast horses whom his friends would like to have beaten. To try to accomplish this, they brought down from the mountains a fine little mare, Maid of the Mountains, owned by Col. Dallas.

In training they found that the Maid did the mile in 1:55 in training shoes, so they matched her against Sparrow's Judy Coon for $5000 a side at one mile. The exciting race came off today. Judy took the lead in the first 200 yards and led at the finish by 10 yards in 1:53.

In a second race, one mile for $1000, the sorrel gelding Gen. Cass beat the gray gelding, Blue Crane, the favorite, by six yards in 1:51½.

SHORTAGE OF RAIN IDLES GOLD MINERS

STOCKTON, Dec. 11, 1850—There is a great outcry for rain through the southern mines. It is calculated that the daily loss from lack of that liquid which the miners need to wash their gold is at least $100,000.

Up-river cities are in despair because of the enforced inactivity.

Ferrymen too have no trade becaus the river beds are still dry. The only good news arising out of the lack of rain is that roads to the mines are hard and in good shape, but the miners would sooner see them muddy if only they could get the badly-needed water.

---o---

Gold Digging Stopped On Christmas Holiday

SACRAMENTO, Dec. 25, 1850 — Gold, the chief reason for their being, was laid aside, though of course not completely forgotten, through the California mining camps today.

It was a complete holiday for the miners. Many of them spent it in fun-making at town and camp saloons, while others gathered together what delicacies of food could be obtained to duplicate as best they could the Christmas dinners they enjoyed in their former homes.

---o---

Gold Vein Is Found At Grass Valley

GRASS VALLEY, Dec. 5, 1850— A great vein of gold-bearing quartz has been discovered here. It is so rich that the whole vein has been staked off in claims not more than 10 feet square.

Good wages have been made by men who had no other tools than a common hammer and used it to break up the rock and pick out the gold in lumps varying in value from a bit to one dollar.

---o---

Ladies Fair A Success

SAN FRANCISCO, Dec. 20, 1850 —The Ladies' Sewing Society netted more than $2100 at a fair they held for the benefit of the First Presbyterian Church in the rooms of the First California Guard at the corner of Jackson and Dupont streets.

It was a great success. The only marring note was when some prominent men appeared at a late hour in company with "women of the town" as companions. The society immediately closed the fair.

CHRISTMAS FETED LIKE JULY FOURTH

SAN FRANCISCO, Dec. 25, 1850 —Christmas here today was observed as a miniature Fourth of July. Guns, pistols and fire-crackers were freely fired on the Plaza and in different parts of the city through the entire day and into the evening.

It was glorious weather, and the whole town was out on holiday. There were many parties, and not a few of the citizens were observed to be carrying quite a load before day was done

---o---

How to Get Rich

STOCKTON, Dec. 14, 1850—Five months ago a trader named Mr. Zacharia took over a store on the levee measuring only 6 by 10 feet. He invested $50 in clothing. Since then he has turned over $215,000 and enlarged his place of business. He is now on his way East to bring his family to this golden country.

JEWELRY OFFERED AS LOTTERY GIFTS

SAN FRANCISCO, Dec. 15, 1850 —Jewelry—watches, chains, fobs, bracelets and necklaces of gold and diamonds—is what appeals most to the Californian as a holiday gift, as gauged by the season's prizes being offered by several lotteries.

These lotteries of "holiday souvenirs" are being heavily advertised by their proprietors. One offers jewelry with a total value of $20,000. Tickets are $5 each (the common figure), and 800 prizes will be drawn from 4000 tickets. Top award is a gold hunting watch and chain valued at $550.

Another lottery, which offers $15,000 in jewelry, with a first prize of a diamond bracelet which the donors declare is worth $1200, has a total of 200 prizes. A ticket here also costs $5.

Each of these lists each and every award, but there are others which declare only that they have "grand prizes."

---o---

SPECIAL LOCKS PUT ON DOORS OF JAIL

SAN FRANCISCO, Dec. 14, 1850 —Because of the frequent escapes that have been made from the city prison by unlocking doors, the authorities have had special locks put on them.

They engaged William Dunn to install his celebrated "Double Acting Cam and Lever Locks." These locks resist all attempts at picking, being locked and unlocked by numbers.

---o---

PLENTY OF GAME

SACRAMENTO, Dec. 2, 1850—In a single day John Cockrell and two other men brought into market here seven elk, three antelopes, 100 brace of quail, four dozen geese and 62 ducks. Four of the elk were shot within the space of an hour. Cockrell and his companions are operating on the Sacramento river about 40 miles from here.

---o---

SAN FRANCISCO, Dec. 5, 1850— A sidewalk has been laid down Battery street from Sansome to Cunningham's Wharf. This is just a sample; every part of the city should be provided in like manner.

THE GOLDEN GAZETTE
1851

Battle With Indians

SAN JOSE, Jan. 19, 1851—An express rider from Mariposa county today brought news of a battle between 400 Indians and 50 to 60 whites commanded by Capt. James Burney.

The whites attacked a fortified Indian village, and the battle lasted for three hours. The Indians lost 60 killed, and 10 to 20 wounded. Eight Americans were wounded, two fatally.

Troubles with the Indians have magnified in the last few months because the settlement of the valleys has driven the Indians' game from their usual haunts. Thus the Indians have faced shortages of food, and have turned to robbery and murder against white men.

Seventy-two whites are reported to have been massacred in Rattlesnake Creek. The men were surprised by Indians after they had stacked their arms and were working in a gulch.

———o———

Article in Herald Leads to S.F. Duel

SAN FRANCISCO, Jan. 12, 1851—A duel took place today in a small valley off Mission road between W. H. Graham and William Walker of Louisiana, one of the editors of the San Francisco Herald.

The affair grew out of an article in the Herald. Graham used strong language in protesting the item, and Walker challenged him. Weapons chosen were revolvers at ten paces for the first shot, with each party to advance one pace at each shot until the five barrels were exhausted. Each man fired two shots. Both of Graham's shots hit Walker, one near the knee and the other in the thigh. The affair was conducted with the utmost propriety and decorum.

Pioneers' Festival Greets New Year

SAN FRANCISCO, Jan. 1, 1851—The California Pioneers Society held a Grand Festival today in honor of the New Year. With the California Guards as an escort, members formed a procession at 11 a.m. that marched to the Plaza. There they heard a moving address by Capt. John Frisbie and a salute of 31 guns in honor of the fact that California is the 31st state of the Union.

Tonight the pioneers prepared a collation at the Guards' armory. Guests filled four rows of tables, and drank to 13 regular toasts, each of which was accompanied by an apt selection of music. Gen. Mariano G. Vallejo, noted Californian, was called upon and gave a speech in his native tongue.

———o———

Levee Completed

SACRAMENTO, Jan. 12, 1851—The entire levee around the city, extending for nine miles, is now completed. Total cost of the project, designed to protect the city from floods, has cost between $160,000 and $170,000.

NEW GOVERNOR FOR CALIFORNIA

SAN JOSE, Jan. 9, 1851 — Gov. Peter H. Burnett, the first governor of the State of California, resigned today shortly after he had submitted a lengthy message to the legislature, and Lt. Gov. John McDougal was sworn in to succeed him. David C. Broderick was made president of the state senate upon McDougal's advancement.

San Jose fitted up the state house for the legislative session at a cost of over $1000. The building was newly painted, and new floors and carpets were laid, and committee rooms fitted up. A plank sidewalk has been laid two-thirds of the way from the hotels to the state house.

———o———

ESCAPES GRIZZLIES WITH SLIGHT WOUNDS

SAN JOSE, Jan. 1, 1851—Charles Packwood is recovering today from wounds he received in an encounter with two grizzly bears near Murphy's rancho, 25 miles south of here.

Mr. Packwood came upon the grizzlies while he was hunting his mules. Dismounting from his horse, he went to a tree to climb it and shoot the bears. As he commenced climbing, the largest of the two bears grabbed him by the heel and dragged him down.

In his fall Mr. Packwood dropped his rifle, but he thrust his right hand into the mouth of the grizzly. Finally, he got hold of his rifle and shot the largest bear at a distance of two feet. His shot killed this grizzly, and the other ran off. Packwood's wounds are not too serious.

———o———

YUBA CITY, Jan. 2, 1851—Snow 12 to 14 feet deep is reported on the head waters of the Feather river. It is reported 18 of a party of 19 men froze to death in one night.

31

ACCUSED PAIR ESCAPE LYNCHING

SAN FRANCISCO, Feb. 24, 1851 —The city was relatively quiet today after a turbulent weekend in which two accused robbers narrowly escaped being seized by citizens and hanged.

The affair began five evenings ago when two men entered the store of C. J. Jansen on Montgomery street, knocked him senseless with a slung-shot and made off with $2000. The next day two suspects were arrested, and identified.

One of the men gave his name as Thomas Burdue, but is believed to be James Stuart, who escaped some time ago from the Sacramento jail where he was held for murdering Sheriff Moore of Auburn. The other is known as Windred. Both denied complicity in the Jansen robbery.

On Saturday, the 22d, 5000 citizens gathered around the City Hall, and handbills urging the two men be turned over to "Judge Lynch" were circulated. A crowd rushed into the courtroom where a hearing was in progress, but the Washington Guards cleared the room and hustled the prisoners to safe-keeping. At dusk there was another gathering of the people, and a committee named to consult with the authorities. Sam Brannan, one of the committe, urged a quick hanging, but his proposal did not carry.

Eight thousand people assembled again on Sunday, and a committee headed by William T. Coleman took steps to conduct its own trial. The hearing lasted from 2 p.m. to midnight, when the jury named to try the suspects reported its vote was nine to convict, and three doubtful. The crowd was disappointed and raised cries of "Hang them, anyhow; a majority rules."

But peace was maintained, and the crowd gradually dispersed. A legal trial will be held later.

---o---

43 Steamers Now Serving California

SAN FRANCISCO, Feb. 1, 1851 — The wonderful, almost magical growth of California is shown by the increase in the number of steamships on the coast and rivers.

Scarcely two years ago, a journey to Sacramento was a sail of six or eight days, and the only possibility of traveling along the coast was by transient vessels. Now there are 43 steamships serving California, as follows:

Eight steamers in the Pacific Mail Steamship Co. line: four in Law's line; two, the Gold Hunter and Sea Gull, between San Francisco and Oregon; three to Gold Bluff and Trinidad Bay; two, the Constitution and Ohio, to San Diego and intermediate ports; eight, from San Francisco to Sacramento; seven, to Stockton; three to San Jose; nine, Sacramento to Marysville.

---o---

MANY VALLEY FIRES

SACRAMENTO, Feb. 13, 1851 — The horizon has been lighted for several days by fires on the plains, above and below on both sides of the river. The dry weather has continued so long the grass is like tinder.

---o---

SCHOONER IS LOST

HUMBOLDT BAY, Feb. 10, 1851 —The schooner Burnea Dea, R. H. Hughes master, of New Bedford, Mass., capsized on the Humboldt Bay bar today.

ARMY POST ASKED FOR CAJON PASS

LOS ANGELES, Feb. 4, 1851 — Citizens are ca   g loudly for the establishment of a U. S. military post at Cajon Pass as the result of recent Indian outrages.

About 13 men were reported massacred at Four Creeks when Tulare Indians killed the parties of Dalton and Capt. Dorsey, who were driving cattle north. Several hundred strong, the Indians also attacked French's ranch with bows and arrows. An emigrating party of 40 Americans happened to be at the ranch and repulsed the Indians, killing some forty of them.

Utahs in the valley drove off 75 horses belonging to Jose Maria Lugo. They were pursued by 15 Paisanos and Sonorians 100 miles from Cajon Pass. But in the attack the Indians, about 50 in number and armed with rifles and revolvers, killed one of the Sonorians.

DROUGHT DELAYS MINING FOR GOLD

ROUGH AND READY DIGGINGS, Feb. 14, 1851—Because of the great drought little gold dust has been secured recently from this rich mining camp. Millions of bushels of earth have been thrown up by miners, but there is no water to wash it.

Some of the miners plan cutting a canal from Deer Creek for a distance of two or three miles to aid them in their work.

At Nevada City a rich find of gold quartz is reported. A tunnel is under construction and is already turning out much good quartz. No less than 2000 claims have been staked off in a short time. From one pan full of dust recently $1000 was taken out.

---o---

Bay Waters Recede As Streets Filled In

SAN FRANCISCO, Feb. 22, 1851 —Clay street has been filled up with earth down to Sansome street. The "Old Niantic," used as a warehouse, now has terra firma around her instead of water.

Many years hence it will be a matter of astonishment when the newcomer is told that where some splendid structure is the ocean once rolled or a mountain reared up its head. Only a year ago Montgomery street was the shore of the bay; today it is Sansome street.

---o---

HOUSE ON TELEGRAPH HILL

SAN FRANCISCO, Feb. 19, 1851 —Streets and buildings are gradually creeping up the slopes of San Francisco's lofty hills. One small zinc house has sprung up on the crest of Telegraph Hill, perched on slim supports. It looks as if a strong wind would whirl it into the bay.

---o---

FUN ON SUNDAY

SAN FRANCISCO, Feb. 9, 1851— Two men, Brady and Finly, amused themselves today by riding down Kearny street on the same horse and smashing all the lamps they could. They were lodged in jail.

Midnight Fire Burns Nevada City Homes

NEVADA CITY, Mar. 12, 1851—A great fire, believed to have been of incendiary origin, last night destroyed from 150 to 200 homes here. Total damage is estimated at $1,000,000.

The blaze started in the ball alley of Gates and Smith on Cayota street and spread rapidly. Luckily, only one life was lost. Citizens today organized a hunt for the suspected incendiaries. It will go hard with them if found.

RACE SEASON OPENS

SAN FRANCISCO, Mar. 24, 1851—The spring race meeting opens today at the Pioneer Race Course at the Mission Dolores. It is expected to be well attended, with a grand match for $500 between the gelding Ito and the filly Mary Snow to be a feature.

Management of the races is under persons who have acquired great celebrity in such affairs in the Atlantic States. Badges to the Club stand and field are available at the Pioneer Club Saloon.

A special event will be slow races between mules. The different riders will exchange animals, and the hindmost wins.

GAMBLING BILL PASSED

SAN JOSE, Mar. 18, 1851 — The legislature today passed a bill to license gambling in the state.

In San Francisco and Sacramento fees will be: house with more than three tables, $1500 every three months; house with three or less tables, $1000 for each three months. In other counties, tables will be licensed for $85 a month each.

STEAMERS ARE BURNED

SAN FRANCISCO, Mar. 3, 1851—The steamer Santa Clara was completely destroyed and the steamship Hartford badly damaged by fire early today while they were tied up at the end of Central Wharf.

The flames broke out in the fire room of the Santa Clara, and spread with such rapidity that at least two crew members were trapped and burned to death.

Rich Quartz Mine At Grass Valley

GRASS VALLEY, Mar. 12, 1851—Great excitement is being created among the miners here as result of the success of quartz mines in this vicinity. Three thousand claims have been made within three days, covering ground for four or five miles around this place.

Major cause of the rush is the strike made in the vein of the Sierra Nevada Company. At a depth of 40 feet this company hit upon a regular defined vein of gold six inches wide.

The company is running a drift into the side of the hill to construct a railroad to carry ore from the vein to its crushing machine. Machines now in operation here are buying up rock which does not show gold to the naked eye for $40 a ton.

Fast Riders Fined

SAN FRANCISCO, Mar. 3, 1851—Four men were fined $50 each today for furious riding through the streets. Such drafts of these upon the treasury of some of these gentlemen will cool their ardor, and learn them not only to show mercy to a brute, but also to have some regard for the lives of their fellow-creatures.

First Newspaper For Los Angeles

In Two Languages

LOS ANGELES, Mar. 17, 1851—Plans to publish a weekly newspaper here, starting next month, were announced today by John A. Lewis and E. Gould Buffum, the latter a former officer in the Stevenson Regiment who is well known throughout the state. It will be called the Los Angeles Star and Southern Pioneer.

"The importance which the southern portion of the state of California has already assumed," the publishers declare, "has rendered it necessary that there should be established in it a newspaper which shall represent the interests of that region. The tide of empire which has already flowed Westward until it has been stayed by the surges of the Pacific, is now turning in a Southerly direction, and the rich agricultural and mineral resources of Southern California are rapidly being developed by American enterprise."

The Star will have a Spanish language section. Terms are $10 a year, in advance.

One Man Is Killed in Battle Over Land

SONORA, Mar. 13, 1851—Dispute over claims to thirty acres of land believed to contain a rich gold deposit led today to a fatal affray.

Joshua Holden has claimed the land, a flat area into which three ravines empty, and has been cultivating it. Miners have repeatedly tried to claim it, but unsuccessfully.

This time a group of men decided to test the matter fully and began work. Holden organized a party to evict the miners. In the battle which developed the squatters killed one of Holden's party and wounded four others.

COAL IN OREGON

PORTLAND, Mar. 8, 1851—Capt. George Drew has discovered a vein of coal on the Cowlitz river. It is two feet thick and half a mile wide.

Dragoons Prevent Bloody L. A. Riot

LOS ANGELES, April 29, 1851—Arrival of Major Fitzgerald's Dragoons today luckily prevented the outbreak of what was feared would be a bloody clash.

The affair resulted from the arrest of five members of the well-known Lugo family on a charge of murdering a white man and a Cherokee Indian in the Cahoon Pass three month ago. A jutice examined them and committed them for trial, refusing the Lugos bail.

Then a habeas corpus writ was obtained, and the district judge after four days of testimony determined to permit bail. This angered a group of men who came down here a short time ago from the up-country. Planning to prevent release of the Lugos, they placed an all-night guard around the jail.

On the other hand, natives and friends of the prisoners gathered in large numbers just outside town and prepared to protect the Lugos. On the arrival of the dragoons, they were summoned as a posse and escorted the Lugos to the courthouse for the signing of $10,000 bail bonds each. The soldiers kept the muttering opposition party in check and then accompanied the Lugos out of town.

MACHINE TEARS AWAY SAN FRANCISCO HILLS

SAN FRANCISCO, April 16, 1851—A curious machine, the steam excavator, moving as if imbued with a spirit of intelligence, has been put into operation here and found to work admirably.

It is fixed on First street, reducing the sand hills on one side and filling water lots on the other. The huge scoop, carrying a hogshead of sand at a time, empties into cars which run on rails. It fills a car in two minutes: 30 men could not do it in the same time.

The machine, powered by a steam engine of 30 horsepower, will excavate 1000 cubic yards a day.

The first United States boy to be born in Los Angeles was born April 15, by name John Gregg Nichols.

UNUSUAL PHENOMENON

LOS ANGELES, April 20, 1851—It is now about six days that we have in this and the surrounding country been the spectators of an unusual phenomenon, which, from its peculiarity, has given occasion to manifold surmises, conjectures, speculations, and rumors. The atmosphere has been so filled with smoke as to confine the vision within a small circumference. And as the smoke was wanting in those aerial properties which affect the eyes and nostrils, there were not wanting many who denied the assertion that it was smoke.

Fast River Trip

SAN FRANCISCO, April 1, 1851—The steamer New World today made the quickest trip on record from Sacramento to San Francisco, 6 hours, 40 minutes from dock to dock.

VALLEJO DAUGHTER WED

SONOMA, April 3, 1851 — Capt. John B. Frisbie was married last night to Donna Epiphania Vallejo, eldest daughter of Gen. Mariano G. Vallejo and Donna Francisca Benicia Carrilla de Vallejo. The ceremony was performed by Father Dumas at the Vallejo residence.

AGAINST GAMBLING

SAN JOSE, April 12, 1851—Citizens of Santa Clara, a very pious and moral community, have petitioned the legislature for laws against gambling.

---

29 SHIPS IN ONE DAY

SAN FRANCISCO, April 5, 1851—Twenty-nine vessels entered the Golden Gate today, one steamer, 22 square-rigged vessels and six schooners. They were of many nationalities and came from Oregon, Atlantic ports, Chile, the British Isles, Bremen, Hamurg, Peru, Manila and Mexico.

A few days ago four steamers left for Panama on the same day, the Tennessee of the Pacific Mail Steamship Co. with the mails, Columbus of Law's line, the Eudora and McKim.

REPORT ON CENSUS IS INCOMPLETE

SACRAMENTO, April 10, 1851—J. Neely Johnson, the United States census agent for California, today made a preliminary report on the 1850 census, but said returns from deputies were still not completed.

No returns have been received from some counties, such as Los Angeles, and others are still only partial. According to Johnson, because of all the difficulties involved the enumeration, even when finished, will probably fall short by a third or even a half of the entire population of the state.

Returns by counties so far are: Trinity, Shasta and Colusa, 1152; Butte, 4786; Yuba, 19,032; Sutter, 3030; El Dorado, 20,785; Sacramento, 11,000; Yolo, 1003; Napa, 414; Sonoma, 561; Mendocino, 56; Marin, 323; Solano, 580; Calaveras, 16,884; San Joaquin, 4000; Mariposa, 4400; San Francisco, 21,000; Contra Costa 722; Santa Clara, 3502; Monterey, 1872; Santa Cruz, 674; San Luis Obispo, 336; Santa Barbara, 1185.

Improvements Made In San Francisco

Montgomery St. Lighted

SAN FRANCISCO, April 1, 1851—Montgomery street, from Telegraph Hill to Rincon Point, now is handsomely lighted at night by a number of lamps placed at convenient distances. They dispel the pall of darkness that overhangs the other streets.

The lamps were erected, and will be maintained by Mr. Crooks by private subscriptions of property owners. Plans are afoot to light more streets.

The aldermen today authorized A. D. Merrifield to lay pipes through the streets from a reservoir to be built on the line of Pacific street two miles west of Stockton street to contain 500,000 gallons.

Merrifield is to furnish water to the fire department, hydrants in various parts of the city and water for a fountain in Portsmouth Square. The city is to pay $30,000 a year for 25 years, and Merrifield is allowed to charge citizens for water at not over 1 cent per gallon.

Fifth Disastrous Fire Hits San Francisco

SAN FRANCISCO, May 4, 1851— On the anniversary of its second great fire San Francisco had its fifth conflagration—and the losses have exceeded in gross volume the total of all previous fires.

For eight months the city had been free of disastrous fires, until a blaze broke out at 11 o'clock last night in a paint store on the Plaza. From that point it spread, with the result that several lives at least have been lost and damage done running to 10 or 12 millions of dollars.

Many buildings erected in recent months had been thought fireproof, but their walls crumbled in the flames. Falling walls caused some deaths in addition to those caused directly by the fire.

The blaze is believed to be the work of an incendiary. The wind at the start was strong from the northwest, and the fire swept several blocks along Kearny street. Then it suddenly shifted to the south, an in a few hours the whole business section was in flames. A wide area was one immense fiery field, and the glow could be seen for many miles. The efforts of dauntless firemen were futile.

Houses were blown up, but fire jumped the gaps. Within ten hours between 1500 and 2000 houses were ruined. When the fire finally burned out, 18 squares and parts of half a dozen more had been devastated. Only five of the brick buildings on Montgomery street escaped. Some old store ships hauled up on the beach burned, including the Niantic, long fixed at the corner of Clay and Sansome streets. In lieu of water, 80,000 gallons of vinegar was used to save the DeWitt and Harrison warehouse.

---o---

Many Chinese in S.F.

SAN FRANCISCO, May 17, 1851 —Attracted by tales of wealth from early Chinese arrivals in California, Chinese are beginning to throng the streets of this city. Four hundred have arrived in the past month, and more are on the way.

Usually they are dressed in their national costume — wooden-soled, turned-up slippers, tights, a kind of shirt frock usually indigo colored, and a small skull cap -— but sometimes one is seen decked in bright colors.

A man named James Clark was fined $100 the other day for cutting off the queue of a Chinese for sport.

---o---

Ferry Disaster

MARYSVILLE, May 28, 1851 — Thirteen men drowned at the ferry crossing at Park's Bar. The rope guiding the ferry broke, and the boat capsized. Only 6 men escaped.

---o---

SAN FRANCISCO, May 9, 1851— The schooner yacht Betty Bliss arrived here today, 32 days from Tahiti, with a cargo of 100,000 fresh oranges. They are to be sold by John McCarthy, corner of Broadway and Sansome St.

COLLECTOR'S "ARMY" GIVES CITY A LAUGH

SAN FRANCISCO, May 28, 1851 —The Hon. T. Butler King, collector of customs, today provided San Franciscans with their biggest laugh in months.

Mr. King is a former eastern congressman who came to California with hopes of becoming one of this state's first senators. A rather pompous individual, he failed in this ambition but later accepted the customs appointment.

In the late fire, the custom house at Montgomery and California streets was burned, but treasure amounting to over $1,000,000 was saved in the official safe. Today the Hon. Mr. King undertook to remove the bullion and dust to a new building fitted up at Kearny and Washington streets.

The excessive care and military display employed by the collector caused high amusement and loud laughter. King assembled thirty gigantic, bearded fellows armed with carbines, revolvers and sabres to guard the treasure. Then King, with a huge Colt in his hand, marched at the head of his army in broad daylight along Montgomery street to the cheers of the crowd of watchers who gathered.

By nightfall, a humorous song about King's army was being sung in the city's barrooms to much applause and laughter. Only one thing was needed to make the triumphant march a complete success, half a dozen big guns from the Presidio.

Treaties Made With Oregon Indian Tribe

PORTLAND, May 5, 1851—A land treaty has been concluded by the commissioners with the Callappoiah Indians who live on the west side of the Willamette Valley.

The land purchased is about 80 miles long by 15 to 20 miles wide. A small tract is reserved for the Indians, whose band numbers 155 individuals. Terms of the sale are $2500 annually for 20 years, payable $500 in cash and the remainder of $2000 in blankets, pantaloons, coats, shoes, shirts, hats or caps, calicoes, linsey plaids, shirting, blanket shawls and handkerchiefs.

Another treaty has been made with the Tuality Plain Indians for over a million acres. The price is in 2 yearly installments of $500 cash and $1500 in goods.

---o---

Scouts Meet Indians

LOS ANGELES, May 25, 1851—A scouting party led by Dr. Hope had an engagement with Pah-utah Indians about 80 miles beyond the Mohahve and killed 13 Indians.

Dr. Hope and his men, numbering only five in all, were attacked, but luckily they were in a natural fort which luckily had a supply of water. They were besieged for five days before the Indians finally withdrew.

---o---

QUARTZ MILLS BOOM

NEVADA CITY, May 27, 1851— Two steam gold quartz-crushing mills are in operation here, and five more are building. One will have six stamps and crush about 10 tons a day.

Near Grass Valley a mill with the heaviest machines in this area is being put up for Judge Walsh. It will have 18 550-pound stamps to start, capable of 40 tons a day, and there are plans to enlarge it to a battery of 40 stamps.

---o---

POND USED FOR LAUNDRY

SAN FRANCISCO, May 5, 1851— The pond over the hills toward the Presidio has been converted into a huge washtub.

Hundreds, mostly females, are seen around its edges. It is the great laundry of the city. The business is conducted on a very extensive scale by one or two establishments. Washing is still pretty high, running $5 a dozen.

'Sydney Cove' Man Hung by Vigilantes

SAN FRANCISCO, June 11, 1851 —John Jenkins, one of the "Sydney Coves" who have been molesting San Francisco, was hanged by the Vigilantes Committee at 2 a.m. today in the Plaza, to the cheers of a large crowd.

The Vigilantes Committee has been quietly organized among the city's leading citizens because of the bad conditions here. Many of the fires which have caused such loss are believed to have been set by arsonists, followed up by bands of plunderers.

There have been many burglaries, assaults and murders. No one has been safe on the streets after dark, yet not one criminal has been executed by trial.

Last night Jenkins entered a store on Long Wharf and stole a safe. He was seen with a load on his back, and was pursued. Jenkins tried to escape by jumping into a boat and rowing out into the bay, but 12 men followed him. As they came up to Jenkins, they saw him throw a load into the water; it was drawn up and found to be a safe.

His captors then took Jenkins to the Vigilantes Committee rooms on Battery street, near Pine. At 10 o'clock the bell of the Monumental Fire Company was tolled, and 80 committee members assembled.

For two hours the committee questioned the prisoner and the evidence. At midnight the death sentence was passed. An hour later, Sam Brannan addressed the crowd in the streets and announced the sentence, which met with general approval.

Armed committeemen took Jenkins to the Plaza. There a rope was thrown over a projecting beam, and a score of persons dragged Jenkins up on it. His body was still hanging several hours later.

———o———

BUSSES START RUNNING

SAN FRANCISCO, June 1, 1851 — Omnibusses, imported from the East, began running today from the California Exchange to the Mission. They were well loaded on their first trips.

The city is not yet extensive enough to support many lines, but it appears as if a line from the foot of Long Wharf to Stockton street would pay.

SONORA HAS A REAL BUSY, EXCITING DAY

SONORA, June 15, 1851 — Today was an exciting day here, even by the standards of this bustling mining town.

Two of the men who had murdered and robbed their former employer, Captain Snow, were arrested in the morning. They were taken out to Shaw's Flat where Snow had lived, and a jury was empanelled. After the verdict the two men were marched by a guard of 1000 men to the scene of the murder and were hanged.

The other incident involved gunfire on the main street. Marshal McFarland had arrested a man in a Chilean house after a row. While he was taking the culprit to the jail, a Mexican fired at the marshal. McFarland shot him, and a melee followed in which three other Mexicans were wounded, one of them fatally.

———o———

Explosion On River

SACRAMENTO, June 3, 1851—At least five passengers died this evening in a steam explosion on the New World as she was sailing down river towards San Francisco.

The ship's steam chimney gave way at the boiler, and a great blast occurred. Several passengers leaped overboard, and three are known to have drowned. Fifteen persons were badly scalded, two fatally

The steamer Wilson B. Hunt was only 50 yards behind at the time of the explosion and rendered aid.

———o———

Indians Raid Horses

LOS ANGELES, June 7, 1851 — Immigrants say they met Walker, the Utah Indian chief, and 12 of his men with 150 California horses. The people of Los Angeles expect another visit from this horse thief when he has disposed of his present plunder.

John Irving & Gang Are Finally Killed

LOS ANGELES, June 1, 1851— John Irving and ten members of his gang, who have been terrorizing this region for some weeks, have been killed by Indians in the Canada of Santa Maria.

Armed with pistols, the gang marched up to the ranch of Jose Mario Lugo to plunder it, and with the announced intention of killing his sons. They broke into his house and gathered up some loot, though they did not find any of the Lugos.

As they left to search further for the Lugo family, they were attacked by between 300 and 400 Indians living in the vicinity whose aid had been sought by property owners. In a running fight with bows and arrows against the pistols of Irving's men, the Indians finally killed all the party. Irving was killed, and two or three wounded.

A coroner's jury today returned a verdict of justifiable homicide in an inquest.

———o———

ANOTHER S. F. FIRE!

SAN FRANCISCO, June 22, 1851 —The city's sixth great fire today leveled ten entire squares and large areas of six others, with losses estimated at $3,000,000.

The blaze broke out about 11 a.m. in a house on Pacific st. near Powell, and winds quickly spread the flames. Firemen were hampered by the fact the water reservoirs were nearly empty.

The Alta California building was destroyed, and the City Hall at Kearny and Pacific sts., bought last year for $150,000, was lost. Thomas Maguire, proprietor of the Jenny Lind Theatre, lost everything a sixth time by fire.

Many of the city's new buildings showed fire resistance because of solid brick walls two or three feet thick; double iron shutters and doors, and tanks of water installed on the roofs.

———o———

Criminals Flee City

SAN FRANCISCO, June 18, 1851 — The Vigilantes Committee has been distributing orders to obnoxious persons to leave the city, and many have gone to "take the country air.'

MINERS, FARMERS RIOT; 3 KILLED

SACRAMENTO, July 12, 1851 — Dispute over a dam on the farm of Jared Sheldon on the Cosumnes river, 24 miles from here, cost the lives of Sheldon and two other men today.

Sheldon had built the dam to irrigate his farm, but miners working higher up the stream bitterly objected to it. To defend the dam Sheldon erected a cannon on it.

When Sheldon was absent, miners came and spiked the cannon and took a guard left by Sheldon as a prisoner. Getting the news on his return, Sheldon organized a group of 11 friends and went to the dam.

Miners with axes were ready to start cutting the dam away when Sheldon warned them they were trespassers. He would kill the first man to strike a blow at the dam, he shouted.

One of the miners' group, which numbered more than 40 men, then shot and killed James M. Johnson, a friend of Sheldon. More guns were then fired, and shots killed Sheldon and Edward Coty. Two others were wounded.

The miners charged the Sheldon party, which had a total of three guns, fired first. They took some of the farmers prisoners but later released them.

Another Hanging By Vigilantes

SAN FRANCISCO, July 11, 1851 — The Vigilantes Committee acted with determination again today, hanging James Stuart to a derrick at the end of Market street wharf. The affair came just a month after the Vigilantes executed John Jenkins.

Stuart, an Englishman who had been transported to Australia for forgery and came to California in the Gold Rush, was the real man for whom Burdue was mistaken in a robbery case several months ago. In the Vigilante trial Stuart confessed a murder for which Burdue was convicted at Marysville, along with various other crimes.

HIGH PRICES LEAD TO SHEEP DRIVES

SAN DIEGO, July 17, 1851 — Because of the great demand for meat and the high prices in California, thousands of sheep are being driven into this state from Mexico.

A party of Mexicans from Sonora is nearing this town by a new route with 6000 sheep. They have lost only 400 on the way. Some Americans are reported at the old Indian ferry with 4000 sheep from Durango, bound for Los Angeles. The sheep cost only $1 a head in Mexico.

Still another group of Americans had bad luck, losing 2800 sheep at Cariso creek, near Warner's Ranch, from eating a poisonous weed. The loss to the owners is figured at no less than $20,000 because of the high price the animals would bring.

———o———

PEARS HARVESTED

LOS ANGELES, July 19, 1851 — Three thousand bushels of pears, mostly from Mission San Gabriel, have been sent to San Pedro for shipment to the San Francisco market. The whole crop was purchased by Dr. Shaw.

———o———

465 VESSELS IN PORT

SAN FRANCISCO, July 24, 1851 — Now lying in port are 465 vessels, according to Harbor Master George Simpton. Among them are 119 ships, 145 barks, 106 brigs, 50 schooners and 45 storeships.

At 9 a.m. the customary bell sounded, and the committee assembled at its rooms for the trial. Stuart was convicted and sentenced to death. The verdict was announced to the crowd by Col. J. D. Stevenson.

Two hours' grace was given Stuart, who was calm and apparently indifferent. Once he remarked it was "tiresome."

Two abreast, arm in arm, the Vigilantes marched him slowly to the execution place. At his own request Stuart was not blindfolded. He kept his hat on his head, but after he had been hanging for a few minutes the breeze blew his hat off.

After some time the city coroner was allowed to remove Stuart's body. Several physicians tried to revive him as his neck was not broken and there appeared to be a spark of life.

The Vigilantes Committee has claimed the right to enter any premises where they have good reason to believe there is evidence to carry out their object to drive out "all criminals and abettors of crime." Many malefactors have fled the city. The Vigilante movement has spread to other communities which have been organizing similar groups to control crime.

———o———

WOMAN HANGED AT DOWNIEVILLE
Shows No Fear

MARYSVILLE, July 8, 1851 — A woman known as Juanita has been hanged at Downieville for the murder of a man with whom she had quarreled, according to reports reaching here today.

After the killing she was immediately arrested, tried, convicted and then hanged. Juanita did not exhibit any fear. She walked up the small ladder to the scaffold before a crowd of over 500 witnesses and put the rope around her neck with her own hands.

Asked if she had anything to say, Juanita replied, "Nothing, but I would do the same again if I was so provoked." She also asked that her remains be decently taken care of.

TWO MORE HUNG BY VIGILANTES

SAN FRANCISCO, Aug. 24, 1851 —The Vigilantes Committee acted again today with dramatic decision.

The group had taken prisoner Samuel Whittaker and Robert McKenzie, two of the most notorious rogues in the state, and elicited confessions to many crimes. A few days ago Sheriff Jack Hays took from the Committee rooms on a writ of habeas corpus issued by Gov. John McDougal and lodged them in the jail.

This Sunday afternoon the Rev. Mr. Williams was holding religious exercises in the jail yard when 36 members of the Vigilantes Committee broke into the jail. Several shots were fired, but no one was hit.

They seized Whittaker and McKenzie, put them into a carriage waiting nearby at the corner of Dupont street and Broadway. The carriage sped up Broadway to Stockton street, over to Washington and down to the Committee headquarters on Battery street.

The Vigilante bell rang, and in a short time ropes were hung from beams jutting out from the second story rooms. The ends were taken inside. Nooses were made and put around the necks of the two prisoners, who were then led through the door-like windows and dropped.

After they had hung there for half an hour, Sam Brannan came to a door and addressed the crowd which had gathered, declaring that the committee could not act otherwise.

———o———

To Settle Carson

SACRAMENTO, Aug. 26, 1851 — An expedition of 75 men, led by Gen. Winn, plans to leave soon with the intention of making a permanent settlement in Carson Valley on the other side of the Sierra Nevada.

Sacramento Has a Triple Hanging

SACRAMENTO, Aug. 22, 1851— Only two hangings were officially scheduled, but three took place today in one of the city's most exciting days.

This day had been set for the execution of three convicted highwaymen, by name Gibson, Thompson and Robinson, but Governor McDougal gave a reprieve for Robinson to September 19, to the anger of the citizenry.

All business in the city was suspended and the streets were deserted as everybody assembled at the scaffold erected at G and 4th streets. Sheriff Ben McCullough conducted the first two executions. A delegation, however, took Robinson from his guards and hanged him at the same spot afterwards— the sheriff and his officers having retired from the scene.

A citizens' meeting tonight, on the motion of Sam Brannan, who has been a Vigilantes leader at San Francisco, unanimously called for the resignation of the governor.

———o———

LOS ANGELES NOTES

LOS ANGELES, Aug. 1, 1851—A challenge to a match horse race has been issued to the northern part of the state by Dons Pio Pico and Teodosio Yorba.

The county has adopted an ordinance appropriating not over $50 a month for any educator instituting the teaching of the rudiments of the English and Spanish languages.

A voluntary police has been organized, at no expense to the city.

———o———

SOUTH ADVOCATES STATE DIVISION

SAN DIEGO, Aug. 30, 1851—The smouldering desire of many citizens of the southern part of the state to divide California came to a head at a public meeting here today.

Behind the move is the feeling that the northern part of the state, in which the gold mines, industry and population are centered, does not give due regard to the welfare of the southern counties, which are largely dependent upon agriculture and cattle grazing.

Its adherents maintain that the south can always be outvoted by the north, and that any revenue law bears heavier on the lower country

FLYING CLOUD IN RECORD TRIP

SAN FRANCISCO, Aug. 31, 1851 — The clipper ship Flying Cloud sailed into San Francisco Bay today, only 89 days from New York, a record for passage around Cape Horn.

Under command of Captain Cressy, famous skipper of the East India trade, the beautiful ship left New York at 6 p.m. June 2. She made Cape Horn in 50 days, and ran from the Horn to San Francisco in 39 days.

On her voyage Flying Cloud made some remarkable time. Her best run in 24 hours was 374 miles, the greatest ever made by a sea-going vessel —an average of 15¾ miles per hour. While making this run, she was carrying top-gallant sails with the wind one point forward of the beam.

In one three-day stretch, the clipper made 992 miles. On one occasion during a squall, 17 knots of line were not enough to measure her speed. The shortest day's run was 40 miles.

Flying Cloud's record is all the more sensational when it is considered that when only 10 days out on the voyage she sprung her mainmast head, rendering her mast very tender for the rest of the voyage.

The Flying Cloud, built by Donald McKay at East Boston, Mass., has three cabins—the first containing the pantry and office rooms; the second or main cabin, splendidly wainscoted with mahogany, satin and rosewood; the after cabin, fitted up elegantly for a drawing room or accommodation of families.

On her trip she carried a varied cargo of merchandise.

———o———

because of the great difference in the value of the dollar in the two sections.

A committee was appointed at today's meeting to arrange for a convention of delegates from the southern counties, with the suggestion that it be held at Santa Barbara in October The purpose is to get underway a move to set up a territorial form of government for Southern California if the consent of the north and of Congress can be obtained.

The San Diego vote is in line with feelings which have been expressed in Los Angeles and other southern regions.

JOHN BIGLER IS ELECTED CALIFORNIA GOVERNOR

SAN FRANCISCO, Sept. 19, 1851 —With nearly all the state returns in from the election of September 3, it became certain today that Col. John Bigler, Democratic candidate, was chosen next governor of California over Pearson B. Reading, Whig.

The latest returns show: Bigler, 22,476; Reading, 21,331. The race has been extremely close, with each man holding the lead at different times since vote counting began.

The total vote polled is estimated at about 45,000. This is reckoned a slim vote, but it gives no data to estimate California's present population because there are many resident foreigners, who are not entitled to vote. It is usually conceded that now California has 200-250,000 population, mostly male adults.

Public Showing of New Gold Crushing Machine

SAN FRANCISCO, Sept. 19, 1851 —Horatio Blasdell showed publicly today the new gold quartz crushing machine he invented, and built at the Pacific Foundry.

With a 6-horsepower engine, it will crush 35 to 40 tons in 24 hours. The machine is of an entirely new type. Broken quartz is thrown into a ribbed iron basin. In the center is a fluted iron cone called a "nut," which revolves rapidly and crushes the quartz.

The quartz then falls onto flat plates of iron which reduce it to a fine powder. In a demonstration today it appeared to work much faster than the stampers and Chilian mills generally used at the gold quartz mines.

STOCKTON MERCHANTS PROTEST $2 CITY TAX

STOCKTON, Sept. 16, 1851 — A new city ordinance levying a tax of $2 a ton on all merchandise landed at Stockton was bitterly protested today by the city's merchants.

Speakers at a mass meeting declared that this law would tend to impede the commerce and further growth of Stockton, and warned that any attempt to enforce it would meet with determined opposition.

Oregon Explorers Are Murdered by Indians

PORT ORFORD, Ore. Ter., Sept. 19, 1851—The story of a murderous Indian attack upon a group of men trying to locate a road to the upper Rogue country was told today to Dr. A Dart, superintendent of Indian affairs for Oregon.

Col. W. G. T'Vault, leader of the exploring party of ten men, and one other man, Mr. Brush, were the only survivors. The attack came when they were canoeing down the Coquille river after traveling north when their supplies ran low. Brush was partially scalped, and T'Vault was also wounded.

Twenty soldiers are soon expected here to be stationed at a post on the Rogue River. This point, about 15 miles north of the Rogue mouth, is attracting considerable attention. The town includes three sections of land, a large stockade fort, two large block houses, several pieces of artillery and other firearms.

A lumber mill is soon to be erected. It is thought this point will ultimately be the principal inlet and outlet of a large portion of California.

Ice From Boston!

SAN FRANCISCO, Sept. 27, 1851 —The Bark Barrington has just arrived, 180 days from Boston, with a cargo of ice. The market has lacked this luxurious article for sometime past, so the Barrington comes just in season. Her ice appears as solid as when first taken from the lake.

Revolver Duels Mark Weekend

BENICIA, Sept. 13, 1851—Messrs. William H. Graham and Frank Lemon came up from San Francisco this afternoon to fight a duel about two miles from the United States Barracks here.

The affair was with revolvers at ten paces. Both men fired five times times without hitting anything. They then reloaded their guns. In two more shots Lemon still missed, but Graham's seventh shot hit Lemon in the shoulder. It was a painful, but not serious wound.

Both principals and their friends are returning to the city tonight on the steamer.

SAN FRANCISCO, Sept. 13, 1851 —Capt. Schaeffer and James Wethered went out on the Presidio road today to settle a difficulty with shotguns, loaded with buckshot, at 15 paces. In the first fire neither was hurt. Then the authorities appeared and stopped the duel.

JUDGE KILLS CLERK IN BALLOT DISPUTE

JACKSON, Sept. 14, 1851—A difficulty here last night between Judge Smith of the county court and Capt. Lewis T. Collier, county clerk, resulted in the death of the latter.

Judge Smith, who had been ill in Sacramento, returned to Jackson and found that the recent election votes had not been counted as Collier, being a candidate, was disqualified from counting. Yesterday was the last day for a legal count, so the judge went to the house where the ballots were deposited and proceeded to count them.

Collier heard of this. Much excited, he went to the house and had high words with the judge. Pistols were drawn, and Collier was fatally wounded.

RAIL SURVEY IS PLANNED

SAN JOSE, Sept. 10, 1851—Plans were made today at a meeting of the San Jose and San Francisco Railroad for an early beginning of a survey of the proposed rail line between these two cities. David Divine was named president of the company, and J. Alexander Forbes, vice president. William J. Lewis was appointed chief engineer.

STEAMER DISASTER IN FOG IS AVERTED

SAN FRANCISCO, Oct. 6, 1851— Saved from disaster after striking a rock in the dense fog near Golden Gate yesterday morning, the steamship Republic was towed in to her wharf by the steamer California. All her 200 passengers from Panama were in good condition, though very tired.

While proceeding slowly in the fog, Capt. Hudson of the Republic thought he was directly off the Gate and pointed his ship eastward. Hearing surf, he was convinced he was still too far south. He first turned north and west, but again heard the surf nearby. To get completely clear, he swung his ship to the southwest, but she struck.

The engines were reversed and drew the Republic free easily. There appeared to be no damage, but 25 minutes later water rushed in and put engine fires out. Anchors were let go, and pumping attempted. Pumps, however, were choked, so the crew and passengers were organized into bailing parties. Lifting of the fog showed rocks close by, so Captain Hudson had his vessel edge farther out. The ship's purser was landed to give the alarm.

When word reached the city, the California was ordered out and met the Republic at midnight about 20 miles south of Golden Gate. Despite the heavy swell, she got a line to the Republic and towed her into the harbor in about seven hours.

———o———

Honolulu Prisoners Rise

HONOLULU, Oct. 23, 1851—Sixty prisoners, employed on the reef cutting stone, staged a revolt last night.

Usually they are returned to the fort at night, but they were placed in some native houses last evening to take advantage of an early morning low tide. They made an escape from their overseers.

Police and soldiers traced them to the Punch Bowl, where the prisoners had broken into the magazine and taken some large guns. An attack scattered them. Only the lack of fire prevented the prisoners from firing their guns, which were pointed at conspicuous buildings in town.

All except two were recaptured, or gave themselves up, by 9 o'clock this morning.

4 Southern Counties Seeking Separation

SANTA BARBARA, Oct. 23, 1851 — In a four-day convention concluded today 31 delegates elected from San Diego, Los Angeles, Santa Barbara and Monterey counties voted to push actively for their separation from California and formation of a territorial government.

The counties of Santa Clara and Santa Cruz had also chosen representatives but they were absent from the meeting because of uncertainty as to its time and place.

The move to withdraw from statehood is prompted by the feeling strong in these "cow counties," that their interests are widely different from those of the gold mining and commercial north and will not receive proper attention from the state government.

Proceedings of the convention will be transmitted to the state legislature by the representatives of the counties concerned, with instructions to seek definite action. There was some difference of opinion as to a boundary between California and a new territory of Southern California. Most wanted to see it located no further north than Monterey county, but some wanted it to extend to Santa Clara county's northern border.

Guns were fired in front of the convention rooms at the conclusion. This evening Santa Barbara delegates, led by Don Pablo de la Guerra and Don Jose Covarrubias, gave the visitors a ball, which was attended by an array of beautiful and graceful senoritas.

———o———

Challenge from Oregon

LAFAYETTE, Ore., Oct. 15, 1851 —Thomas Hubbard of this place challenges any person who dares take it up, in the sum of $500, that he can raise 300 bushels from one peck of oats.

———o———

TUOLUMNE, Oct. 12, 1851—A company here is getting up a menagerie to show in Mexico and eastern United States. The collection will include 12 grizzly and other California bears, and all other animals of the county. There will also be some of the most beautiful gold specimens found in California, from the finest gold dust to a lump weighing 28 pounds, 5 ounces.

Brutality Is Charged To Clipper Captain

SAN FRANCISCO, Oct. 31, 1851 —Seafaring men stormed through San Francisco streets today looking for Capt. Robert (Bully) Waterman of the clipper ship Challenge and his first mate as a result of stories of brutality to crew members on a voyage from New York.

Only the promise of city officials that Waterman and George Douglass, the mate, would be brought to trial, together with the power of the Vigilance Committee, prevented the excitement from developing into a riot. This afternoon the United States marshal issued a warrant against the two men charging murder and other crimes on the high seas, and offering a $500 reward for their arrest.

The Challenge arrived two days ago, 108 days from New York—one of the fastest runs yet made. She is a magnificent ship and made one run of 300 miles in 24 hours, averaging 14 knots. Captain Waterman reported three men were lost off the mizzen topsail off Cape Horn, and six died of disease.

Even before he was brought to berth, stories spread of terrible conditions on the voyage, of the mutilation of sailors' limbs and even worse things. A large crowd gathered at the wharf. But Waterman had previously left the ship; and Mate Douglass fled in a boat. He was pursued, but escaped.

———o———

HORSE THIEVES CONVICTED

STOCKTON, Oct. 24, 1851—Frederick Salkmar, alias Flat Foot, and James Wilson, alias Mountain Jim, today were convicted of horse stealing and sentenced to death.

Two confederates were sentenced to prison for 10 and 7 years. These men formed the gang whose depredations have caused much excitement. Once they barely escaped lynching.

———o———

Female Immigrants

SAN FRANCISCO, Oct. 15, 1851 —The female portion of our population is gradually increasing, from almost every nation. Two vessels are now expected shortly, one from France with a number of French girls and the other from Germany with 30 damsels.

HIGH WAGERING AT HORSE RACE

SANTA BARBARA, Nov. 19, 1851 —One of the greatest horse races ever held in Southern California was run off here today, with at least $20,000 in wagers at stake.

The race, between the American horse "Old Breeches" owned by Alfredo Robinson and the California horse "Buey de Tango of Francisco de la Guerra," had been on tap for the past month and aroused tremendous interest up and down the coast.

Jack Powers, noted horseman residing here, was in charge of Old Breeches.

Original stakes put up by the backers of the two horses consisted of ranches, cattle, etc., of a value estimated at $10,000. An equal amount was put up by other parties.

The distance was about 280 yards over a course laid on a level piece of ground adjoining the beach. A straight fence of light sticks separated the two horses. The whole town turned out, and many visitors from surrounding ranches. On one side was a decorated tent to provide shade and a place to drink; on the other side a row of ox-carts which had carried senoras and senoritas to the scene.

Caballeros rode to and fro, offering their bets, sometimes offering their horse, saddle and bridle. The horses had no gear other than a light bridle and surcingle to serve their youthful riders as stirrups.

The race was run after several false starts. Old Breeches won by two lengths in 14 seconds. There was much cheering by Los Americanos, while the natives without a murmur and with quiet dignity surrendered the stakes.

———o———

Steamer Operators Stop Races on River

SACRAMENTO, Nov. 1, 1851 — An agreement has been made between the owners of the steamers Senator and Confidence that they will not engage in any more races on the river run to San Francisco.

Both boats are sufficiently tested to make them favorites with travelers, and continued rivalry might lead to accidents. Now on alternate days, one boat will leave five minutes ahead, and keep ahead all the way down.

South Threatened By Indian Attack

LOS ANGELES, Nov. 29, 1851 — Residents of Los Angeles and San Diego counties are fearful of a general attack by Indian tribes, led by

———

Bear Valley Scene Of Big Gold Find

BEAR VALLEY, Nov. 20, 1851— Several thousand gold-hungry miners have rushed here in the last few days as a result of a tremendously rich strike made on a hill about a mile off the main road from Stockton to Mariposa.

The discovery was made by a party of six Sonorians headed by an experienced miner named Don Ramon, who had been prospecting along a stream. Their attention was attracted to the hill, and they began tunneling into it from the stream bed.

In four days they took out $220,000 worth of gold. They took in five Americans to protect them from being driven off by other miners.

There are no gold lumps, but much fine dust. One sack of 70 pounds of earth yielded between $2400 and $3000.

———o———

Farmer's Rich Crop Wins Award at Fair

SAN FRANCISCO, Nov. 14, 1851 —In a well attended ceremony last night at Shelton's Agricultural and Mineral Fair Mr. Horner of Santa Clara Valley was given a silver goblet as a premium for his services in advancing the agricultural interests of California.

On his 800-acre farm, with the average aid of 60 laborers and at a cost of $50,000, Mr. Horner has produced a crop worth $200,000 at present prices. His harvest totaled: potatoes, 120,000 bushels; onions, 6000 bushels; table beets, 4000 bushels; turnips, 1000 bushels; tomatoes, 1200 bushels; barley, 5000 bushels; pumpkins, 30 tons; cabbages, 108,000 head; 600 chickens, 1200 dozen eggs, and several hundred pounds of various seeds.

Antonio Garra, an Indian raised at San Luis Rey Mission.

Antonio is estimated to have gathered a force of 400 to 500 men, and can muster at least 3000 within a few days. They have many arms as well.

At Aguas Calientes another party has killed several men visiting the springs for their health, and driven J. J. Warner from his rancho. The Indians stole his cattle, pillaged his house and killed his chief vaquero. Warner and his family have escaped to San Diego.

Indians residing at Temacula have refused to join Antonio, however, and are moving their families and stock to San Diego.

Available forces in the area have been put in the field, and an appeal has been sent north to Gov. John McDougal for aid. Los Angeles has named a commission of five citizens to equip a force to fight the Indians: Abel Stearns as chairman, Pio Pico to get horses, Augustin Olivera and Gen. J. H. Bean to get arms, and Francis Mellus to obtain provisions.

The Indians uprising is believed to have been caused by the killing of a half dozen Indians at Los Angeles in a row developing out of their playing their favorite game of Peon. They attacked a sheriff's patrol which attempted to arrest one Indian, and fighting ensued.

———o———

BUSINESS IS POOR

SAN FRANCISCO, Nov. 24, 1851 —Business is dull here because the recent arrival of many clipper ships has thrown large quantities of goods on the market. Much merchandise was shipped from the East in anticipation of shortages here after last May's fire.

Country buyers currently are few, and act with great caution. Coffee has been as low as 9¾ cents a pound. Ten cases of butter in jars sold at 10-11 cents a pound; hams are quoted at 18-20 cents.

Coals are held firmly and have an upward tendency. Sales have been made at $23 a ton for Welsh coal, and $20 for English coal. Lumber is in a more healthy state. Pine plank retails at $85-90 a thousand feet, and rough one-inch Oregon boards at $50.

Prisoners Escape Jail On Christmas Night

JACKSON, Dec. 26, 1851 — Four prisoners in the county jail took advantage of Christmas night celebrations by making an escape. Apparently supplied with tools, they cut a hole through the jail door.

The men who escaped are John Green, serving three years for horse theft; John Small and George M. Brown, committed for murder, and James Clark, an old Texas Ranger, committed for attempt to kill.

The latter is the most dangerous of the group. He was held for trial after stabbing an old man at a fandango in Mokelumne Hill. When brought to jail here, he escaped injury when the stage overturned though his guard was hurt badly.

Two prisoners awaiting trial refused to leave the jail when the others fled.

STORES FALL INTO BAY

SAN FRANCISCO, Dec. 12, 1851 — Three men had a miraculous escape last night when two stores fell into the bay at Rincon Point in a great crash.

Built on piles, the stores owned by Messrs. Hussey, Bond and Hale held about 1200 tons of merchandise. Between them and the bank was a wharf holding 2000 tons of coal which collapsed and fell against the stores.

Three men were sleeping on the second floor of one store but escaped unharmed.

BALL AT VALLEJO

VALLEJO, Dec. 25, 1851 — A well attended Christmas ball was held here tonight, with many attending from San Francisco and Sacramento. The steamers Sophie and Express made special trips from Central Wharf in San Francisco with guests to the party. Last boat for the returning celebrants will be the C.M. Weber, leaving at 5 a.m. tomorrow.

MINE CLAIM DISPUTE

CARSON HILL, Dec. 20, 1851 — A serious difficulty has arisen between two mining companies over a mining claim, worked by Morgan & Co. but contested by another party of miners. The county court ruled for Morgan, but the others threaten to take possession anyway.

S.F. Requires Many Public Improvements

SAN FRANCISCO, Dec. 5, 1851 — San Francisco is an unfortunate city in matters of public accommodations, the editor of The Alta California, the city's leading newspaper, complained in an editorial today.

Wharves are exposed to tempestuous northers, to ravages of the worm and to numerous other destroying agencies. Improvements at the water line are often damaged because piles are forced out of line by the pressure of sand used to fill other water lots. The tide converts part of the waterfront into a filthy lake.

Streets are narrow and obstructed, and sidewalks so irregular pedestrians are driven into the middle of the street to take their chances on being ridden over or trampled under by recklessly driven mules, horses and wagons.

Careless driving should be strictly punished, the editor urges, and storekeepers required to keep walks passable.

---o---

ESCAPES DROWNING TO ENJOY CHRISTMAS

SAN FRANCISCO, Dec. 25, 1851 — J. McCann, a visitor from Mariposa county, was able to enjoy Christmas after a narrow escape from drowning last night.

A watchman and a private citizen heard cries near Clay and Sansome streets, and found McCann struggling and almost exhausted in seven feet of water. In going to his lodgings in the Texan House on Long Wharf, McCann mistook Clay street for Commercial street in the dark and walked off the dock.

---o---

RAILROAD IS URGED

STOCKTON, Dec. 19, 1851 — The business done between Stockton and the mines would seem sufficient to support a railroad. Trade of this town is increasing by 100 per cent every 12 months.

At least 500 teams are trading to the mines, along with 1500 pack mules and a dozen daily stages. Steamers and river craft land nearly 200 tons of merchandise daily.

4 INDIANS EXECUTED ON CHRISTMAS DAY

SAN DIEGO, Dec. 1851 — Four Indians involved in the uprising of tribesmen in the southern part of the state were shot to death today for the murder of four invalid Americans at Aguas Calientes a month ago.

They were Francisco Mocato, chief at San Ysidro; Luis, alcalde of Aguas Calientes, and Jacobo and Juan Bautista of the same place.

The four were executed in the presence of 80 Indians, including squaws and children, after sentence was passed by a council of war made up of Col. Magruder, several other officers, Dr. O.M. Wozencraft, Indian agent, and State Senator J.J. Warner, who was driven from his ranch in the Indian trouble.

Twenty soldiers made up the firing squad. After graves were dug, the prisoners knelt by them and then were shot.

This execution is believed to have ended the serious threat of Indian trouble in the South. The Indians were captured after soldiers and volunteers had advanced on the Rancho of Los Coyotes and fought the Indians, killing several of them.

---o---

Duelist Convicted

NEVADA CITY, Dec. 3, 1851 — E.B. Lundy was convicted today in county court for violation of the state statute against duelling as a result of the encounter in which he shot and killed Lieut. Dibble.

The jury recommended Lundy to the mercy of the court because strong provocation and mitigating circumstances were proved, and Lundy had attempted to avoid the whole unfortunate affair. Lundy's counsel intends to file for an arrest of judgment on the ground that the grand jury was illegal in having 24 members instead of 16.

---o---

Street Lights Coming

SAN FRANCISCO, Dec. 30, 1851 — This city will soon have some lighting on its streets. Messrs. Perry and Dexter are erecting a line of lamp posts on Montgomery, Jackson and California streets. There will be two or three lamps to each post, each containing four oil burners.

THE GOLDEN GAZETTE 1852

JANUARY 1852

NEWS ARRIVES AT RECORD SPEED
26 DAYS FROM EAST

SAN FRANCISCO, Jan. 18, 1852 —The steamer North America arrived here today with news from New York up to December 26 — brought through the Nicaragua route in 26 days. This is three days shorter than the fastest time ever made before from New York to San Francisco.

The North America left San Juan del Sur January 5. Besides news of the eastern states she carried news from Paris up to December 5, which was only six weeks on the way.

WELLER IS ELECTED AS STATE SENATOR

SACRAMENTO, Jan. 30, 1852 — After three days of balloting, members of the state legislature today elected Col. John B. Weller, Democrat of San Francisco, to be U. S. Senator for a six-year term, dating from last March 4, succeeding John C. Fremont.

Weller's election was assured when other Democratic candidates, headed by David C. Broderick, withdrew. The final vote was 71 to 17 for P. B. Reading, the Whig candidate, who was also the defeated candidate for governor of California last fall.

Sessions of the 'egislature were moved to this city from Vallejo, the designated capital, after the inauguration of Gov. John Bigler because the buildings and accommodations provided at Vallejo were not considered adequate.

MINERS' WAGES DROP

STOCKTON, Jan. 25, 1852 — Wages in the southern gold mines have dropped within the past two weeks because of new arrivals from the East, and the northern mines.

Previously the rate has been $100 a month and board, but wages are now $3 to $5 by the day, with some men working for $2.

Mining Town Forms Vigilance Committee

MOKELUMNE HILL, Jan. 10, 1852—The long series of outrages in this vicinity has led to the organization of a Committee of Vigilance here because civil law has proved powerless.

Large numbers of property holders and miners have signed as members. A constitution has been adopted, officers chosen, a meeting room arranged and alarm signal provided.

A system has been worked out for the instantaneous trial of criminals by an impartial jury of 12 men, for deciding the method and amount of punishment and for putting the same into speedy execution.

To promote the peace and quiet of the community, committee members have agreed to refrain from the discharge of firearms after sunset, except where necessary for self-defense. A reward of $300 has been offered for the arrest and delivery of James Campbell, perpetrator of a recent murder who was let go free by civil authorities.

———o———

WHERE'S STATE LINE?

SALEM, Ore. Ter., Jan. 24, 1852— The Oregon territorial legislature has asked that a survey be made to determine whether Shasta, Butte City and neighboring country are in Oregon or California. If they lie within Oregon, they will add several thousand to the population.

FIREMEN PARADE NEW YEAR'S DAY

SAN FRANCISCO, Jan. 1, 1852. — Members of two of San Francisco's finest fire companies, Sansome Hook and Ladder Company and Howard Engine Company, put on a grand display today in observance of the New Year.

Led by a band, they paraded together through the streets. Sansome, strongly and handsomely equipped, whose never-tiring and prompt exertions at fires have won high fame, were in full uniform. Their new apparatus, truck, ladders and hooks, shone in gleaming white and gold paint.

Howard men wore their uniform of blue shirts, glazed caps and helmets, and black pantaloons. After the parade they tested the power of their machine in the Plaza. They bore down on the pumps with such might that two times they threw a steady stream over the Plaza's lofty flag pole and the third time shot an unbroken stream 40 feet clear of the top.

———o———

Ex-Gov., Editor Duel

SAN FRANCISCO, Jan. 12, 1852 —John McDougal, who has just recently retired as governor of the state, and A. C. Russell, editor of the Picayune, engaged in a hostile meeting today. The former governor challenged the editor as a result of criticism he had penned in the columns of his paper.

In the first exchange of shots Russell was hit in the hand, and slightly wounded. The matter was terminated there when both men shook hands.

———o———

MAIL FROM SALT LAKE

SACRAMENTO, Jan. 10, 1852— Mail arrived here today from the Salt Lake, brought by a party of 10 men led by S. Hanson, who left on their journey November 1.

Several times on the trip they had to fight off Indian attacks.

Oregon Shipwreck Takes Lives of 42

ASTORIA, Ore., Feb. 1, 1852 — Search was pressed today for bodies of the 42 victims of one of the most disastrous shipwrecks in the history of the Pacific Coast. There was no trace of the steamer General Warren, which sank after she was beached in desperation on Clatsop Spit.

The steamer sailed from here two days ago for San Francisco. After discharging the pilot who got her safely across the Columbia river bar, the General Warren got into trouble in the high seas, losing her fore topmast.

Capt. Charles Thompson then tried to put back into port, and got the pilot on board again. The steamer was leaking, but the pilot considered that the waves at the bar were too heavy to cross. Capt. Thompson was afraid the storm would drive him north, and induced the pilot to try the bar crossing.

It was safely accomplished; but the weather then shut in foggy and dark. After striking two or three times in 16 feet of water, the ship began taking water rapidly. She was headed for Clatsop Spit to beach her.

Despite all attempts to lighten ship, the surf broke over the General Warren. Passengers and crew huddled on the forecastle and in the rigging. Finally one boat was sent to shore with ten men to get help. When a whaleboat was obtained and return made to the Warren, there was not a trace of steamer or people.

---o---

JUDGE TEFFT DROWNS

SAN LUIS OBISPO, Feb. 6, 1852 —Judge H. A. Tefft lost his life today in a harbor tragedy here, which also took the lives of three members of the crew of the coast steamer Ohio.

The judge had come up on the vessel from Los Angeles, and was being rowed to shore to pick up his wife preparatory to continuing on to San Francisco to start a trip to his old home in the East. The Ohio's boat was overturned in the surf 100 yards from shore. A second boat went to the rescue, but it also capsized, although the occupants were saved.

HILO IS THREATENED BY VOLCANO'S FIRES

HILO, Hawaii, Feb. 26, 1852 — This beautiful town has been threatened for several days by the rivers of lava pouring from Mauna Loa in the volcano's first great eruption in nine years.

Mauna Loa gave its first warning when a light appeared at its top early on the morning of the 17th. Soon bright columns of lava began shooting up into the air. Within two hours the lava had flowed down the mountain side a total of 15 miles.

Three days later fire began issuing half way down the mountain. The lava moved towards Hilo, but was temporarily diverted. Two days ago another eruption occurred, accompanied by many explosions, and has continued ever since.

---o---

FAITHLESS PARTNER IS GIVEN 50 LASHES

MOKELUMNE HILL, Feb. 6, 1852 — For robbing his partner a miner named Phillips was taken out by the Vigilance Committee today and given 50 lashes on his bared back, then ordered to leave town.

The affair began a couple of weeks ago when the canvas house occupied by Phillips and his partner, Bohrer, was robbed of a trunk containing $800. The trunk was found, broken open and empty. Some Mexicans were arrested as suspects, but proved their innocence.

A day or two later, Phillips went to San Francisco. On his return Bohrer's suspicions were aroused, and communicated to the Vigilance Committee. It was discovered that Phillips had a fresh certificate of deposit for $820 in a San Francisco bank. Although he protested his innocence, the verdict was that Phililps had staged the robbery.

---o---

THEATRICAL STARS

SAN FRANCISCO, Feb. 5, 1852— More theatrical stars from the East are turning their attention to California. On the steamer Pacific today there arrived Mrs. Alexina Fisher Baker and Lewis Baker, who have drawn high praise from critics; and also the New Orleans Serenaders, whose popular performances are well known.

PLACERVILLE PLANS FIFTY-MILE CANAL

PLACERVILLE, Feb. 27— The South Fork Canal, the most important work of its kind in California, is in a fair way to being built.

Preliminary surveys have been made by Colonel Platt and J. F. Edgerton, engineer, and a company organized with a capitalization of $500,000. The canal is to be 10 feet wide, 3 feet deep and over 50 miles long. Twenty-six miles will be covered with 2-inch planking.

This canal will be of great advantage to the country. Not only will it provide a good supply of water to the gold mines in this vicinity, but it will open new surface diggings along it to provide employment to thousands of men.

The company intends to extend it from Placerville to most of the mines, and eventually to the adjoining plains, which will stimulate agriculture.

Citizens are subscribing handsomely to the company.

---o---

TIDAL WAVE REPORTED

HONOLULU, Feb. 2, 1852—A remarkable phenomenon of the sea is reported at Waialua. Without warning the sea rose rapidly until the tide reached 20 to 25 feet higher than normal for a period of ten hours.

Five houses were swept away, and a small vessel at anchor was completely submerged. It is believed that the high tide was the result of a submarine eruption. The effects were felt at Waialua only.

Sacramento Levee Is Broken By Flood

SACRAMENTO, Mar. 7, 1852— Low lands of the city were inundated today when the rapidly rising river burst through the city levee in two places.

Under heavy rains the river had risen many feet in the past 24 hours. The authorities gave notice last night the alarm bell would be sounded to announce any failure of the levee and summon citizens to help repair the damage. The deep tones of the bell were sounded between 1 and 2 a.m. At 5 o'clock the public crier went through the streets calling on all able-bodied men to help at the scene of disaster.

The city bridge on Third Street was swept away shortly after the flood rushed into the slough. It is believed a man was on the bridge at the time, and lost his life. Several houses built on piles near the slough were carried away. Fears are felt some of the occupants met a watery grave.

Rain has been falling with unabated fury.

Marysville Lively As Mining Activity Reopens

MARYSVILLE, Mar. 31, 1852 — Streets of this city present a very lively appearance these days. They are thronged with pack mules and teams loading for the gold mines.

The reopening of the Downieville road will improve trade substantially. Marysville merchants anticipate that in another week trade will be fully reopened.

Failing S.F. Newspaper Sold for $15 in Auction

SAN FRANCISCO, Mar. 12, 1852 —The San Francisco Evening Picayune was sold today under a deed of assignment at Payne's Auction Room for $15, subject to the payment of a mortgage amounting to $8,525.

It was bought by Mr. Judah as agent for other parties. Rumors had persisted for some time The Picayune, published by Mr. Russell, was in difficulties and might suspend.

STEAMER WRECKED BELOW ACAPULCO

SAN FRANCISCO, Mar. 15, 1852 — The steamer Tennessee has brought news of the total loss of the steamship North America, which was overdue here for several days past on the run from Panama.

The North America, one of the best ships in the line, went aground 50 miles below Acapulco, Mexico. Passengers were rescued.

Accusations of negligence have been made against the ship's master, Capt. Bléthen, who has always had a very high reputation professionally and personally.

---o---

Legislators Hit

Sacramento, Mar. 5, 1852

Dear Editor:

I am sorry to observe that the public journals seem not to scrutinize and comment with freedom upon the doings of our legislature.

Recently that honorable body, with an eye to the interest of the State, made an appropriation of all money on hand to pay themselves $300 each. This modest appropriation, we are informed, is based on necessity: That is, many of the members are so much in want of funds that, unless the money is taken by them to the exclusion of all other State creditors, they must very soon adjourn.

Such action would leave the State without the benefits of their wise enactments, for which the last two months of doing nothing have shown them so admirably suited.

Yours truly,
Pro Bono Publico.

---o---

FIGHT BLOODLESS DUEL

SAN FRANCISCO, Mar. 5, 1852 —Two Frenchmen, supposed to be the same pair who previously applied to the Marshal for official permission to settle their differences in a quiet manner with small swords, engaged in a duel this afternoon near Mission Plank Road.

They used pistols instead of the swords originally preferred. They exchanged shots from a distance of about 20 yards, without any injury. A conference was held after the first firing to such good effect that the opponents embraced in the most affectionate manner and ended their differences.

Most Brutal Murder At Mining Town

MOKELUMNE HILL, Mar. 21, 1852—One of the most cold-blooded murders ever committed on this renowned gold hill was perpetrated last night.

The victim was Miguel Huguez; the murderer, Juan DeSoto. The latter has been in the constant habit of living with him. Yesterday he threatened to take her life.

The woman appealed for protection to Huguez and William Pierpont, his mining partner. They locked her in a room in their house for safety. DeSoto swore he would kill the two men.

During the evening DeSoto came upon Huguez by surprise and plunged a large Bowie knife nearly 18 inches long through his body. DeSoto made his escape by brandishing his bloody knife.

Huguez died about half an hour afterwards. No trace has been found of his murderer.

---o---

CALIFORNIA WEATHER SUPERIOR TO EAST'S

SAN FRANCISCO, Mar. 2, 1852 —While our friends in the Eastern States have been freezing under the chilling influence of a terribly rigorous winter, we have been enjoying the softest, mildest, most genial climate that ever a country was blessed with.

The bight sky, warm and cheerful sunshine and deliciously agreeable temperature have made our winter more like spring merging into summer.

Accounts just received from the Atlantic States indicate the weather in January was the coldest on record for many years past. The Hudson, Delaware, Susquehanna, Potomac, and even the James River, were frozen over from shore to shore, so that pedestrians and even vehicles could cross on the ice without difficulty.

Good Returns Given By Gold Quartz Mills

QUARTZBURG, April 9, 1852—Some of the quartz machines in this area are paying off handsomely.

The Washington Mill yesterday yielded 125 ounces in the amalgam. This is equal to $800 and gives a net profit of $700 per day, the expenses being $100 per day.

The Baltimore and Quartzburg Mill is more than paying expenses even though it is handicapped by the fact the cams on the main shaft are too short and do not raise the stamps adequately. This mill, however, is being completely remodeled and should return much higher profits when used in connection with the improved Godard amalgamator.

Placer diggings in this vicinity are paying fair wages also

Citizens Stop Robberies

SAN FRANCISCO, April 13, 1852—The sudden and complete cessation of robberies and burglaries during the past three weeks is a subject of general remark and congratulation.

Previously, not a night passed without two or three houses being entered and robbed. The complete impunity the villains enjoyed induced the belief that they would continue their depredations until some fearful examples were made.

The citizens, who had long endured these outrages, finally roused from their inactivity and gave evidence of a determination before which the robbers quailed. Taking counsel of wisdom, the villains at once ceased their enterprises, and the city once more enjoys tranquillity.

Delegates Sail East

SAN FRANCISCO, April 1, 1852—California's delegates to the national convention of the Democratic party leave for the East today by way of Panama, some on the steamer Pacific and some on the Golden Gate.

The population of Los Angeles County is estimated at 7831: 4043 whites, 3693 Indians and 295 foreigners.

Flood Destroys Dams

NORTH FORK, American River, April 23, 1852 — The early spring freshet has swept away the massive, expensive dam erected at Oregon Bar.

The New York dam just below withstood the early flood, but was destroyed by the freshet early this week. The breakwater, however, is still standing.

The North Fork is to be flumed this summer from the bend above Oregon Bar for three miles to a point midway between New York Bar and Manhattan Bar. The bed of the river between these points has proved in the past to be immensely rich in gold.

---o---

EXPEDITION TO JAPAN

SAN FRANCISCO, April 7, 1852—Californians are taking keen interest in the naval expedition the federal government is sending to Japan.

Its purpose is to try to open commercial relations with that extraordinary country. The naval force, under the command of Commodore Perry, will consist of several steamers, backed by a frigate and one or two corvettes.

One of the main objectives will be to negotiate for the protection of American sailors who may be wrecked on the coast of the Japanese Empire. Pacific mariners have been afraid to sail near the Japanese shores in the past because shipwrecked sailors of the United States and other countries have been treated in very harsh manner.

---o---

GOLD FOUND ON ISLAND

OREGON CITY, Ore., April 20, 1852 — Intelligence from Queen Charlotte's Island confirms the rumors of the existence of valuable gold mines there.

The Indians had large lumps in their possession. They were so hostile to the expedition that attempted to settle on the island that its members were compelled to return to Oregon for arms and assistance. A considerable emigration to this island is taking place. No less than five vessels filled with armed miners have sailed for that destination in the past months.

HUGE WAGERS ARE LAID ON L. A. HORSE RACE
SYDNEY MARE WINS MATCH

LOS ANGELES, April 1, 1852—All Southern California is talking about the great match race between the Sydney mare "Black Swan" and the California horse, "Sarco," won by the fomer.

Run over a nine-mile route at the track two miles southeast of town, it was the longest and most exciting race ever held in California. The crowd that collected, not only from this county but also from all parts of the south, was such as has seldom been seen here.

The native population thought "Sarco" invincible, and many did not hesitate to stake all their property on him. "Black Swan" had a big reputation in the northern part of the state.

Both animals were in good condition. "Sarco" led by two lengths in the early stages, but "Black Swan" soon came up and won by 75 yards. Time for the nine miles was 19 minutes, 20 seconds.

The principal stake was 1000 head of cattle and $2000 in cash, but it is reliably estimated that at least $50,000 changed hands on the race.

$200 IS WAGERED ON A BAKING CONTEST

SACRAMENTO, May 4, 1852 — The proprietors and journeymen of the Sacramento Bakery and the establishment of Mr. Smith on L street engaged in a baking match for a wager of $200. Quantity, rather than quality, was the goal.

Four persons were engaged in each shop. The contest was a warm one and resulted in victory for the men of the L street bakery. They worked up 11½ barrels of flour, out of which they made 31 barrels of crackers, while the Sacramento Bakery team worked up only eight barrels of flour.

The next contest, we learn, is to be an eating match for double the sum of money.

SLOOP ARRIVES HERE FROM TULARE LAKE

STOCKTON, May 20, 1852 — The sloop Argo, commanded by Capt. Sacket, has arrived at the port of Stockton from Tulare Lake, with a cargo of produce.

This is the first time such an occurrence has happened and is significant of what will take place in the future. The distance is some 250 miles, and there are numerous ranches all along the borders of the San Joaquin River.

The agricultural trade of the upper settlements of the San Joaquin will shortly be of sufficient importance to employ a steamer from Stockton. In fact, it is surprising that no boat has yet been put on the route. The navigation is good during all seasons of the year as far as Tulare county.

Phrenology

Prof. Pinkham will deliver a course of 24 lectures on Phrenology at the Phrenological Hall on Clay street, opposite the Plaza, commencing on Tuesday evening, May 25, at 8 o'clock. The lectures will be illustrated with a large collection of Drawings, Paintings, Busts and Skulls, and close with the public examinations. Admittance, 25 cents.

Those wishing Examinations, Charts or written Delineations can be waited upon at the hall.

Price of an examination, $1; with a Chart, $2; for a written Delineation, $3.

Service to Shipmasters

SAN FRANCISCO, May 17, 1852 — Messrs. Barrett and Sherwood of the City Observatory will have a ball dropped every day at mean noon from the Telegraph Hill signal pole. As this can be seen from all parts of the city and bay, it will enable shipmasters to check their chronometers for correctness. As the ball will be dropped on mean time, it will of course be of no use for regulating watches unless one knows the difference between mean and apparent time on a given day.

Gold Found in South

LOS ANGELES, May 12, 1852 — Gold has been found near Andres Duarte's farm at San Gabriel, about 18 miles from Los Angeles.

Several specimens of silver ore have been found recently in the southern country. Placers have been located within 75 miles of this place.

New San Francisco Map

SAN FRANCISCO, May 1, 1852 — Alexander Zabriskie, formerly an officer of the engineers corps in Poland, has just completed a new and very perfect map of San Francisco. It contains the names of all important localities in the city, and will be of great use as a ready reference. Copies may be purchased from Cook and LeCount, or Mr. Zabriskie, northeast corner of Montgomery and Washington sts.

Weather Disagreeable

SAN FRANCISCO, May 10, 1852 — The climate here has been excessively poor for the past several days. Cold, damp and misty, it has been the opposite of the mild and genial weather with which we were favored during the winter.

Newcomers here might well imagine that the seasons are reversed in California as the spring months have been decidedly colder than the winter. The same raw disagreeable weather, varied by occasional rains, appears to be prevailing throughout the interior valley as well.

Telegraph Sought Across Continent

SAN FRANCISCO, May 2, 1852 — Henry O'Reilly, the indefatigable builder of telegraphs, is busily promoting his favorite project of extending his system from the Atlantic states to the Pacific.

He is hopeful of being able to have a line in operation as far as San Francisco in 18 months, provided Congress will grant him a right of way through the wilderness and protection to his wires.

It is very much to be desired that California be connected by telegraph with the Eastern states. We are now perfectly isolated from the rest of the Union. Were we under any form of government than that to which we are so much attached, and so distant from the seat of government, the people would soon shake off their allegiance and proclaim California a separate union.

In their pursuit of gold and wealth, the people of California have not forgotten they are still a component part of the great American confederacy.

If Congress will only listen to Mr. O'Reilly, we shall have the pleasure, before two years, of placing before our readers in every morning's issue the news and abstract of the proceedings of Congress the day previous.

NUGGET IN STREET

SONORA, May 25, 1852 — A lump of gold weighing $1173 has been dug out of the main street of this town.

GIGANTIC STEAMER

SAN FRANCISCO, May 1, 1852 — News has been received here of one of the most extraordinary schemes offered to the public which might bring these shores within a month's reach of London.

Two London promoters propose building iron steamers 720 feet in length, with 90 feet of beam and 36 in depth, with four engines of 1000 horsepower, and a screw. In addition, there will be eight masts, with huge latteen sails. The vessel is to be built of iron and will be not only shot-proof but fire-proof.

LOLA MONTEZ TO VISIT CALIFORNIA

SAN FRANCISCO, June 18, 1852 — The celebrated Lola Montez, Countess de Lansfeldt, will in all probability visit California during the present season.

Her arrival will doubtless create a great excitement among all classes of our society and make her the observed of all observers. Should she come, the public need not expect to find her an artiste of the first order. As a danseuse she is without grace, all her accomplishments in that line being strictly mechanical and acquired.

In beauty Mme. Montez has nothing to boast of, and but for the peculiarity of her eyes and mouth, which are both fascinating, she would not excite remark. In fact, on observing her anyone is surprised that she should have such power of controlling others as is attributed to her.

She is very vain, and very desirous—like others in her profession and like many theatrical persons of mediocre capacity—of being puffed in the newspapers for talents and acquirements she does not possess.

---o---

FIRST TIMBER RAFT

SACRAMENTO, June 15, 1852— A raft of 7000 feet of timber from the mountains of Shasta arrived yesterday, the first of this species of craft to come to the port of Sacramento.

The timber was cut and rafted on the Sacramento River above Shasta City by Messrs. Benjamin Jones, George Welch, W. A. Jones and J. Philips. They may justly be called pioneers in this business.

---o---

STAGE TEAM RUNS AWAY

SACRAMENTO, June 8, 1852— One man narrowly escaped injury here today when he tried to stop a runaway stage team on J street.

The horses of one of the country stages suddenly became unmanageable, and the driver lost all control. A man rushed into the street to try to check their speed. He was knocked down, and horses and stage passed entirely over him. By some miracle he escaped without hurts. The driver of the team maintained his self-possession and finally succeeded in bringing the horses up without damage.

Floods in San Joaquin Cover the Low Lands

STOCKTON, June 6, 1852 — A flood now covers the banks and bottoms of the San Joaquin River to an extent nearly equal to that of 1849-50. The waters are still on the rise.

The consequences are most disastrous to the crops, with many totally destroyed. Only a few will be able even to raise late crops.

This has put such a blight on the settlement of these low lands that, unless the legislature will adopt some wise and practical plan of reclaiming them or permit the settlers to reclaim them, the whole must be abandoned.

---o---

WAGONS AT SALT LAKE

MARYSVILLE, June 11, 1852—A gentleman just in from the mountains reports that 34 wagons of the advance cross-country emigration have arrived at Salt Lake.

The teams arrived there in good condition. Members of the party said the emigration this year will be double the amount of any previous year. This train is coming through Marysville and may be expected here in two or three weeks.

---o---

Reward for Murderer

SACRAMENTO, June 12, 1852— Governor Bigler has offered a reward of $1000 for apprehension of A. B. Hetherby for the murder of Solomon Sharp in this county earlier this month. John Sharp, brother of the deceased, has added $500 "for the recovery of the perpetrator, dead or alive."

Hetherby's accomplices, now in jail, say he is connected with a band of robbers who plan to locate in Carson Valley or on the Humboldt to murder and rob emigrants. Hetherby, about 25 years old, is 5 feet 7 inches in height and has black hair and eyes.

---o---

Man Killed, Scalped

MARYSVILLE, June 9, 1852 — The body of D. Comstock, who has been missing nearly a month, was found between Deer Creek and Bridgeport. Arrows were shot through the body, and he had been scalped. Identification was made from the clothes and a ring.

10,000 IMMIGRANTS ARRIVE IN MONTH

SAN FRANCISCO, June 2, 1852 — California's population, drawn from every quarter of the globe, continues to increase with astonishing rapidity.

During the month of May, 10,641 passengers landed at this port by steamers and sailing vessels as follows: from Panama, 4561; from China, 2445; from San Juan del Sud, 1743; Chile, 791; Mexico, 603; France, 201; Oregon, 107; from New York and Boston direct, 89; Sydney, 55; Sandwich Islands, 36; Society Islands, 10.

Departures on outgoing vessels have probably totaled not more than 1500. When the immense number of emigrants crossing the plains begin to come in, an average of 10,000 newcomers each month will be fully sustained.

It may be safely estimated that the population of California will increase at least 100,000 during the present year.

---o---

Gold at Los Angeles

LOS ANGELES, June 26, 1852— Although the result of the latest explorations is not as favorable as anticipated by the over-sanguine, gold placers have been discovered, of considerable extent, in the vicinity of San Gabriel. They are rich enough to pay for working, although as yet but little prospecting has been done.

Coal Is Discovered Near Los Angeles

LOS ANGELES, July 11, 1852 — Several veins of coal have been discovered in this county near the sea coast.

The experiments which have been made justify the claim that it will be esteemed above any imported coal. It is bituminous, easily kindled, and glazes and burns briskly. It gives little or no cinder, and leaves a fine ash.

An experienced blacksmith who has tested the coal states that it is fully equal to the best coal he has ever used for welding iron or fusing metals.

Four or five distinct seams or veins have been found. Plans are being made for a thorough exploration.

―――o―――

Holiday Fire Feared

SAN FRANCISCO, July 4, 1852— Unless precautions are observed in the use of crackers and other fireworks over the July Fourth holiday, it is feared there may be another of those disastrous fires which have devastated this city on several occasions.

Great care, therefore, needs to be taken by all who indulge in burning gunpowder in celebration of the occasion. Serpents, chasers and all other kinds of fireworks which cannot be controlled should not be used. Even the common Chinese crackers should not be let off except in places where they could not possibly do any harm.

―――o―――

GAME VIOLATORS FINED FOR SELLING QUAIL

SAN FRANCISCO, July 16, 1852 —Two dealers in game and meats in the New World Market were fined $50 today by Justice Bailey on a charge of offering a quantity of quail for sale.

We trust this will be a lesson to others as there is a society of our citizens who are determined that the laws for the protection of game shall be enforced.

―――o―――

New diggings have been discovered above the Downieville Buttes. The quartz leads have been tested and show rich ore.

CALIFORNIA DEMOCRATS SWING INTO ACTION

SAN FRANCISCO, July 16, 1852 —The Democrats have all the fun to themselves at present, and the Whigs have nothing to do but look on.

Nomination of Franklin Pierce for the presidency appears to be very acceptable to the Democrats throughout the state. In their estimation any person who throws a doubt on his election has but poor judgment.

It will soon be time for the Whigs to make a noise. The next mail steamer should bring news of the Whig national convention and the name of their nominee. It will then be their turn to fire guns, make speeches and cause a commotion.

Between the two parties it will be hard indeed if the country is not saved at the next election. The political temperature will soon be at a point indicating fever heat. It is rising fast now.

―――o―――

REDISTRICTING CITY

SAN FRANCISCO, July 1, 1852— A resolution was passed today by the Board of Assistant Aldermen providing for the preparation of a plan to change the present division of the city into wards so that the population of the various wards will be nearly equal.

At present the Eighth ward has as great a representation as the Third although it polls only one-eighth as many votes and pays less than one-hundredth as much in taxes.

―――o―――

First Suspension Bridge To Span Consumnes River

SACRAMENTO, July 27, 1852 — The first wire suspension bridge to be built in California is in the process of erection across the Cosumnes river; a little above the dwelling house on Daylor's Ranch.

W. D. Wilson is the sole proprietor and architect of the bridge. It will have a 150-foot span, be 12 feet in width and 28 feet in height.

Mr. Wilson was owner of the bridge over the Cosumnes which was washed away by the last flood. The new bridge, when completed, will be a strong and beautiful piece of mechanism.

SHOOTS GRIZZLIES WITH HARPOON
WHALING GUN USED

STOCKTON, July 30, 1852 — Oliver Allen, the inventor of "Allen's Patent Whaling Guns," who is now engaged in farming near the mouth of the Tuolumne river, has developed a new way of dispatching grizzly bears, using one of his whaling guns as the instrument of death.

Mr. Allen loads his gun in the same way as for shooting whales, with a harpoon and line attached. The gun is then secured to a tree. The end of the line attached to the harpoon is tied to a broken limb or some movable object, and a bait is tied to a string hanging from the gun so that the instant it is touched the gun discharges.

The gun is set up so it cannot be approached except in a direct line with its muzzle. Sure destruction awaits whatever dare touch the bait, which is usually a piece of fresh meat or fish. Mr. Allen has killed several bears in this way. One of them was of enormous proportions, weighing between 1200 and 1500 pounds.

―――o―――

Girls Feature Parade

SACRAMENTO, July 4, 1852 — Among the most beautiful features of the Fourth of July procession here was the appearance of 31 girls, all dressed in white, to represent the 31 States of The Union.

Panama Canal Comes Nearer to a Reality

PANAMA, Aug. 4, 1852—Dr. Cullen, who has devoted himself for years to the opening of a ship canal across the Isthmus of Panama, left here today much encouraged at the prospects for success.

After going to Washington, Dr. Cullen will proceed to London to lay before the English government the result of his negotiations with the government of New Granada concerning the project. He won a grant in the face of strenuous opposition from the Panama Railroad Company.

Many of the first noblemen and men of talent and enterprise in England are said to be among the friends and promoters of this great undertaking to connect the Atlantic and Pacific oceans by this canal.

A New Resort Across The Bay Now Ready

OAKLAND, Aug. 10, 1852 — The magnificent Lovegrove House, combining all the advantages of the most popular and favorite resorts in the Atlantic States, is now ready for the reception of visitors at this Contra Costa spot.

George H. Lovegrove, the proprietor, plans to keep a first-class house worthy of the approbation of all who call. Pleasure parties visiting Oakland will find superior accommodations here. In addition to the public dining table and bar, dining rooms are fitted up for private parties.

A bowling saloon, with double alleys, is connected with the Lovegrove House.

MANY FIRES REPORTED

SAN JOSE, Aug. 12, 1852—An unusually high number of fires are reported sweeping through the parched grass and timber in every part of the state.

Marin County has been desolated. Now Contra Costa is suffering. A dense smoke has been rising for some days from the plains along the San Francisco Bay. This indicates fire has taken hold of the dry grass and is spreading to the hills. It is hoped that it may not reach the crops and numerous farm houses in that vicinity.

Noted S.F. Editor Fatally Shot In Duel

SACRAMENTO, Aug. 2, 1852 — Edward Gilbert, senior editor of The Alta California, leading San Francisco newspaper, was killed in a duel at Oak Cottage near here early today.

He was shot in an encounter with James W. Denver as a result of a letter commenting on one of Gilbert's political editorials.

Gilbert, only 33, was highly esteemed in California. A native of New York state, he was trained as a printer, but joined the New York Volunteer Regiment to come to California in 1847. He served as a lieutenant.

Active in political affairs, Gilbert was a member of the constitutional convention and elected one of the first two congressmen from the state.

Chinese Theatre Planned

SAN FRANCISCO, Aug. 12, 1852 — A number of wealthy Chinese residents are said to have sent to China for a dramatic troupe.

The troupe, expected to arrive soon, numbers upwards of 100 performers—tragic, comic and musical—who have made a reputation at home. They are provided with full theatrical costumes, decorations, scenes and all the singular contrivances with which they fit up their theatres in Canton.

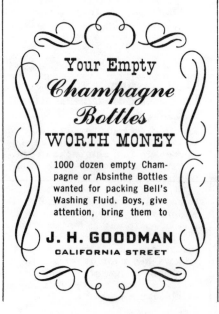

AUSTRALIAN GOLD LURES EMIGRANTS

SAN FRANCISCO, Aug. 16, 1852 — Even this state of fabulous golden riches is feeling some effects from the glowing accounts of the gold fields in Australia.

Several ships have sailed hence with passengers intending to try their luck there. In general, they are men of the type who are always ready to leave one place, no matter how prosperous, for the prospect of greater wealth in a new one.

Some of our far-seeing and adventuresome merchants, always on the lookout for a new market, have also shipped considerable amounts of goods to Sydney and Melbourne.

UPRISING IS RUMORED IN BAJA CALIFORNIA

SAN DIEGO, Aug. 2, 1852—Active preparations are under way to proclaim the independence of the Baja California peninsula and hoist the "Bear Flag," according to reports received on reliable authority.

Don Manuel Castro, a native of Monterey and formerly an officer in the Mexican army, is said to have been quietly enlisting men in both San Diego and Los Angeles counties to proceed to Baja California for that purpose. Rumor has it that he has been quite successful.

Followers of Castro are believed to be making their way over the border with the plan of uniting at some given rendezvous and then marching on Santo Tomas and La Paz.

Daguerrotype Studios Are Very Successful

SAN FRANCISCO, Aug. 10, 1852 —There is perhaps no other city in the Union where the Daguerrean art is so frequently patronized for the procurement of likenesses to be sent home as souvenirs to absent friends and families.

Large numbers are sent off by every steamer, through the mails and the various expresses, to be treasured by the recipients in remembrance of those who are toiling in a far-off land. The art has been carried to such perfection now that painted miniatures are almost superseded.

Fire Insurance Ready For Buildings in S. F.

SAN FRANCISCO, Sept. 8, 1852— The firm of Case, Heiser & Co. has been appointed agent of the Niagara Fire Insurance Co. of New York and is ready to receive proposals for insuring first-class buildings, merchandise and personal property in this city.

This is an important and significant feature in the city's history. After the dreadful losses which our business community and citizens generally have suffered from fire, the simple announcement of an eastern insurance company establishing an agency here imparts a refreshing feeling of confidence and reliance. It will also have a favorable effect on business.

As a result of the rebuilding following the four big fires, the city contains a large number of buildings fire-proof "from turret to foundation." Walls are of great massiveness; roofs are of brick work and cement; windows are protected by iron shutters.

In addition, many buildings have wells and pumping systems. Construction has required an immense outlay of money because of the high price of materials and labor.

———o———

Telegraph Hill Cut To Fill Battery St.

SAN FRANCISCO, Sept. 19, 1852 —The work of filling in the foot of Battery street is making rapid progress. Telegraph Hill is being fast cut away under the repeated extracts of material from it. A communication between Griffith's Wharf and Market street will soon be fully established.

New Record for Clipper In Unloading Cargo

SAN FRANCISCO, Sept. 19, 1852 —The great clipper ship Flying Cloud holds another record today.

Not only has she made the quickest passage from New York to this port, but now she holds the record for the fastest discharge of cargo from a vessel of her large tonnage. Under the management of Messrs. Allen and Ruggles, her entire cargo has been landed without accident or damage in the remarkable time of eight days.

The clipper's cargo included all sorts of merchandise and heavy machinery, and measured 100,000 cubic feet, or 2500 tons.

———o———

Mule Train Arrives From Ohio, Indiana

COLUMBIA, Sept. 13, 1852—Columbia has been enlivened by the arrival of 14 wagons, with four mules each, from the plains with about 75 emigrants, mostly from Ohio and Indiana.

The train made the journey to Columbia in about 130 days. Its members report the route to the southern gold mines seems preferable to any yet traveled. They found grass and water at convenient distances all the way through.

No sickness struck the company, and all present a hardy and rugged appearance. Four ox teams of this train, containing the women and children, are behind and expected to reach the settlements in a few days.

———o———

CAMPAIGN WITH SONGS

SAN FRANCISCO, Sept. 12, 1852 — Songs, the more ridiculous the better, seem destined to play a prominent role in political campaigning in California this fall.

The chorus of one Whig song runs:

"Hurrah, hurrah, hurrah!
Whene'er the chance permits
With warm Scott soup and
Graham bread
We'll give the Demos fits."

In reply the Democrats sing:

"Alas poor Cooney Scott,
'Tis too late in the day,
You never can be President
We hear the people say."

LARGE SHIPMENT OF GOLD DUST

SAN FRANCISCO, Sept. 1, 1852— The Pacific Mail Steamship Company steamer sailed for Panama today with $2,132,847 in gold dust, the second biggest gold cargo of the year.

Total shipments by steamers and sailing vessels from January 1 to the present time have been $29,195,965, which is at the rate of $43,793,947 for the year.

From today's immense shipment it will be seen that our mines hold out, and that there is no denger of their being exhausted. From the accounts daily received from the mining regions, there is every reason to believe that the gold deposits are so extensive they will give employment to thousands of miners for a hundred years to come.

With the mining population increasing, it is not unlikely the gold shipments from this port will be double what they are now.

———o———

Competition Melts Price of Import Ice

News has been received of the clearance from Boston, Mass., of another cargo of ice for California notwithstanding the competition in this market by shipments from the Russian settlements to the north which caused price to drop from 20 cents to 6 and even 4 cents a pound.

The Boston and California Ice Company, it seems, is not disposed to flinch from this source of competition. It has two cargoes on the way, and another scheduled for next month.

———o———

SAW MILL AT AUBURN

AUBURN, Sept. 22, 1852—A mammoth saw mill is in operation six miles from here.

It has an engine of 80 horsepower, runs two perpendicular saws and has a lath machine. Installation of other machinery is planned. Though the mill has a daily capacity of 15,000 feet of lumber and 10,000 laths, the demand is greater than the supply.

———o———

SAN FRANCISCO, Sept. 1, 1852— The scarcity and high price of rice, their staple diet, is causing concern to the Chinese residents of the city.

Prominent Hotel Is Destroyed by Fire

SACRAMENTO, Oct. 13, 1852 — The large and beautiful hotel "The Pavilion," together with its stables, outbuildings and fences surrounding it was totally destroyed by fire this afternoon.

The blaze began in the hotel kitchen after the cook built a fire in the stove, on which was a quantity of land. This took fire and ignited the paper on the walls. In a few minutes the entire room was ablaze.

Despite the valiant efforts of neighbors, the hotel was an immense heap of smoldering ruins within 20 minutes after discovery of the blaze. Some 300 tons of hay stored nearby were saved, however.

The hotel was built in 1850 at a cost of more than $30,000 and was occupied by Charles Denman. It was one of the handsomest and most commodious hotels in this section of the state.

---o---

Bloomers Draw Stares On Portland Streets

PORTLAND, Ore. Ter., Oct. 9, 1852—Quite a number of Bloomers, worn by women just arrived from over the plains, have made their appearance here in the past few days. Being the first examples of the genuine Bloomer costume ever seen in Oregon, they of course attracted much attention.

Fast, New Steamer Ready For Service

SAN FRANCISCO, Oct. 7, 1852—The new steamer Cortes, built for Pacific Coast service, attracted much attention on her arrival today from New York by way of Cape Horn. She is a beautiful ship and has proved one of the fastest on record by average 250 miles a day on her run from Valparaiso to Panama.

During her stopover at Valparaiso she was visited and closely examined by the English admiral and many of his officers, including the engineer staff. They agreed with the American officers present that the Cortes is one of the most beautiful specimens of naval architecture and shipbuilding afloat on the oceans.

The Cortes has an engine of 300 horsepower, but consumes only 20 tons of coal per day. She has a wheel 31 feet, 5 inches, in diameter, making 15 revolutions per minute. Her extreme length is 227 feet, and beam is 32 feet. During her trip the Cortes drew only 9 feet, 6 inches of water although she had on board 80 tons of spare machinery and stores for other vessels of the line. Accommodations are provided for 800 passengers.

SANTA CLARA VALLEY DRAWS IMMIGRANTS

SANTA CLARA, Oct. 3, 1852 — Within the past few days this city and county have received a substantial immigration. It is gratifying to note that the newcomers appear to possess more stability than many of the area's population of the last three years.

Trees Would Help To Beautify City

SAN FRANCISCO, Oct. 11, 1852 — Almost every new arrival to this city remarks on the lack of any form of foliage, and on the improvement that would be made if the streets were lined with shade trees.

San Francisco certainly presents a bleak appearance to the newcomer. The sandhills surrounding the city on three sides are not attractive. There is no question but the planting of trees would add a measure of beauty.

It is to be hoped some enterprising property-holders will plant a few trees, such as would thrive in this climate, in front of their dwellings. Such improvements would soon be copied by many others. In a short time every street, especially those removed from the business portion, would be beautified. What a handsome avenue Stockton street would be with shade trees on each side throughout its length!

On the practical side, lots on such an improved street would no doubt sell for 10 or 15 per cent more than they do at the present time.

---o---

Big Grizzly Shot

SACRAMENTO, Oct. 20, 1852—A grizzly bear weighing over 800 pounds was shot yesterday below Grape Vine Ranch on the Sacramento river by Mr. Tier, a resident of that vicinity.

The bear was trying to climb a fence when Mr. Tier dropped him instantly with a single bullet just behind the shoulder. After being dressed, bruin was brought into town to undergo inspection by the curious.

---o---

HUGE GOLD NUGGET

SACRAMENTO, Oct. 1, 1852 — One of the largest and handsomest lumps of gold ever found in California is now on display at the banking house of Mills, Townsend & Co.

This splendid specimen is nearly pure and weighs slightly more than 204 ounces. The firm also has another nugget, perfectly pure, that is worth $500. Both specimens were taken out at Downieville.

Pico Band Members Condemned To Hang

LOS ANGELES, Nov. 29, 1852 — Three members of Salomon Pico's robber band were condemned today to die by hanging for the murder of Gen. Joshua H. Bean, who had served as alcalde and mayor of San Diego and was appointed a major general by the state's first legislature.

Their trial was conducted by a committee of seven men elected by the people after six members of the Pico gang were arrested.

The gang members were caught after being named by a Sonorian woman known to be the mistress of one of Pico's men. Pico himself passed through Los Angeles only two days ago in broad daylight, but being somewhat disguised, was not discovered in time.

One of those condemned, Reyes Feliz, aged 15 or 16, was executed. Though he denied killing Bean, he admitted to other crimes, including murder.

———o———

WAVES DAMAGE WHARF

SAN FRANCISCO, Nov. 5, 1852 — Sixty feet of Law's Wharf at Clark's Point was carried away by the waves in the bay as a result of the norther which has been blowing for two days. For awhile it was feared that the Pacific St. Wharf would go, but it only swayed.

All vessels anchored in the harbor had every inch of cable in use.

———o———

FORT GUARDS VALLEY

STOCKTON, Nov. 11, 1852 — Fort Miller, military post at the point where the San Joaquin river enters the plains, is deemed to exercise an important and beneficial effect on the Indians in this part of the state. The post consists of five commissioned officers, 80 soldiers and one woman. The fort is large, well arranged and convenient.

———o———

LOS ANGELES, Nov. 6, 1852 — Col. Washington and his party left today for San Bernardino to commence survey of the Base Line. A.B. Gray, formerly of the Boundary Commission, is engaged in surveying a range of township lines from San Bernardino to the sea coast.

Sacramento In Ashes— Six Lives Known Lost

SACRAMENTO, Nov. 3, 1852 — A huge section of Sacramento was completely destroyed, and at least six lives were taken by a raging conflagration that broke out shortly before midnight last night.

California's First Presidential Vote

SAN FRANCISCO, Nov. 22, 1852 — Practically all returns, even from the most remote areas, are in from the state's first opportunity to vote for the presidency.

It now is certain that the Democratic nominee, Franklin Pierce, has carried California over Gen. Winfield Scott, the Whig leader, by a majority of between 9500 and 10,000 votes despite the fact that both San Francisco and Sacramento voted Whig. The total vote throughout the state is estimated at approximately 70,000.

Published returns have brought to light some oddly named localities: in Siskiyou, such as Lower and Upper Humbug, Greenhorn; in Shasta, One Horse Town, One Dog Town; in other counties, Jackass Gulch, Pine Log Cross, Shingle Machine, Yankee Jim's, Greaserville, Mud Springs.

———o———

MINERS PROSPERING IN COLUMBIA AREA

COLUMBIA, Nov. 15, 1852 — An inspection trip covering this town, Shaw's Flat and Springfield shows strong evidence of the commencement of stirring times among the miners.

Recent rains have swelled the rivers and creeks, thus affording a good supply of water to the ditches, which are the main means of providing the miners with constant employment. The winter's work may be said to have fairly commenced.

The Sullivan's Creek Race is flowing well and affords facilities for gold washing to many patrons along its route of several miles. The great Tuolumne ditch and its numerous branches have much more water.

Population in this area has more than quadrupled within the last year.

The fire started in a millinery shop on J street near Fourth. In five minutes the fire spread from building to building and up and down, and across the street. The flames carried the fire along both sides of J street to Eighth.

For a time it appeared that the hook and ladder firemen had arrested the fire. Then the wind, which had been blowing toward the levee, increased to a gale and changed to the north, thus turning the fire broadside on. In a few minutes it had spread to M street.

Inmates of the hospital, 70 in all, were taken to the levee and thence to a suitable house by Drs. Brierly and Williams.

Everything was gutted to Eighth street on the north and Ninth on the south side of J street, to Twelfth on K, down to N on the southeast and through N and M to the levee. At 5 a.m. the fire was nearly out.

At least six lives were lost in the blaze. Mme. Lanos of the millinery and dry goods shop perished in bed, and three members of No. 3 Engine Co. fell with a building roof and were swallowed up.

Total losses are initially estimated as at least $5,000,000. The ballots cast in the city yesterday's presidential election were destroyed. It is reported over 3500 votes were cast and that the count for presidential electors, which had just been completed, showed a Whig majority of 500.

———o———

CONSTRUCTION BEGINS ON TELEGRAPH LINE

SAN FRANCISCO, Nov. 12, 1852 — Work of erecting poles for the first magnetic telegraph line in California got underway today. The starting point is the corner of Montgomery and Merchant streets.

The intended route of the California Telegraph Co. line is by way of San Jose, Stockton, Sacramento and Marysville. Already one man here has complained that the poles are unsightly.

This is just the commencement of a vast and continuous line of communications, and, no doubt, will be continued until the shores of the Atlantic and Pacific oceans, as it were, are brought together.

The company was formed on a monopoly granted by the legislature to Messrs. Allen and Burnham.

First Legal Hanging Held in San Francisco

SAN FRANCISCO, Dec. 10, 1852 — Ten thousand spectators today witnessed the first execution to be held under the sentence of a lawful tribunal in the county of San Francisco. There have been other hangings, but under vigilante aspices.

The man executed was Jose Forner, who stabbed and robbed to death a Mexican, Jose Rodriguez, in Pleasant Valley last September.

TWO MEN DROWNED ON CHRISTMAS NIGHT

LOS ANGELES, Dec. 26, 1852 — Two men sailing from Catalina Harbor to San Pedro in a small craft lost their lives last night when they were caught in a southeast gale and driven on the rocks northwest of San Pedro. A third member of the party managed to fight his way to safety ashore.

The gales have carried away the brick storehouse at San Pedro, and destroyed a large amount of government stores. The mountains around Los Angeles are white with snow.

Fremont Title Confirmed

SAN FRANCISCO, Dec. 27, 1852 — The federal board of land commissioners issued an opinion today confirming Senator John C. Fremont in his title to the rich mineral lands in Mariposa county known as the Fremont claim.

Fremont's title has been regarded by the public as questionable, and the opinion will cause much dissatisfaction. Difficulties may arise from attempts to enforce it as many men have prospected and worked gold quartz claims within the possible limits of this grant of ten square leagues. Within the claim are four towns, Mariposa, Agua Frio, Guadalupe and Carson's Creek, with a total population of about 3500.

Many Attend Christmas Concert

SAN FRANCISCO, Dec. 25, 1852 — Although the day and evening were cold and rainy from some of the most inclement weather of the season, the Christmas night concert given by the popular singer, Miss Kate Hayes, was well attended.

Forner was convicted in a regular trial last month despite his plea of self defense. He claimed that Rodriguez had tried to rob him and had wounded him in the leg in their struggle.

A gallows was set up on the slope of Russian Hill out of the view of any houses in the city, but a crowd of 10,000 including many women turned out. A company of volunteer riflemen was summoned to clear a space about 200 yards square around the scaffold.

Forner was closely guarded as he was brought to the execution scene in a wagon from the county jail about three quarters of a mile distant. The prisoner calmly smoked a cigar on his last journey, and in a final statement repeated his declaration of innocence.

SALINAS VALLEY FLOOD

MONTEREY, Dec. 25, 1852 — This section suffers much from the floods in the Salinas Valley, which has caused great loss to farmers. The river rose nine feet in one 12-hour period.

Late today this town was hit by the worst storm of all. Hurricane winds ripped roofs from many houses and damaged the church. Adobe walls have been so saturated with water that they threaten to dissolve.

At Santa Cruz the southeast gale which blew for several days drove several anchored vessels onto the northern shore, including the brigs Virginia, Androscoggin and Emily Bourne, and the schooners Curlew, Sophia, Guadalupe, Emperor and Sarah Lavinia. It is feared most of them will be totally lost.

How badly the storms have hit this general area is shown by the fact that it took the mail rider six days to reach San Juan from San Jose, a distance of less than 50 miles.

Slayer Lynched

SACRAMENTO, Dec. 25, 1852 — A hanging by the people took place today at a ranch two miles up river from here.

The man executed was William K. Jones, and the hanging occurred on the place of the man he was convicted of killing, Peter McGaffing. Jones had been held in custody by some neighbors since the fatal quarrel between the two men several days ago.

Miners Celebrate

NEVADA CITY, Dec. 25, 1852 — Despite the constant rain and snow which have put a halt to almost all activity, Christmas Eve was celebrated by a joyous gathering of people from almost every section of this region.

Rough, long-bearded gold miners left off their slouched hats and corduroys to dress as close to the mode as they could and join in dancing the polka. If there are no turkeys or plum pudding for Christmas dinner today, it is not for lack of gold to pay for them.

RAIN & SNOW MAR CHRISTMAS SEASON

It is a gloomy Christmas, from the weather standpoint, for practically all of California.

There has been continuous rain, with snow in the mountains, for the entire week. Snow may be seen even on all the mountains surrounding San Francisco Bay, while many mining districts toward the Sierra are almost completely isolated because mountain trails have been blocked by snow. There are reports that several men who have tried to transport food on their own backs have been frozen.

Rivers in the valley region have all gone over their banks. Sacramento, Stockton and Marysville are all flooded. Between the towns and the mountains are vast areas of standing water. There are food shortages and much distress in many communities.

OREGON TERRITORY HAS A WHITE CHRISTMAS

PORTLAND, Ore., Dec. 25, 1852 — For the past two weeks Oregon Territory has had the coldest weather ever remembered. Snow covers the ground a foot deep, and the mercury has dropped to only four degrees above zero.

As a result of the severe weather, there is much suffering and destitution among the immigrants who arrived from the eastern states late in the fall. A large number of cattle is reported to have died in outlying ranches.

THE GOLDEN GAZETTE 1853

JANUARY 1853

Wild Horses, Elk Abound in Valley

STOCKTON, Jan. 16, 1853—Wild horses are almost innumerable on the San Joaquin plains, driven to high ground by the bad weather and floods.

Many thousands are ranging in the area between the Merced and Mariposa rivers. Hunters are taking them with the lasso by the hundred. The horses are easily caught when they are driven to low lands where they bog down in the mud.

There is a great abundance of elk meat in the market. Elk are found in bands of five to 20 animals corralled by the flood. The rancheros are living almost entirely on elk meat.

Large numbers of elk, with huge antlers, have been shot in the country bordering the Calaveras river. Hunters anticipate having fine sport in the spring months when the elk will be in best condition.

Bad Roads Require Use of Pack Mules

STOCKTON, Jan. 15, 1853 — Because the bad roads prevent the use of teams, Todd's Express is operating with a train of 30 pack mules to Sonora.

Rates are $30 per passenger, with the demand brisk. On one trip the mule train brought in 230 pounds of gold dust from Sonora for shipment to the Atlantic states.

RIVER STEAMER SINKS

BENICIA, Jan. 7, 1853 — Two women and a child were drowned when the steamer Camanche sank after colliding with the steamer Bragdon near here in rough and hazy weather last night. The ship went down in eight minutes.

Refugees Arrive After Rugged Trip

SHASTA, Jan. 8, 1853 — Eighty men, refugees from Yreka, arrived here today after taking 18 days to fight their way through the snow. Twenty-seven of the men were more or less frozen, two of them critically.

It took the party 36 hours to make the one 16-mile stretch with only parched barley to eat. Three men had to be left at Martin's ranch because their feet were frozen, two of them critically.

The group report not more than 200 people remain at Yreka and that there has been no flour there for 40 days. Many residents have gone north to Oregon.

Snow is four or five feet deep at the Trinity and two feet here.

Pilot Boat Lost

SAN FRANCISCO, Jan. 7, 1852— The pilot boat Sea Witch was lost in the harbor last night as a result of the heavy fog.

Earlier in the day she was outside the Heads with one pilot on board, the others being engaged in bringing ships in or out. At dark she was making for the harbor when she saw the ship Huntress flying a jack and in a dangerous position.

The pilot boarded the Huntress and ordered the crew of the Sea Witch to follow her in. In the fog the pilot boat lost sight of the Huntress and struck on Little Alcatraz. Her crew just managed to get off safe in a small boat.

BEEF TO BE SOLD

STOCKTON, Jan. 2, 1853 — A drove of 40 beef cattle, owned by D. J. Hope, arrived today from Santa Barbara. He intends to slaughter them for the market, and asks 50 cents a pound.

Citizens of Calaveras Hunt Joaquin's Band

STOCKTON, Jan. 27, 1853—Calaveras county citizens are up in arms over a band of Mexican marauders, said to be led by a robber named Joaquin, concerned in the murder of four Americans at Turnersville.

The bandits have been active through the winter months, and in the past week there have been at last four killings. Joaquin has levied his "black mail" generally upon the Chinese.

A general search for Joaquin and his villains has been begun by 300 armed miners. They have posted guards at the ferries on the Stanislaus and Calaveras rivers to prevent escape. One of the gang was caught at Yankee Camp and another at Cherokee Landing. Both were strung up.

Americans have driven the entire Mexican population from the San Andreas region and the forks of the Calaveras. The greatest excitement extends in every direction.

Flood at Sacramento On New Year's Day

SACRAMENTO, Jan. 1, 1853 — The New Year was ushered in by a flood that covered almost the entire city as a result of unprecedented warm rains that fell for 48 hours.

Boats drawing 6 to 10 inches can float along practically every street. J street was covered at times today by up to 500 boats of all descriptions. Despite the flood, the city was not down-hearted. Ladies still made their New Year's calls. Boatmen engaged in numerous impromptu races, cheered on by many who sat at their second-story windows to see the show.

WASHINGTON FETE RIOT KILLS 2, WOUNDS 2

LOS ANGELES, Feb. 23, 1853 — A Washington's Birthday ball here broke up with gunfire in which two men were fatally shot and two others were wounded.

The party was given by several men at the home of Abel Stearns, one of the city's most prominent citizens. Others who were not invited determined to break it up. During the evening a cannon was carried from the Plaza to a point near the Stearns house and discharged at 11 p.m. At the same time a mob of 15 to 20 men started ringing gongs and throwing firecrackers into the house.

After considerable noise they retired, and all was quiet until shortly after 1 a.m. when one of the men at the party started home. As he went out, he heard sounds which indicated another attack and quickly closed the door. Immediately the men outside threw themselves against the door and tried to break in.

Several of those inside wished to attack the rioters at once, but were persuaded to refrain until the ladies present could retire. While they were waiting, a shot from outside passed through a window blind and slightly wounded Judge Myron Norton in the shoulder. Those inside returned the fire through a window and wounded Robert Moore, a gambler formerly of Santa Barbara.

Despite more shots from the outside, Colonel Watson and Judge Norton led a sortie against the rioters and fatally wounded Elias Cook and Dr. J. T. Overstreet.

Settlers Meet Bandits Who Brag of Killings

LOS ANGELES, Feb. 11, 1853—A party of 20 French settlers who arrived here from Sonora today said that at San Fernando, Lower California, they had met up with two men who claimed to have committed many assassinations in the California gold regions.

One of the men was named Guadalupo Valdez and the other Ramos. Valdez said he alone had murdered over 30 Americans and displayed 15 Colt's six-shooters he said he had taken from his victims.

JOAQUIN'S BAND IN MANY KILLINGS

STOCKTON, Feb. 28, 1853—From the mining regions the news of the diggings is favorable, but it is overshadowed by the series of atrocities, unexampled for villainy and cruelty, that are being committed with impunity.

Joaquin still pursues his career of crime. Daily there are new stories of his doings. As may be imagined, there is little police organization in the mountains. Communities are isolated, and the roads are just mere trails. The wonder is that such an organization has not sprung up before. Americans are said also to be acting with Joaquin.

Despite all the advantages these bandits possess, it is thought they soon will be caught and punished. They will be hunted down like wolves and receive as little mercy.

Six Chinese Killed

BIG BAR, Feb. 8, 1853—A party of five men, believed to belong to Joaquin's band, attacked a Chinese camp at these Cosumnes river diggings today. They killed six Chinese and made away with $6000.

Near French Camp the bodies of three murdered men were found secreted in a hole and covered with brush.

River Rates Cut

SACRAMENTO, Feb. 17, 1853 — Competition between the steamers running to San Francisco is so great that a price war is on. Passage down river has dropped to $1 on most ships, and in some cases as low as 50 cents.

LOS ANGELES HAS DAY OF MUCH ACTIVITY

LOS ANGELES, Feb. 9, 1853 — Each day impresses on one the fact that this city of Los Angeles is one of the fastest-moving localities on record.

As for instance, yesterday was a busy day. There were four weddings, two funerals, one street fight with knives, a lynch court, two men flogged, a band serenade, a fist fight and one man tossed in a blanket.

If any of the flourishing up-country towns can hold a candle to that, let them do it or else hold their peace.

YELLOW FEVER HITS STEAMER PASSENGERS

SAN FRANCISCO, Feb. 23, 1853 — There has been heavy mortality from yellow fever aboard the last two steamers to arrive from Panama.

The Golden Gate lost 23 passengers, and the Winfield Scott, which arrived yesterday, suffered 41 deaths. The disease reached its full virulence after the ships left Panama. No case is reported as arising in this city.

Oregonians Build Steamer

PORTLAND, Ore. Terr., Feb. 8, 1853—A stern wheel steamer is being built at Milwaukie near here to run between Portland and Oregon City. She will be 116 feet long and 16 feet in beam, and have two engines.

Plank Road Planned

SACRAMENTO, Feb. 20, 1853 — Peter H. Burnett, first governor of the state of California, is leader in a movement to promote the sale of stock in a proposed plank road from Sacramento to Nevada City by way of Auburn and Grass Valley.

FLOUR PRICES DROP

SAN FRANCISCO, Feb. 28, 1853 — Flour prices have dropped in the past fortnight from around $12 to $9 a barrel as a result of the arrival at this port of cargoes totaling 50,000 barrels. Stocks in the city and state are now estimated at 80,000 barrels.

Steamer Aground Off Of the Golden Gate

SAN FRANCISCO, March 6, 1853—The Pacific Mail steamer Tennessee went ashore this morning in a dense fog in Bolinas Bay, north of the Golden Gate. Her 600 passengers, including 100 women and children, have all been safely landed.

The ship, which left Panama February 19, had steamed back and forth outside the heads during the night because of the fog. Almost without warning she struck broadside on the beach at 9 a.m. Only a short distance ahead and astern of the place where the Tennessee grounded were cliffs which would have shattered the ship with probably heavy loss of life.

After she hit, the first mate went overboard with a cable and was able to make the ship fast to a cliff, and to organize a means of getting the passengers safely ashore. It is feared the Tennessee will be a total loss though cargo and machinery may be saved.

The Tennessee had no word to report of the steamer Independence, long overdue from Panama. The Independence was last seen February 13 off Cape San Lucas, and it is thought she must have met with disaster.

SHEEP, MULES, WAGONS DRIVEN FROM SANTA FE

LOS ANGELES, March 24, 1853—Mr. Aubrey and a party arrived here today from Santa Fe, New Mexico, with ten wagons, 3500 sheep and 100 American mules.

They will immediately proceed to the northern part of the state to sell the sheep and the mules in the markets there. The party started the drive on November 18. Sheep were said to be scarce in New Mexico, bringing $2 to $3 a head.

On the Gila the Aubrey group ran across an old camp around which were strewn the bones of eight or ten persons. It is supposed some party of emigrants was cut off and destroyed by Indians.

Road Surveys Begun

LOS ANGELES, March 16, 1853—The board of supervisors has appointed surveyor; to locate roads connecting Los Angeles with San Bernardino, Santa Anita and San Pedro,.

FISHING INDUSTRIES HAVE POSSIBILITIES

SAN FRANCISCO, March 20, 1853—In the rush for gold the fisheries of California are often overlooked. Rivers, bays and estuaries are alive with salmon.

It is estimated there are 400 boats, valued at $60,000, engaged in fishing on the Sacramento river alone. Nets have a value of $80,000 and Seines of $6000. Average haul of the boats during the season is $30 a day, while hauling seines will make $100 daily. The catch supplies all northern California markets, with 5000-6000 pounds a day now coming into this city.

Fishing smacks are also busy outside Golden Gate. Monterey Bay is famous for the number of sardines, but so far no fishing is done for them commercially.

Many Chinese engage in fishing. In the vicinity of Mission Creek they get about 5000 pounds a day, and sell to the Chinese population at $5 a hundred pounds.

EXPANSION FOR THE ALASKA ICE TRADE

SAN FRANCISCO, March 5, 1853—The arrival of the brig Consort from Sitka last night with 220 tons of ice marks a new era in the ice trade of the Pacific Coast.

The Consort is owned by the American Russian Commercial Company, which has engaged vigorously in supplying the various markets on the coast with ice from Sitka. With the rapid advance of civilization, this article is becoming a necessity of life, especially in the summer months.

It is fortunate a supply of ice is near at hand, within 15 days' sail of San Francisco. The lake from which the company gets its ice can furnish 15,000 tons a year and is easy of access, being 1500 yards to the ship landing. The company has sent engineers and a working force to get out the ice and build ice houses an a railway to the shore to enable loading ships all year.

Shipments of ice may now be expected to arrive here every two weeks. This supply from Sitka will annihilate the ice trade that has existed between Boston, Mass., and this port.

State May Offer Big Reward for Joaquin

BENICIA, March 28, 1853—A resolution was introduced in the legislature today by Assemblyman Herbert to pay a $5000 reward to anyone capturing the notorious bandit Joaquin and $1000 each for his associates. The proposal was referred to the Committee on Military Affairs for consideration.

To account for the simultaneous reports of Joaquin in various parts of the state, there must be several Joaquins, or people must magnify every ferocious-looking character they meet into the robber.

Only a short time ago it was reported he was committing atrocities in Mariposa. Now one report has it he was seen a few days ago near Mokelumne Hill, while the Shasta Courier affirms that he is in that neighborhood.

LIGHTHOUSES FOR COAST

SAN FRANCISCO, March 28, 1853—It is gratifying to navigators and merchants that several lighthouses are being erected along the coast of California and Oregon for the protection of shipping.

The lighthouse on Alcatraz has been completed and will be put in operation on the arrival of the latest type of revolving lantern from France. The lighthouse at Fort Point at the entrance to the harbor is half completed. One at Point Pinos near Monterey is under construction, and work will soon begin on a light on the Farallones.

SANTA ANA, March 19, 1853—Indians, believed to be Pah-Utahs, have been engaging in several forays in this southern country.

The Bandit Joaquin is Seen Near Monterey

MONTEREY, April 15, 1853—Reports have reached here that the bandit Joaquin and two of his gang surprised residents of a house on the Salinas Plains in the night time by knocking on the door and asking for refreshment.

The leader of the group was about 21 years old, tall and handsome with a beard and mustached. He carried four revolvers and a large bowie knife. Acting and talking courteously, he at length admitted that he was Joaquin and declared, "No man takes me alive."

Joaquin gave the reasons for his career of crime. After he had been oppressed by Americans at the gold placers, robbed of $40,000 and flogged, he determined to get revenge. Having heard a large reward was offered for him, he said he had ridden into Stockton in disguise and saw a poster offering $5000 for him. Underneath it, according to his story, he wrote, "I will give $10,000 myself—Joaquin."

After eating, Joaquin paid his fare at the house before leaving at about 1 o'clock in the morning.

———o———

Reward Proposed for Capture of Joaquin

BENICIA, April 14, 1853 — The legislature's judiciary committee today reported out a bill authorizing a state reward of $5000 for the arrest or capture of Joaquin the robber.

———o———

Horse Thieves Hanged

SAN JUAN BAUTISTA, April 8, 1853 — Citizens of the town today hanged two Mexican horse thieves, who had stolen stock from the rancho of David Spencer on the Salinas River.

After a pursuit they were found hiding in a clump of bushes near Gilroy's. Bound and brought here, they were committed to trial at Monterey. But the citizens, who have suffered much from gangs of thieves, took them from the officers and hung them on a hastily erected gallows. The two men claimed they had bought the horses from an Indian.

Many Lives Are Lost By Steamer Disasters

SAN FRANCISCO, April 12, 1853 —The populace of San Francisco has been shocked by three steamer disasters, two involving ships bringing passengers from the Atlantic States and one bay steamer.

BLOODY OUTBREAK KILLS TWO IN SANTA BARBARA

SANTA BARBARA, April 30, 1853 — Two men were killed, and the county sheriff was critically wounded in a fight in the town Plaza today arising out of a land ejectment suit.

Claiming the land is theirs, Dr. Nicholas Den and Daniel Hill obtained a court order to eject the well known horseman, Jack Powers, from the Arroyo Burro Ranch.

Sheriff William W. Twist had summoned a large number of citizens to assist him in serving the writ in the belief he would meet opposition. While the posse was assembling, a man identified only as "Mickey" threw a lasso over a brass cannon in the Plaza and started dragging it away. The sheriff ordered him to stop.

At that moment someone fired a shot which fatally wounded John A. Vidal, a former justice of the peace. An Indian named Leyva then drew a knife and stabbed the sheriff, who turned and shot him dead before slumping from his own wound. General gunfire followed, in which at least two other men, members of the opposition party, were slightly wounded.

The situation remained tense in Santa Barbara tonight, but there was no further shooting.

———o———

New Marine Hospital

SAN FRANCISCO, April 7, 1853 —The cornerstone of the new $100,-000 U. S. Marine Hospital on Rincon Point was laid today at well attended ceremonies.

The four-story building, 182 by 96 feet, will accommodate 800 patients. It will be supplied with bath houses, proper ventilation and all modern improvements. It will be built of California brick, with interior woodwork of New York manufacture. Grounds will run to the water's edge.

On April 1 news reached here of the loss of the long-missing steamer Independence of the Panama service with 125 passengers and crewmen. She struck a reef on the island of Margarita off the coast of Lower California February 16. Captain Sampson got her off, but she began to leak badly and was run ashore. After the ship burst suddenly into flames, many people leaped into the surf in panic. Relief was given to the 300 survivors by some whaling ships anchored on the other side of the island.

The steamer S. S. Lewis of the Nicaragua line went ashore near Bolinas Bay in a dense fog in the early morning of April 9. She was too far north of the Golden Gate to hear the warning sounds of Sweeny & Baugh's Fog Bell. Despite high surf all 385 on board were saved, but the ship is a total loss.

Yesterday the boiler exploded on the steamer Jenny Lind in the bay off Pulga Rancho on her run from Alviso to San Francisco. Of the 125 people on board, at least 25 were killed and over 30 injured; it is feared others may have drowned from being blown into the water.

The accident occurred while the company was getting dinner, and the escaping steam swept through the dining salon.

———o———

GREAT CANAL BUILT IN MINING DISTRICT

SONORA, April 22, 1853—One of the wonders of this mining district is the canal of the Tuolumne Hydraulic Association.

It starts out from a dam 25 feet high and 85 feet long that has been built across the Tuolumne River 20 miles above here. A timber flume extends along the high rocky banks of the river for several miles and then runs into a canal. The section to Sonora, Campo, Seco, Yorktown and Poverty Hill is complete, and work is progressing on the branch to Montezuma and Chinese Camp.

When complete, the entire canal will be 40 miles long. It guarantees ample water for the dry season, and should greatly increase both mining and farming activity in this region.

REWARD FOR JOAQUINS VOTED BY LEGISLATURE

BENICIA, May 15, 1853 — A bill providing for a reward of $5,000 and authorizing Capt. Harry Love to raise a company of rangers to pursue and capture the Joaquin bandits was passed by the state legislature today. Vote in the senate was 15 to 9.

Originally naming only "the robber Joaquin," the bill was amended to include "all the companies of robbers commanded by five Joaquins, viz.: Joaquin Muriata, Joaquin Carrillo, Joaquin Ocamarenia, Joaquin Valenzuela and Joaquin Botillen and also other leaders of predatory bands and their members."

It is provided that all cattle, horses, mules and other recovered booty shall be restored to the counties where they were stolen, and also that any captured bandit shall be returned for trial to the county where the crime was committed.

———o———

NEW FIRE ENGINE ARRIVES

SAN FRANCISCO, May 28, 1853 — Members of Columbian Engine Co. No. 11 paraded today in celebration of the arrival of their new engine. It is one of the neatest and most tastefully decorated machines in the city.

Body of the engine is white, set off with blue and yellow lines. On one side of the "jacket" is painted a handsome representation of the ship Golden Light burning at sea. On the other side is Neptune gliding over the sea in his chariot shell. Behind is a painting of a fireman in the Columbian uniform advancing through clouds of dense smoke.

———o———

French Girls Arrive

SAN FRANCISCO, May 28, 1853 —The ship Sacramento arrived today from France with a number of passengers, including 68 young ladies. The voyage from Le Havre took 150 days.

———o———

Northwest Road Planned

OLYMPIA, Wash. Ter., May 21, 1853—Citizens of this territory are hopeful of adopting measures to open a road this season across the Cascade Mts. to Fort Walla Walla for the benefit of the coming immigration.

Three Men Rob Office Of Express Company

SACRAMENTO, May 3, 1853 — Details of the daring robbery of the office of Adams & Co. express at Mormon Island have been received here.

The agent, Mr. Nichols, had retired to his room for the night and left his two assistants to close up and go to bed in the main room. Before they locked the door, three men entered and pretended to search for letters.

As the assistants went to wait on them, the men drew pistols and knives. Failing to find the keys to the safe after binding the assistants, the robbers compelled them to call Mr. Nichols. When he answered, they bound him too and took the keys from his possession. They took all the contents, valued at $7,000.

During the whole operation the bandits were very cool. One read a newspaper, and all three enjoyed some cigars they found in the office, though they complained of their quality. It is believed they were aided by confederates who served as sentinels outside.

Adams & Co. has offered $2,000 for arrest and conviction of the robbers and 25 per cent of the amount of money recovered.

———o———

VISITOR IS THE VICTIM OF A BOLD ROBBERY

SAN FRANCISCO, May 14, 1853 —Three men are held in jail today as suspects in the particularly bold robbery of a visitor from Sacramento.

On arriving at night on the boat from Sacramento, the traveler declares, he was decoyed by a man who offered to take him to a suitable hotel. While they were passing along Front st. near the Pacific Wharf, he was suddenly knocked into the water.

There, a boat was waiting to receive him, and he was immediately gagged and bound on being picked out of the water. The boat then passed under a building built on piles. A trapdoor was opened, and the victim was hoisted into a room above, where he was robbed of $400 before being let go.

The Famed Lola Montez Arrives on Steamer

SAN FRANCISCO, May 21, 1853 — The beauteous Lola Montez, Countess of Lansfeldt, famed for her association with the King of Bavaria and connection with various escapades in Europe, was among the passengers arriving today on the steamer Northerner.

Mme. Montez attracted more attention than the many other notables on board, including Sen. William M. Gwin, who returned from Washington. Everybody was in a fever to catch a glimpse of her.

The countess will make her debut at the American Theatre Thursday evening in the role of Lady Teazle in "School for Scandal," and will perform her famous "Spider Dance" at a subsequent performance. The minimum price of seats for her opening night is $5 for the dress circle and parquette, with $3 for the family circle. First tickets brought a premium of $65 at an auction.

———o———

Many Chinese Fish for Large Shell Species

MONTEREY, May 14, 1853—Large numbers of Chinese are engaged near here in catching a large species of shell fish that is found on the rocks. They dry them and put them up for shipment to China, where they are esteemed a delicacy and command a high price.

The steamer Sea Bird brought down 150 more Chinese from San Francisco to join in the business.

IRON WORKING FIRMS FLOURISH IN S.F.

SAN FRANCISCO, June 8, 1853 —Great progress has been made on the shores of the Pacific Ocean in the working of iron. The expense of transporting heavy machinery from the east has led to building up of flourishing manufactories here.

Iron works in this city are mostly found in the Happy Valley area. The principal ones are Donahue's Union Iron Works, at First and Mission streets; Eagle Iron Works, Alta Foundry, Vulcan Foundry, Pacific Foundry and Sutter Iron Works.

The Union Iron Works, founded in 1850, has grown into a business doing from $15,000 to $20,000 a month, employing between 75 and 100 men. It makes steam engines and boilers, mining and agricultural machinery, sawmills, grist mills, etc., as well as castings of iron and brass for many uses.

Facilities of the Union Works are extensive. It has its own pattern shop, foundry, finishing shop, blacksmith's shop with five forges and a crane, and a boiler shop that has very complete machinery. One of the Union's distinctions is that it has the only steam-riveting machine in the West.

Much work is being done by the Union Works now for the San Francisco Gas Company, such as retorts and purifiers. It is safe to predict that the metalworking industry in this area will keep expanding to meet the needs of this rapidly growing state.

U.S. SENATOR GWIN ENGAGES IN DUEL

SAN FRANCISCO, June 1, 1853 —A duel was held today over the county line between U. S. Senator William M. Gwin and the Hon. J. W. McCorkle as a result of certain offensive remarks made by the latter at the racetrack.

Mr. McCorkle won the choice of weapons: rifles at 30 paces, the combatants to wheel at the word and fire. A number of spectators on the field saw three shots fired without effect, although one of Senator Gwin's shots passed almost through McCorkle's hair.

The affair ended when McCorkle withdrew his remarks, and the dispute was then settled amicably.

News of Joaquin

MARIPOSA, June 6, 1853—Capt. Harry Love's Company of Rangers, empowered by the state legislature to pursue and capture the bandit Joaquin, has been raised here.

——o——

SAN LUIS OBISPO, June 16, 1853 — Private advices have been received here to the effect that without doubt the bandit Joaquin is in this county.

He is reported rusticating on one of the county's ranches with from 15 to 18 compatriots. Joaquin declared that he would do no harm if he is left alone, and that he planned to leave when ready for Mexico.

Citizens of this county do not consider themselves strong enough to attack Joaquin in his hideout.

——o——

COLUMBIA, June 4, 1853—Pedro Sanchez, known as a lieutenant of the bandit Joaquin, was killed last night by a Spaniard named Albino Teba after a dispute at a fandango house.

——o——

SNOW TURNS BACK PARTY

SONORA, June 10, 1853 — The company of 25 men who recently started for Walker's River were turned back after undergoing hardships ascending the mountains over snow and ice.

They got within six miles of the summit of the Sierra Nevada when they came across snow running 40 feet deep. It was in such condition from the commencement of thawing that it could not support the weight of their pack animals.

About half of the company have returned, and have left for Placerville with the intention of crossing the mountains by way of the Carson road. It is believed the others may have killed or left their animals behind to attempt crossing at night on snow shoes when the snow is crusted by the evening cold.

——o——

Stages in Rate War

LOS ANGELES, June 15, 1853— The stages running between Los Angeles and San Pedro are in such strong competition that the fares have been cut to 50 cents from $1. At that, considering the present price of shoe leather, it is cheaper riding than walking.

QUARTZ MILLS BOOM IN GRASS VALLEY

GRASS VALLEY, June 23, 1853 —This section claims to be the most extensive of all the gold-bearing quartz areas of California.

Four quartz mills are now in active operation here. The biggest is the Empire Company, on Wolf Creek. It has a steam engine of 60 horsepower, that drives 16 stamps which will crush twenty tons of rock per day. The company uses one of the new patent amalgamators, which works well, and its rock is rich. Besides its mining machinery, the Empire group operates a sawmill.

Next in size is the Agua Frio Company, a stock company largely owned by Englishmen. It has a capacity of fifteen tons a day. Rock is taken from a 40-foot tunnel and brought out by small rail cars.

One of the other two mills took out $13,000 in gold during the last week. The Grass Valley Company's mill is not yet in operation, and will add to this region's take in gold.

——o——

LOTS OF LIQUOR IN S.F.

SAN FRANCISCO, June 3, 1853 —By actual account the Christian Advocate has found that the number of places in the city where liquor is sold is 537.

OUTLAWS THREATEN PEACE OF SOUTH

LOS ANGELES, July 16, 1853— The county of Los Angeles is practically in a state of insurrection. A gang of outlaws, many of whom have been expelled from the mines for crime, are daily committing robberies and murder.

At a meeting held at the El Dorado, citizens of the town resolved to organize a mounted police force for protection. Companies are being formed here and at the Monte and San Bernardino.

Two murders have been reported within the last couple of days, and there are reports of two men killed on Pio Pico's ranch. A band of robbers, supposedly led by the bandit Joaquin Carillo, attacked a party of New Mexicans near Temecula. The New Mexicans had in their possession $70,000 that they made from the sale of 25,000 sheep, and this amount of gold was a powerful lure to bandits.

A hired vaquero named Vergara shot and killed his employer, David Porter, former Virginia and Texas lawyer, while riding from San Pedro to Los Angeles two days ago.

INDIANS ARE HOSTILE ON ROGUE'S RIVER

SALEM, Ore. Ter., July 14, 1853— Reports from the Rogue's River are that the Indians on Grave Creek are on the watch for whites along the trails. It is dangerous for one man to travel alone, though there is little danger if whites proceed in parties of three or four.

Old Taylor, chief of the Indians, and three others have been hung. Captain Bates is at the head of 40 whites in pursuit of the Indians. Old Taylor and his tribesmen are said to have killed seven whites last winter and then reported that they drowned in the river in a storm.

A rumor that there are white women near Table Rock in the custody of Indians is generally believed. A search party went out to investigate. They found nothing definite but killed six Indians.

SAN FRANCISCO, July 20, 1853 — Undersheriff John A. Freaner was shot and wounded today while trying to secure the ejectment of a squatter, Redmond McCarthy, from a house and lot on Mission street.

LONGSHOREMEN STRIKE FOR HIGHER WAGES

SAN FRANCISCO, July 25, 1853 —The longshoremen, or "lumpers" as they are sometimes called, began a strike today for higher wages.

About 400 longshoremen met at 7 a.m. and decided to raise their wages from $5 to $6 as well as limit their work day to nine hours. They went from wharf to wharf, first asking any hands at work discharging vessels to quit work. In case of refusal the strikers forced the workers to retire.

A group boarded the brig Dudley, and the captain appeared with a pistol and drove them off. By late in the day the strike became general, and the wharves were as deserted as they are on a Sunday.

Lola Montez Marries

SAN FRANCISCO, July 2, 1853— The famous dancer Lola Montez was married to Mr. Patrick P. Hull at 6 a.m. today in the Church of the Mission Dolores. A number of gentlemen witnessed the ceremony.

This afternoon Madame Montez left for Sacramento to start on a tour through the interior.

CORNERSTONE LAID

SAN FRANCISCO, July 17, 1853 —Bishop Alemany today laid the cornerstone of St. Mary's Church at California and Dupont streets in an imposing ceremony attended by a great throng. The church will measure 75 by 130 feet, and be 200 feet high to the top of the cross on the spire.

The Bandit Joaquin Is Slain By Rangers

STOCKTON, July 30, 1853—The famous bandit Joaquin, whose name is associated with a hundred deeds of blood, has at last been captured and killed.

Capt. Harry Love, commander of the company of State Rangers, today brought in to Stockton the head of Joaquin and the hand of one of his lieutenants, as well as one prisoner. Another prisoner drowned himself in the San Joaquin River.

The Rangers have been diligent in their search for the bandit gang. Recently they got information that Joaquin was lurking in the wilds of the Tulare Valley. They met up with the robber chief at the head of his band a few days ago. In a running fight the Rangers killed Joaquin, his lieutenant and captured two others, while three robbers managed to make their escape. Several of the band's horses were also taken.

The victors in the battle cut off Joaquin's head and placed it in spirits to bring in proof the veritable robber himself had been killed.

Overland Arrivals

SACRAMENTO, July 4, 1853 — The first of the overland army of 1853 arrived here today, just one day later than the first arrivals of last year.

The party of 12 men from Galena, Ill., headed by Capt. Isaac Evans, left St. Joseph, Mo., April 20 with four wagons and 25 horses. This side of the South Platte they were attacked by about 80 Crow Indians, but managed to escape with the loss of only a little stock. The weather along the overland route was very severe.

This is the third overland trip for Captain Evans since the gold immigration to California commenced.

Santa Barbara Robberies

SANTA BARBARA, July 10, 1853 A band of robbers was active in this vicinity this week.

They knocked down and tried to rob Mr. Stedman and another person. They also stole two saddled horses from in front of a citizen's house.

BOY TAKES WILD RIDE IN RUNAWAY BALLOON

OAKLAND, Aug. 30, 1853—Joseph Gates, 16-year-old San Francisco newsboy, yesterday inadvertently took a ride in a balloon that carried him from this town to a landing in the Suisun Plains above Benicia.

Three steamers were busy at work carrying hundreds of people across the bay yesterday morning to see a balloon ascension announced by Mr. Kelly. The balloon, about 40 feet in circumference, was in a small yard on Third street near Broadway. While the bag was inflating, several small balloons were sent up and a collection taken.

About 3:30 p.m. Kelly took his seat in the balloon car, but the bag just dragged down the street, banging Kelly around. A lighter man then got in, but the balloon still didn't work. The car was replaced by just a board without results.

At this point the crowd began hooting it was all a fake. Then young Gates, known by the nickname of "Ready," who had come to sell oranges, offered to take a ride, supposing it would be for only a few feet if at all. But the balloon rose quickly and disappeared over the hills to the northeast. It was feared his life would be lost, and Kelly started off on horseback in the direction the balloon had taken.

Although he knew nothing about managing a balloon, the boy finally managed to make it descend by cutting into its side with a knife to allow its gas to escape. His only injury came when he sprained an ankle in jumping when the balloon got close to the ground.

———o———

CLIPPER SHIPS REACH S. F. IN "DEAD HEAT"

SAN FRANCISCO, Aug. 12, 1853—The famous clipper ships Flying Cloud and Hornet arrived here today in a "dead heat" from New York, each taking 105 days for the voyage.

The Hornet actually made port about 40 minutes ahead of the Flying Cloud, but left New York several hours ahead of the other ship. She was becalmed outside until the other ship came up. It took the Hornet 19 days to reach the Equator and 48 more to Cape Horn; the Flying Cloud's times for these two laps were 17 and 46 days, respectively.

Both ships were caught in heavy gales for more than three weeks, the Flying Cloud losing her chief officer and a seaman overboard. Though the Flying Cloud has made the quickest trip on record from New York to San Francisco, these passages are the best of this season so far.

———o———

THIEVES 'STEAL' SAILORS

SAN FRANCISCO, Aug. 9, 1853—Sailor thieves are greatly inconveniencing ships here.

The practice in this port is for sailors shipping out to get two months' pay, $30 or $40 a month, in advance. After the sailors receive this money, the thieves then board the ships and help the crewmen to get away.

Squatter Row Killing

SAN FRANCISCO, Aug. 4, 1853—Dr. John Baldwin, well known citizen, died today of wounds received by gunshot from Joseph Hetherington in a dispute over ownership of a lot in the North Beach section.

Trouble with squatterism is spreading in the city. Today the neighborhood found to its surprise that a fine lot at Stockton and Green streets, next to the Clarendon Hotel, was in the possession of a new tenant, named Cheesebrough. He decided to appropriate the lot, and hastily erected a fence and a house.

In the afternoon F. B. Gray, who had paid $10,000 for the lot and held undisputed title previously, assembled a party of workmen to eject Cheesebrough and demolish his structures.

———o———

IMMIGRANTS FROM TEXAS

SAN DIEGO, Aug. 15, 1853—Word has been received here from Capt. Brown, commanding the U.S. Army post at Vallesito, that 50 immigrants from Texas have passed there. They said there are many other people on the trail behind them, well supplied with cattle.

———o———

SAN JOSE, Aug. 1, 1853—A dispute caused by the epithet of "liar" today ended in the death of Thomas Piles and the wounding of three other men at Piles' farm near here.

Bandit's Head on Display

SAN FRANCISCO, Aug. 19, 1853—The head of Joaquin Muriata, the robber of Calaveras who was captured and killed last month by Capt. Harry Love's Rangers, is now being shown in a saloon here and drawing large crowds.

Several people have definitely identified the head as being authentic. It is the impression of ex-Senator Warner of San Diego and Don Andres Pico of Los Angeles that it is the veritable robber chief himself. The latter had 50 horses stolen by Joaquin in Los Angeles county last month, although the bandit later returned 43 of them.

The head is in a fine state of preservation and bears the impress of the character of the famous robber. Messrs. Black and Nuttall of Love's troop brought it here a few days ago with the object of obtaining the rewards offered all over the country for Joaquin. They have with them certificates of identity for the head.

A letter, allegedly from the bandit Joaquin Carrillo, has been received by newspapers here stating, "I still retain my head, although it is proclaimed through the presses of your fine city that I was recently captured and became very suddenly decapitated." It is thought to be a hoax.

———o———

Indians on Rampage

YREKA, Aug. 26, 1853—A fierce four-hour battle was fought two days ago in the Rogue River Valley country between a force of whites and Indians led by Chief Sam.

The whites lost three men killed and eight wounded, including Gen. Lane and Col. Allen, out of a force of 96 men. Ten Indians were killed and 30 wounded out of some 250. At the end of the fighting Chief Sam agreed to a parley.

Cause of the expedition was the murder of several white settlers in the valley by the Indians.

JURY IS DIVIDED AFTER LONG TRIAL

SANTA BARBARA, Sept. 2, 1853 —One of the longest trials ever held in California has just ended here, with the jury unable to reach a verdict.

Although the incident took place last January, Patrick H. Dunne was indicted and put on trial before Judge Joaquin Carrillo for the shooting of Francis Fontaine in a quarrel. It took ten days to get a jury, and the testimony lasted for two weeks.

In his plea to the jury Edward S. Hoar, Dunne's attorney, referred in stirring fashion to Dunne's heroic part in the attempt to rescue the ill-fated Donner Party in the high Sierra in 1846 during which he lost all his toes by freezing.

The jury voted seven for a complete acquittal and five for finding Dunne guilty of manslaughter. At the conclusion Judge Carrillo ordered a second trial to be held in Los Angeles.

SWIMMING POPULAR AT SANTA BARBARA

SANTA BARBARA, Sept. 3, 1853 —Sea bathing is one of the elegant luxuries in which the natives of the feminine gender indulge in here to their hearts' content.

In the evening, gay senoritas of the village are accustomed to go to the beach in large numbers.

The senoritas all are graceful and beautiful swimmers. No false modesty prevents them from enjoying the pleasures which a daily ablution affords.

RAIL ROUTE STUDIED

LOS ANGELES, Sept. 20, 1853— Lieuts. Stevenson and Parke returned today from a tour of reconnaisance through the passes of San Gorgonio and Cajon. They report that the former possesses great advantages as a route for a railroad or wagon road, much better than anticipated.

SAILORS, BEWARE OF 'SHANGHAING'

SAN FRANCISCO, Sept. 20, 1853 —The practice of "shanghaing" is beginning to be carried to some lengths in this port.

It consists in drugging, making drunk or otherwise forcing sailors by improper means on board ships about to sail. It is resorted to when vessels find it difficult to get mariners in the ordinary manner.

Last Sunday, a sailor named John Williams was taken from the clipper ship Highflyer, bound for China, on a writ of habeas corpus issued by Judge Lake. An affidavit was given that William was made drunk by a pack of wharf-runners and induced to sign mock shipping articles. He was then knocked down, gagged and taken aboard the ship anchored in the stream.

The Highflyer is taking 250 Chinese back to Hongkong.

FIRST TELEGRAPH LINE ON THE PACIFIC COAST

SAN FRANCISCO, Sept. 22, 1853 —The first telegraph line on the Pacific Coast was opened today, running from the Merchants' Exchange downtown to the outer Telegraph Station on Point Lobos. Its purpose is to carry reports of incoming shipping.

Messrs. Sweeney and Baugh, proprietors of the Merchants' Exchange, held a grant fete at Point Lobos to celebrate this great advancement. Two hundred fifty guests went out to the spot and enjoyed a sumptuous outdoor repast. J. S. Henning, builder of the telegraph line, and the English, French and Danish consuls were among the prominent guests present.

Twelve regular and a number of volunteer toasts were drunk. During the festivities nearly a hundred messages were sent into the city by the telegraph.

OREGON IMMIGRATION

PORTLAND, Oreg. Ter., Sept. 2, 1853—The total immigration into Oregon for this year will probably run to 10,000 persons, and perhaps even more.

The mail carrier on the Salt Lake route reports that the immigration is proceeding under favorable circumstances. He says 200 wagons are already at The Dalles, and that 1300 more had passed Fort Hall.

Hydraulic Method Is Introduced in Mines

CALAVERAS, Sept. 10, 1853—A great improvement in gold mining operation is being demonstrated here. The plan has been adopted by Major Case on his claim on Stockton Hill, and found to be very effective as well as a great saving in labor and expense.

This method consists of the use of the hydraulic principle by which a powerful stream of water is brought by hose to bear on the bank of earth. Force of the water washes the earth away very rapidly. The debris then passes into the sluice where it undergoes the usual processing to recover the gold.

Major Case estimates his hose does the work of ten laborers. All work of moving heavy rocks is done away with as the water washes the dirt from around them, and they then roll out of the way and are so disposed of. Hydraulic will be especially useful on hillside claims.

JAIL BREAK AT L. A.

LOS ANGELES, Sept. 11, 1853— The worthy Marshal of the town and his assistant today locked up in jail 25 Indians supposed to be drunk. No sooner had the officers left, when the door of the jail went crash, and the Indians scattered in every direction.

Telegraph Line Links S. F. with San Jose

SAN FRANCISCO, Oct. 15, 1853— The telegraph is now in operation from San Francisco to San Jose. Though it has not yet been turned over to the company by the contractors, the line is being used daily for transmitting messages.

A gentleman in San Jose telegraphed a friend here, and ten minutes later received a reply requesting him to come up. By sundown the San Jose man was in this city. For this accommodation he was glad to pay $1.50, a price which would be extravagant in the Atlantic states.

The whole line from San Francisco, to San Jose, Stockton, Sacramento and Marysville, is to be completed by November 1. The line from Nevada City to Auburn is in operation, and soon will extend to Sacramento.

FIRE HITS SONORA

SONORA, Oct. 4, 1853—Fire broke out at about 3:30 o'clock this morning and spread rapidly through a sizeable portion of this mining town. The property loss is estimated at $300,000.

The blaze started when a candle that had been left lighted set fire to some curtains. A man saw it in time to stop spread of the fire, but no one would leave the game in the gambling house next door to help.

The Sonora Hook & Ladder Co. and Sonora Hose Co. did valiant work, and the reservoir supplied by ditch from one of the mining canals was of great assistance in stopping the flames before the entire town burned. E. B. Lundy, who was sleeping in the rear of Hollister's Saloon, was burned to death.

MANY SHEEP IMPORTED

SAN DIEGO, Oct. 22, 1853—More than 35,000 sheep that have been driven to California from Sonora were entered at the custom house here this week.

The parties owning this drove report there are 15,000 more sheep on the other side of the Colorado River, and 1,200 Texas beef cattle on the road between the Colorado and San Diego.

Lone Indian Woman Is Found on Island

SANTA BARBARA, Oct. 2, 1853 — Much interest is being shown here in a wild Indian woman taken off the Island of San Nicolas by George Nidever, a trapper.

The woman is believed to have lived alone on the island for many years after other members of her small tribe left for the mainland following a fight with trappers who were taking otters there. She has been seen on the island many times since, but always resisted attempts to rescue her until now.

Appearing to be about 60 years of age, she speaks a language that is different from other Indians dialects of California. Her clothes are of curious manufacture from bird feathers and fishbones.

---o---

FILIBUSTER SHIP

SAN FRANCISCO, Oct. 1, 1853 — William Walker, former San Francisco newspaperman, has sued Gen. E. A. Hitchcock, commander of the Military District, to recover possession of the brig Arrow which was seized by soldiers at the foot of Clay Street wharf.

It is rumored that the brig is to be used in an expedition to seize the province of Sonora from Mexico and make that state a republic. Walker, however, denies that she is fitted out for such a purpose.

Judge Satterlee today ordered the brig returned to Walker. The sheriff went on board to take possession, but the soldier guard remained under order from General Hitchcock.

---o---

Gen. Lane Leaves for Washington

PORTLAND, Oregon Ter., Oct. 10, 1853 — General Lane, territorial governor, has left for Washington, taking with him an Indian lad of 16 or 17, the only son of the head chief of the Rogue River tribes, as a hostage that the Indians will keep the treaty. The wound that the general received in the Indian fighting is nearly healed.

---o---

Wine Production Largest Ever

LOS ANGELES, Oct. 4, 1853 -- A greater quantity of wine will be made up here this year than ever before.

THREE MEN HANGED AT SAN LUIS OBISPO

SAN LUIS OBISPO, Oct. 9, 1853— Three murderers were hung by a party of citizens today at San Luis Obispo harbor.

The three, Ramon Espinosa, Juan Ygera and Manuel Verdez, were brought up from San Pedro on the steamer Goliah. Eight or ten Americans were waiting at the landing. When the prisoners were brought ashore, they decided to hang them at the beach because it was feared the Mexican population in town might attempt to rescue their compatriots.

A hillside spot a little back from the beach was selected. The Americans drove the prisoners there in a wagon. They stopped it under the overhanging bough of a tree and adjusted ropes. As the three prisoners stood up side by side, the wagon was driven out from under them.

Weight of the three men bent the bough but did not allow their feet to touch ground. After hanging for some time, they were cut down and buried.

The three men, together with a woman, were arrested at Los Angeles by Rangers on charges of murder and robbery for killing a French peddler and stealing nine horses at San Luis Obispo. They are believed to have been part of the band formerly led by the noted Joaquin.

A jury of the people tried them in the Los Angeles County court room, with Don Abel Stearns presiding, and found them guilty. It was decided to send the men up to San Luis for execution.

---o---

FIRE DESTROYS THE ST. FRANCIS HOTEL

SAN FRANCISCO, Oct. 23, 1853— The five-story St. Francis Hotel, located at Clay and Dupont streets, was destroyed by fire today. The body of one man was found in the ruins; another man jumped three stories, but survived.

Built in 1850 of wood, with partitions of cloth and paper, the hotel was one of the most combustible buildings in the city. The blaze started on the fourth floor and spread rapidly.

LOWER CALIFORNIA IS SEIZED BY FILIBUSTERS

LAPAZ, Lower California, Nov. 8, 1853—Heading a party of filibusters from California, William Walker, former San Francisco newspaperman has proclaimed the Republic of Lower California with himself as president.

Walker's force of 45 men of the so-called First Independent Battalion, arrived here several days ago aboard the bark Caroline. Within half an hour a party went ashore, took the Mexican governor prisoner and seized the town. In the process they lowered the Mexican flag and raised the new government's flag, consisting of three horizontal stripes — red, white and red — with two stars in the white stripe.

Today the filibusters were making ready to sail north to San Lucas when another vessel came in with a newly appointed Mexican governor. He was taken prisoner as well. But a party of Walker's men ashore was fired on, and the Caroline bombarded the town.

Colonel Walker landed his whole force immediately again, and had a general battle in which his army killed several of the enemy without any losses of its own. The Mexicans were chased out of town.

It is Walker's intention to have his seat of government at Ensenada, about 90 miles south from San Diego, and there wait for reinforcements expected to flock to his banner from California. Walker claims the rancheros of Lower California are pleased with the new government.

Miners Doing Well

SAN FRANCISCO, Nov. 16, 1853 — Gold mining operations through the state are generally encouraging, although the onset of winter will halt much work.

At Foster's Bar on the Yuba claims are paying from $6 to $40 a day. A Wingdam company has paid $80 to $100 per day to each share, and the Golden Falls Company $100 to $200 daily.

Some companies at Kennebec Bar are getting from 20 to 30 ounces of gold daily from each long tom. Five men on North Fork took out of a bank claim $560 in one week. On the Oregon side one claim has paid as high as $1000 a day, and on Jamison Creek $3444 was taken from 17 tons of quartz.

The Mokelumne River mines have not been doing so well on the whole this year, although several companies are getting 20 to 30 ounces a day. One company at James' Bar got $10,000 in two weeks' time. The mining water companies are making great progress in carrying water in every direction to the dry diggings.

———o———

Immigrants Outnumbered

SAN FRANCISCO, Nov. 1, 1853— Two steamers sailed today in gallant style with 970 passengers and $2,755,000 in golden treasure for the eastern states — the California bound for Panama and the Cortes for San Juan del Sud, Nicaragua. The steamer Pacific arrived with 700 newcomers to make up for some loss in population.

———o———

UTILLA, Ore., Nov. 1, 1853 — The Indian agent, who has kept a record of the season's immigration, reports that a total of 6449 persons has passed this point.

———o———

CHINESE SHOOT MEXICAN BANDIT

DRYTOWN, Nov. 2, 1853 — Two Chinese traveling from Dry Creek to Mule Creek were fired on today by a Mexican bandit named Antonio who has been terrorizing their compatriots in this area.

One of the Chinese was wounded, though not fatally, and they managed to give the alarm. Antonio was forced to take shelter in his cabin, whose whereabouts was discovered for the first time. A large crowd of Chinese and Americans gathered outside and called on Antonio to come out, but he threatened to shoot anyone approaching.

A Chinese provided the solution for the ticklish situation, managing to drop a canister of gunpowder down the cabin's chimney. It exploded and set the building on fire, forcing Antonio to come crawling out. He aimed his pistol at the nearest American, but 20 Chinese quickly fired and riddled him with bullets.

———o———

Kit Carson Leading Mountain Men East

SAN DIEGO, Nov. 15, 1853 — The famous scout Kit Carson left today at the head of a large party of mountain men. They had a large amount of money with them and were bound for New Mexico, they said.

The party came down from the north on the steamer Goliah, and created considerable excitement here as it was thought they were on an expedition to Sonora.

———o———

MANY WHALERS MEET AT SANDWICH ISLANDS

HONOLULU, Nov. 5, 1853—Marking the close of the present season of operations in North Pacific waters, 112 whaling ships have arrived in the past two weks at the harbors of Honolulu, Lahaina and Hilo.

All the whalers are American, with the exception of three ships from Bremen, three from France and one from Russia. In Honolulu harbor alone today are 87 whalers and 15 merchant vessels. Among

the latter is the clipper ship Nestorian, which brought from New York one of the largest cargoes ever received here, 1440 tons mostly in stores and provisions for the whaling fleet.

It has been a poor season for the whalers, with the catch only a little more than half what it was last year. There is an average of only 700 barrels of oil for each ship. There is no demand for oil here, which is worth 40 cents a gallon.

Beware of Walking In Wharf District

SAN FRANCISCO, Dec. 25, 1853 —That the loss of life from the poor condition of the streets in the neighborhood of the wharves is so frequent that persons in that section should move with caution was borne out on Christmas Eve.

There were two drownings from this cause. One unidentified man fell through where Jackson and Davis streets open into a dock. He shouted for help, but disappeared before a rescue could be organized. Another unknown person fell in at Davis and Pacific streets, and was lost.

Another man fell through a large opening in the middle of Front street, between Washington and Jackson streets, where the tide ebbs and flows, but fortunately he was saved. William Fallard also fell into one of the man traps on Washington street.

———o———

Big Real Estate Sale Of 122 S.F. Water Lots

SAN FRANCISCO, Dec. 26, 1853 —The holiday season causes no letup in the commercial activities of this metropolis of California. The city put up for sale today 122 subdivided water lots lying on each side of Central Wharf between Clay and Sacramento streets, and Davis and East streets. They comprise two full original blocks. The whole property brought $1,193,750 in the sale.

———o———

Masonic Ceremonies

SAN FRANCISCO, Dec. 27, 1853 — The Anniversary of St. John the Evangelist was observed today by the Masons of San Francisco with a grand parade and other ceremonies.

Some 4000 men were estimated to have marched in the procession, which was a quarter of a mile long. Starting from Masonic Hall then up to Clay to Kearny Street, through Kearny to Washington Street and down the latter to the new theatre, the Metropolitan, where officers-elect of the different lodges were installed.

FILIBUSTERS HOLDING FAST AT ENSENADA

ENSENADA, Lower Calif., Dec. 25, 1853—It was a quiet but watchful Christmas for Col. William Walker, self-proclaimed president of the Republic of Lower California, and his army of filibusters from California.

The president yesterday received a communication from a number of prominent Mexican citizens along the border asking a guarantee of their persons and property and pledging themselves to take no part in the political affairs of the country.

This move followed on Col. Walker's recent proclamation asking the support of the people and declaring he had proclaimed the independence of Lower California to remedy the evils of the existing Mexican government. He asserted all "well-disposed" persons will be protected and banditry put down.

For the moment Walker's hold on the country seems secure. He came here several weeks ago with a small party after first landing at La Paz. Within recent days he has received 230 men as reinforcement by the bark Anita from San Francisco. There was some fighting, in which two of Walker's army were killed but now all is secure with the Mexican leaders, Colonel Negrete and Melendez, having fled.

Walker's troops are kept under strict discipline at his headquarters, Fort McKibben, named for one of his slain soldiers. It is believed General Santa Anna is organizing Mexican forces to attempt to retake Lower California.

THEATRE OPENING ON CHRISTMAS EVE

SAN FRANCISCO, Dec. 23, 1853— Christmas Eve of 1853 will be long remembered for the opening of the new San Francisco Theatre called The Metropolitan, on Washington street. It is an edifice singularly emblematic of our marvelous city in the grandeur of its design, elegance and rapidity of construction.

Beauty, talent, taste and wealth graced the inauguration of the new dramatic temple. More than 1800 persons attended and vigorously applauded the initial presentation featuring Sheridan's "The School for Scandal." Mrs. Catherine Sinclair, the popular leading actress, took the role of Lady Teazle, and Mr. J. E. Murdoch appeared as Charles Surface.

As the seats in the parquette have not yet been built, the space was filled with easy arm chairs. Three tiers of galleries rise above it. To the right of the spacious stage is a fresco painting of Ophelia and Laertes; opposite is a scene from the Spanish play "The Cid". On the arch of the stage is a painting of Shakespeare flanked by the genius of Comedy and Tragedy.

The Christmas presentation tonight will be "Richard the Third" with Mr. Edwin Booth appearing.

———o———

Christmas Race Program

SAN FRANCISCO, Dec. 25, 1853 — Mr. Wilson's gelding pacer C. Spear clearly demonstrated superiority in the Christmas Day racing program at the Union Course. The purse was for $200, best three out of five heats at a mile. C. Spear took the first two heats, and was declared the winner when Mr. Crooks' gelding Ned McGowan was disqualified in the second heat.

———o———

DOUBLE-BARRELED VERDICT

MOKELUMNE HILL, Dec. 20, 1853—At a coroner's inquest here where two men were held for a killing, the jury returned the following verdict: "that the deceased came to his death by his own hands, and that the accused were accessory to the deed."

———o———

SAN FRANCISCO, Dec. 25, 1853 —A white frost so deep that it looked like snow covered the ground here this morning.

THE GOLDEN GAZETTE 1854

JANUARY 1854

159 CHINESE ARRESTED IN RAID ON MEETING

SAN FRANCISCO, Jan. 3, 1854 — The police made a most singular arrest last night, rounding up 159 Chinese meeting in a building on Jackson street.

The raid, in which a force of 20 men participated, was made as a result of an affidavit by Mr. Marcel, the Chinese interpreter of the Recorder's Court, charging that a secret Chinese association was extorting $10 a month from each Chinese woman residing in a public house in order to remain in the city. The group is said to have collected $1000. Information regarding the society was given by some of the principal Chinese merchants, who have also been forced to make contributions.

When breaking into the meeting house, police found the presiding officer of the Chinese group holding a four-foot club over a fellow kneeling inside a large hoop covered with red cloth.

In court today the Chinese, who were held overnight in the jail, claimed they were merely members of a benevolent and fraternal organization called the Hung Gate Society. There being no direct evidence to connect them with extortion, the prisoners were released by the court.

Stage Lines Form 1 Company

SACRAMENTO, Jan. 11, 1854 — Effective today, all the various stage lines operating from here are consolidated into one organization, the California Stage Company. Its capital and value are set at $1,000,-000.

James Birch, the pioneer stage man in California, is president, and he assures the public "speed and accommodation" will be the motto of the company. All stages will leave from and arrive at the Orleans Hotel. Sacramento is the great stage depot of the state, 20 stages leaving every morning for all parts of the country.

Indian Reservation Is Making Good Progress

STOCKTON, Jan. 29, 1854—Lieut. E. F. Beale, the Indian agent is pushing rapidly ahead with the establishment of the Indian reservation at Tejon Pass.

There are now over 2000 Indians concentrated there, and more are coming in each week. Lieut. Beal startd out with 60 Indians. Those in the reservation are savages who have been in conflict with the whites, and not mission Indians.

Already two miles square have been sown with grain, and 24 ploughs are kept constantly at work. Most of the labor is performed by the Indians themselves.

With removal of the source of the fear of Indian depredations, many colonists are moving into the southern San Joaquin Valley, which is well known to be the richest and best for agricultural purposes. The Indian reservation itself is far removed from any white settlements.

50,000 Sheep Arrive

LOS ANGELES, Jan. 14, 1854 — Fifty thousand sheep have arrived in this area from New Mexico, and will be driven on to other California markets.

The celebrated Capt. Aubrey brought in between 14,000-15,000. The journey took him only three months, and he did not lose more than 300 or 400 animals en route. He came by a new way which saved 150 miles.

Among other men who have driven sheep here is Judge A. Otero, who ingeniously worked a scheme to avoid paying the enormous ferrying charges made for ferrying sheep across the Colorado River. He had a flatboat made in New Mexico, and carried in sections on wagons to the Gila River. There he put it together and floated it down to the Colorado. By this boat he got free crossing for his 19,000 sheep and so saved $4500 in charges.

PASSENGERS ARE SAVED FROM GROUNDED SHIP

SAN DIEGO, Jan. 20, 1854 — All persons on board, numbering between 800 and 900, were safely removed from the steam Golden Gate today after 36 hours of terror in one of the heaviest southeast gales to sweep this area in years.

En route from Panama to San Francicso, the Golden Gate stopped here on the 18th to deliver mail and supplies. On leaving the harbor, she went ashore on a shoal just outside because of lack of maneuverability resulting from a mechanical accident to her engines and paddle wheels.

The coastal steamer Goliah, under Capt. Salisbury Haley, went to the rescue. He made valiant efforts to tow the Golden Gate off, but broke two hawsers. Then the Goliah had to give up and leave the scene as the southeast gale came up.

Although the high waves severely damaged the Golden Gate's decks, all on board remained safe with the exception of minor injuries. They could not be taken off until the seas subsided today. The steamer is still fast in about nine feet of water.

The Goliah will take the Golden Gate's mail, 135 bags, and many of her passengers north to San Francisco.

Columbia River Frozen

PORTLAND, Ore. Ter., Jan. 19, 1854 — This has been the coldest winter experienced here in many years. The Columbia River is frozen over for 30 miles from Vancouver down. The Willamette is also frozen.

New County Planned

STOCKTON, Jan. 6, 1854 — Some of the projectors of the new county to be made out of portions of Tuolumne and Mariposa counties propose to call it Stanislaus rather than Washington.

GRAND JURY CALLS FOR HONEST JURIES

SAN FRANCISCO, Feb. 4, 1854—Deploring the readiness with which trial juries set free men accused of crime, including murder, the San Francisco Grand Jury in its report today called for selection of "judicious and honorable men for the trial of capital offenses."

"Of the hundred or more cold-blooded murders which have been committed in this county during the last three years," the grand jury report stated, "but one single solitary case has been prosecuted to conviction and execution!

"In many cases no reasonable doubt could exist as to the guilt of the parties arraigned, but jurors would not convict. The almighty dollar and other appliances have been potent enough to silence the claims of conscience and of solemn oaths. The criminal has been almost uniformly acquitted, and let out again upon society in mockery of all justice.

"There are those amongst us," the report continued, "who boldly assert that no man, however criminal, who has money or friends who can advance it, will ever be hung in this county. The selection of jurors in such cases should be made by the High Sheriff himself from that class of citizens who cannot be bought nor intimidated."

TULE LANDS FERTILE

STOCKTON, Feb. 4, 1854 — The feasibility of the tule lands for agricultural purposes has ben generally doubted, but experiments near here are showing different after highly successful attempts.

Within a few miles of Stockton at least five garden spots have been created along the banks of the San Joaquin River. A year ago they were just rank growths of tules. But a few hardy men cleared the tules away and built up the land with ditches. The soil has proved of the richest description, and three crops of vegetables can be raised a year.

Flees Two Wives

PLACERVILLE, Feb. 2, 1854 — A Dr. Smith who has been residing here with a wife he wed in California had an unexpected visit from a wife and child he left a couple of years ago in the Atlantic States.

First Legal Hanging In Los Angeles

LOS ANGELES, Feb. 13, 1854—The murderer Herrera was hung today in the first judicial execution to be held in Los Angeles County.

A detachment of Rangers, both afoot and on horseback, was in attendance to guard the prisoner. Sheriff Barton was in charge of the arrangements, which were carried out with solemnity and propriety.

Several thousand people witnessed the hanging, and considerable sympathy was shown for the prisoner. Herrera made an address in which he said no justice was possible in our courts.

FILLIBUSTER ARMY FAILS; LEAVES ENSENADA

ENSENADA, Lower Calif., Feb. 12, 1854 — Col. William Walker, self-proclaimed president of Lower California and Sonora, today broke up his camp here and marched southward with 150 men.

Behind him he left his sick and wounded. It is now considered his expedition is a failure as he has suffered numerous desertions as well. The U.S. naval sloop-of-war Portsmouth came into the harbor and humanely took aboard the sick men to carry them to San Diego.

With the naval steamer Columbus, the Portsmouth is keeping watch on the coast and Walker's movements. It is believed Walker's force is likely to encounter an army of 350 Lower Californians.

Oregon Volcano Active

PORTLAND, Ore. Ter., Feb. 27, 1854 — The crater of Mount St. Helens is showing unusual activity. Clouds of smoke and ashes are constantly arising with the smoke appearing to come up in puffs. The smoke is greater than occurred last August, indicating the volcanic fires are increasing within this majestic mountain.

SACRAMENTO, Feb. 8, 1854—On a bet for $50 with Jesse Hambleton, Jerose C. Davis of Putah Creek to day carried in one hand a flask of quicksilver weighing 96 pounds from the Orleans to the Crescent City Hotel.

55 Million in Gold Is Shipped Out in '53

SAN FRANCISCO, Feb. 1, 1854—A comprehensive table prepared by Adams & Co., bankers and forwarders, shows that Gold Dust manifested and shipped from the port of San Francisco during the year of 1853 totaled $54,906,956.74, making it the biggest year in California's gold history. In addition, there was an uncalculable amount taken out by individuals.

By comparison, 1851 shipments amounted to approximately $34,500,000 and 1852 gold to $45,800,000. June was the biggest gold month during the past year. with $6,200,000 going out by steamer and other vessels.

By destination, the gold was distributed as follows:

New York	$47,914,447
New Orleans	390,781
London	4,795,662
Panama	793
Valparaiso	445,778
Sandwich Is.	194,000
China	926,134
Manila	17,430
Calcutta	1,240
New South Wales	38,670

New Gas Lights Streets

SAN FRANCISCO, Feb. 11, 1854 — The principal streets of this city were lighted tonight for the first time from the works of the San Francisco Gas Company. The effect was grand, and the contrast between the new and the old lamps was very noticeable despite the bright moonlight.

Mr. J. M. Moss, president of the company, presided over an elaborate banquet in celebration of the event at the Oriental Hotel. It was attended by members of the city government.

The company so far has laid over three miles of pipe in the city. Workmanship on the 3000 joints that have had to be made is so good that not a single leak has been experienced. The proposed price for the new gas is $15 per 1000 feet.

New Oregon State?

PORTLAND, Ore. Ter., Feb. 15, 1854 — A movement is on foot in Southern Oregon, of considerable significance, looking to the creation of a new territory state.

INDIAN TROUBLES IN WASHINGTON

SEATTLE, Washington Territory, March 5, 1854 — Two residents of this territory have died as a result of difficulties with Indians.

The trouble started when a man named Young was murdered by Indians. Sheriff Russell of King's county, Dr. Cherry and several others went in pursuit to Holmes' Harbor. There they were attacked by a large band of Indians. Dr. Cherry, the sheriff and another man were wounded, but the white party killed nine Indians and drove the others off.

Dr. Cherry died of his wounds soon after returning to Seattle.

---o---

Editors Have Duel

SAN FRANCISCO, March 21, 1854 — A hostile meeting took place at an early hour today near the San Jose road, about 12 miles from the city, between two newspapermen, Mr. Washington of the Times & Transcript and Mr. Washburn of the Alta California.

Long negotiations failed to bring a settlement, so the two fought with rifles at fifty paces. Five shots were exchanged. On the third exchange Mr. Washington's shot went through Mr. Washburn's hat, and on the fifth he hit Washburn under the left arm.

A surgeon promptly extracted the bullet which lodged in Mr. Washburn's back. The wound, though serious, is not considered dangerous.

---o---

SACRAMENTO, March 10, 1854— Dr. Dickson of the Marine Hospital, San Francisco, died early this morning from a gunshot received in a duel yesterday afternoon with District Attorney Thomas of Placer county.

S. F. Branch Mint Ready to Open

SAN FRANCISCO, March 30, 1854 — Having been examined and accepted by the government commissioners, the new United States Branch Mint was turned over today to its supervisor, Dr. L. A. Birdsall, It will open for business to receive gold dust in a few days.

The whole cost of the mint building and equipment is $296,000. It has

Latest Intelligence From Los Angeles

LOS ANGELES, March 18, 1854— The miners at Santa Anita are not in such good spirits as hoped. Difficulty in getting water to the gold placers is discouraging. If the price of mining labor, from $1 to $1.50 a day, is any indication of the richness of the mines, the inducement to work there must be small.

Plenteous rains have fallen in the last few days to remove fear that continued drought would be disastrous to grass and grain crops.

Tree Has Hanging Record

JACKSON, March 20, 1854 — An old oak tree here is gaining wide fame for being the point from which mob-tried criminals make their exit from this life.

---o---

460 Votes Cast in Portland

PORTLAND, Ore. Territory, March 15, 1854 — In the municipal election held here a total of 460 votes were cast.

a sixty-foot frontage on Commercial street near Montgomery and includes three stories and a basement. Front of the building is covered with cement painted and sanded to resemble Connecticut sandstone, ornamented with iron dressings and cornice. A cast iron eagle will surmount the structure. Front doors and windows are protected by double iron shutters.

Completely new machinery was especially built under the supervision of the Philadelphia mint and shipped here for installation.

The charge for assaying and refining gold dust will be 11 cents per ounce, or .6%, and for coining ½%, making the entire charge for assaying, refining and coining 1.1% as compared to a charge of 7/8% at Philadelphia. The charge for assaying and running into bars alone will be ½%, which is the same as levied at the assay establishments here of Wass, Molliter & Co., and Kellogg and Richter.

---o---

OVERDUE STEAMER ARRIVES

SAN FRANCISCO, March 26, 1854 — The long-delayed Nicaraguan steamer Brother Jonathan arrived in port today to end fears she had met with disaster. Public anxiety had been at a high pitch.

She was delayed on her trip south to San Juan del Sud by an accident to her machinery during a gale in the Gulf of Tehauntepec, which forced her to put in at Acapulco.

The Brother Jonathan brought in many passengers, including 197 females as well as 103 packages for Adams & Co. and 64 for Wells Fargo & Co.

Between 20 and 30 passengers who sailed for the East on her last trip lost their lives by drowning when a launch of the Nicaraguan Transit Co. swamped in the waves in taking them out to board one of the lake steamers.

---o---

Denies His Death

THE EDITOR, Dear Sir: In the recent issue of a newspaper I noticed my name, as being killed by the Indians between San Diego and Walker's Camp. I am here to contradict the statement. I am yet living and well; and further, no attack was made on me.

—A. G. Tebbetts

Difficulties Hamper Clipper Flying Cloud

SAN FRANCISCO, April 29, 1854 — Keen alarms over the fate of the famous, record-breaking clipper ship Flying Cloud were raised for awhile through the shipping district here today. It was reported that the clipper, outward bound for Hong Kong, had been driven ashore while trying to beat out of the harbor and was a total wreck.

The Flying Cloud was taken in tow at 5 a.m. today by two steam tugs. After she passed Fort Point, one hawser parted and the roughness of the tide and severity of the gale raging stopped all progress. While the ship anchored about a mile offshore, the two tugs stood by and the U.S. Steamer Active came up to help if needed.

However, by 2 o'clock in the afternoon the Flying Cloud reported she was safe and just waiting for a change of tide to proceed to sea.

Flying Cloud holds all records for speed of passage from New York to this port. When she arrived with 2385 tons of cargo on April 20, she set a new record of 89 days, 8 hours, for the voyage to eclipse her previous mark, set on her first visit to San Francisco, by 13 hours. In two other voyages her times were 114 and 105 days respectively, both respectable marks for the long trip around Cape Horn.

———o———

Walker's Men Desert Filibuster Army

FORT YUMA, April 7, 1854 — A party of a dozen men from the command of William Walker, self-appointed president of Lower California and Sonora, have come up on the Sonora side of the Colorado and crossed the ferry in a nearly naked and starving condition.

It is understood about 50 men, half of the filibuster army, have deserted Col. Walker's party because of difficulties on the march from Lower California to Sonora. Walker is reported to have had to turn back to San Vicente.

San Pedro Prospects For Growth Are Seen

LOS ANGELES, April 8, 1854 — San Pedro, the only marine outlet of a rich and extensive region certainly merits some little notice since it has been constituted a port of entry by the United States Senate.

That San Pedro in a few years will be a city of some size and respectability is apparent to even the most casual observer. Trade already approaches $200,000 weekly. The enterprising firm of Alexander and Banning plan construction soon of a wharf, which will altogether remove the few difficulties existing to prevent the safe and expeditious landing and shipping of goods.

———o———

WASH. TERRITORY GOLD DISCOVERY

STEILACOOM, Wash. Ter., April 4, 1854 — The most intense excitement ever created here occurred today with the unmistakable discovery of gold.

Dr. P. M. Miese of this community took his spade and pan, and went to a spot at the head of high water. There he washed out a pan and found simon-pure ore. The news soon spread, and men and boys hurried to the spot.

Some $25 of gold probably was washed out today from a hole two feet square. Reports have also been heard there is considerable gold being taken out on the Yakima by parties who have been in that region all winter.

———o———

FANDANGO HOUSE PROPRIETOR GUILTY

SAN FRANCISCO, April 4, 1854 — The first court hearing under the new ordinance for the suppression of houses of ill fame, which went into effect April 1, was held today.

Police had descended on a fandango house on Pacific street between Stockton and Dupont, and arrested its proprietor, Charles Walder, eleven men and 14 women. Walder was sentenced to pay a fine of $500 or spend 60 days in jail, while the others were freed as the ordinance provides no penalty for inmates, only the proprietor.

STEAMER DISASTER! MANY LIVES ARE LOST

SAN FRANCISCO, April 15, 1854 — The steamer Secretary blew up in San Francisco Bay today while racing the steamer Nevada to Petaluma in Sonoma county. It is estimated 16 were lost and 31 more injured out of the 60 persons on board.

The two vessels have been engaged in intense rivalry on this run. Today the Secretary left here ahead of the Nevada, which is generally rated faster. The Nevada was just passing when the Secretary's new boiler gave way. It is believed the engineer had tied the safety valve down in an effort to make more speed.

Many of those aboard were on their way to the Russian River mines.

———o———

Lumber Bark Capsizes On Leaving Mendocino

MENDOCINO, April 21, 1854 — The bark Walter Claxton, Capt. Folger commanding, capsized today on leaving port when she ran into a heavy sea outside and took too much water through her fore scuttle. Sixteen men were aboard, and it is feared several were lost. The bark belonged to the California Lumber Co.

———o———

Many Chinese Arrive From Hong Kong

SAN FRANCISCO, April 19, 1854 — The British ship Lord Warriston arrived from Hong Kong today with 780 passengers, 200 of them females. She made a short passage of 48 days, and reported several other ships crowded with passengers were on the way and several more still loading at Hong Kong when she left.

———o———

Chinese Publish Newspaper

SAN FRANCISCO, April 28, 1854 — The first number of a Chinese newspaper was published here today as the organ of the Chinese population. It is called Gold Hills News. The Chinese in the state number about 25,000, and nearly all of them know how to read.

S. F. MERCHANT SEEKS TRADE WITH JAPAN

SAN FRANCISCO, May 11, 1854 — Silas E. Burrows, a prominent merchant of this city, hopes to be the pioneer in the Japanese trade if the reports are correct that Commodore Perry has succeeded in opening the ports of Japan to commerce.

News to this effect was received here just a few days ago, and Mr. Burrows immediately fitted out one of his clipper ships the Race Hound to go to Jeddo. Renamed the Lady Pierce, in honor of the wife of the president of the United States, she sailed from this port today and expects to make the trip in 30 to 40 days.

Mr. Burrows laid in a large cargo of "bijouterie" as presents to the Japanese as well as 2000 gold dollars for those who board his ship. Though her mission is pacific, the Lady Pierce is armed with five small guns for her protection, primarily against the Hong Kong pirates.

There is no question that San Francisco, by virtue of her position, is destined to gain a large share of the benefits from this new field of commercial enterprise.

———o———

DUEL THREAT DISMISSED

SAN DIEGO, May 19, 1854 — A complaint made against Major J. McKinistry of the U.S. Army alleging that he issued a challenge to a duel was dismised today after a hearing by Justice of the Peace D. H. Rogers.

J. Judson Ames of the San Diego Herald had charged that he had received the challenge from the major. He claimed also that he was afraid to leave his house for fear of being shot down, but was brought into court on judicial order. There, several witnesses, as well as Major McKinistry, testified they would not believe Ames under oath in situations where his own interest was involved.

———o———

WASHINGTONIANS DROWN

SEATTLE, May 5, 1854 — George N. McConaha of Seattle, president of the council, and Captain Barstow of Widby's Island, were drowned when the canoe in which they were traveling with a crew of Indians capsized on the way from Olympia to Seattle.

Coastal Steamer Hits Rocks Off Pt. Arena

PETALUMA, May 27, 1854—Captain Pierce of the steamer Arispe arrived here today, overland from Fort Ross, with the news that his ship had struck on the rocks off Point Arena and sunk.

Fortunately, both passengers and crew were able to get off safely on rafts hastily made from spars and casks, when the ship stayed afloat for some time after striking. After leaving San Francisco for Humboldt Bay on May 23, the Arispe ran into heavy weather outside the heads and had some difficulty with her machinery. Captain Pierce blamed his compass as being out of order and so leading to the disaster.

The Arispe was a new steamer of 336 tons, valued at $50,000.

———o———

INDIAN TRIBES BATTLE

GRASS VALLEY, May 24, 1854— Two tribes of Indians engaged in a pitched battle near Rush Creek yesterday.

The fight began with bows and arrows, and then proceeded with rifles. Six are reported to have been killed. The battle started over stealing a squaw.

———o———

Indians On Warpath

YREKA, May 10, 1854 — A band of 56 Indian warriors, with 200 horses, passed through here today from above The Dalles, Oregon, on their way to fight the Shastas, who they claim put to death two small parties from their tribe. The northern Indians will claim vengeance if the Shastas fail to surrender certain of their tribesmen.

———o———

Narrow Escape for Lola

GRASS VALLEY, May 22, 1854— Lola Montez, the celebrated dancer, actress and international figure who has been performing in California during the past year, was thrown from her horse and narrowly excaped with her life. The accident occurred when she was attempting to jump the horse over a wide ditch while she was in search of wild flowers.

Walker & His 'Army' Surrender at Border
ONLY 33 MEN LEFT

SAN DIEGO, May 8, 1854 — The attempt of the filibuster, Col. William Walker, former San Francisco newspaperman, to set up an independent Republic of Lower California and Sonora, came to an end at the boundary line between Mexico and the United States today.

With the remainder of his party, numbering only about 33 men, Walker surrendered this afternoon at the border at La Tia Juana to Major J. McKinistry and Capt. H. S. Burton of the U.S. Army. General Melendrez of the Mexican forces had followed the filibusters in their retreat towards American soil, but there was no fighting as Walker's force crossed the line and laid down their arms. About 40 United States troops had been encamped near the boundary when word was received of Col. Walkers' approach.

Many citizens of this area gathered near the scene in the expectation of seeing a fight between the Mexican forces and Walker before the latter left Mexican soil. Walker's men were taken prisoners as neutrality violators, but were paroled to report to Maj. J. E. Wool at San Francisco.

———o———

NEW DISCOVERIES HINT MORE GOLD

STOCKTON, May 22, 1854 — The public of California has been startled by news of the new discoveries of gold diggings at Iowa Hill, near Grass Valley.

The idea has long been current that the richest deposits of the precious metal in the state lie in the beds of creeks. But if this report is borned out, a new inexhaustible field of mining operations has been found, and richer gold fields than any yet worked will be developed in California.

The heavier masses of the golden metal, as yet untouched, will be sought in the hills. Hundreds of tunnels are being dug by eager miners in the northern mines, and miners in the southern district have almost totally adopted this system of finding their fortune.

Mining Prospers Through California

SACRAMENTO, June 15, 1854— General features of the mining news in California are new gold discoveries and a steady improvement in operations of the water companies.

In Nevada City the tunnel companies are making exceedingly handsome profits. One company, the Empire, is realizing as high as 100 ounces of gold per day from 15 hands. Its tunnel is 1,100 feet long. The ditches in Nevada county are said to be paying from 6 to 50 per cent per month.

Reports of new gold discoveries in the Contra Costa county hill range are not confirmed. The Iowa Hill diggings near Grass Valley are yielding immensely. One company reports it has taken out 20 pounds of gold in a single day.

Pacific University Holds Examinations

SANTA CLARA, June 14, 1854— Examinations and exhibitions of the preparatory department of the Pacific University were held here yesterday and today.

There were 36 pupils in the Ladies' School and 48 in the Gentlemen's. Eighteen young men have been studying Latin and Greek preparatory to a regular college course and two are prepared to enter the college proper in which the first class will be formed at the opening of the next term on July 15.

NEED WOMEN'S INFLUENCE

SAN FRANCISCO, June 26, 1854 —"One of the main causes of the increase of crime in the new States and in our mining districts is the absence of virtuous, intelligent and pious females," the Rev. Dr. Scott declared in a talk before the Unitarian Church last night.

"The life, character and happiness of the miner, the clerk and the merchant emigrant," he said, "would be vastly improved if they were surrounded by their mothers, wives and sisters. If Eve was the first in transgression, her daughters are certainly first in healing the earth's sorrows.

"Nothing is more imperatively needed in California," Dr. Scott added, "than the softening, purifying and elevating influence of women. And sure I am if mothers and wives at home only had a view of the inner life of society in this State, they would fly at once to its shores, plains and mountain cabins."

———o———

STOCKTON EDITOR SHOOTS HIS RIVAL

STOCKTON, June 22, 1854—Joseph Mansfield, editor of the San Joaquin Republican which is published here, was fatally shot today by John Taber, editor of the Stockton Journal.

The shooting arose from an article that appeared in the Journal. The two editors met on the street at about 9 o'clock this morning. After some words passed between them. Taber drew a Derringer pistol and fired at close range. Mansfield succumbed to his wounds several hours later.

———o———

Japan's Ports Opened

SAN FRANCISCO, June 7, 1854— The schooner Restless arrived here today with the news that the U. S. sloop-of-war Saratoga had reached Honolulu with word that Commodore Perry had concluded a treaty of amity with the Empire of Japan on March 28. This means that the ports of Japan will be opened to commerce.

Squatter Riots Rage In San Francisco

SAN FRANCISCO, June 11, 1854 — The most exciting topic of interest here in the last several days has been the squatter riots which have followed a decision of the U. S. Land Commission that has thrown doubt on the validity of land titles in the city.

George D. Smith, of Rochester, N. Y., was killed by a shot through the head in a regular battle that raged for two hours, from 1 to 3 a.m., on First street near the Gas Works a week ago. Participating in the fight were a party of squatters and a force of over a dozen men led by Mr. Canny, agent of Capt. Joseph L. Folsom, who owned the lot in question. Double-barreled guns, Colt's revolvers and axes were the weapons used. Mr. Canny and one of his men were arrested following the fray.

Two nights ago another squatter riot occurred on Green street near Stockton street. A woman bystander was shot through the right lung, and a youth named John Mooney was also wounded. Several men were arrested, but were discharged for lack of evidence.

Yesterday an "association" was formed following a mass meeting for the protection of property, and to hold the squatters in check. Col. David S. Turner was named president. Judge Freelon of the Court of Sessions has charged the Grand Jury to supervise the objects of the association and restrain it from breaking the law.

———o———

San Pedro Lighter

SAN PEDRO, June 12, 1854 — Messrs. Alexander and Banning today launched a new lighter, named the San Bernardino, capable of discharging 40 to 45 tons of freight.

———o———

New Alcatraz Light

SAN FRANCISCO, June 2, 1854 —The new light house atop Alcatraz, or Bird Island, which has just been put into operation, can be seen 12 miles at sea.

———o———

SAN FRANCISCO, June 26, 1854 — For a wager of $1,000 William Walker last night completed the feat of walking for 80 consecutive hours, without stopping or sleeping.

DEMOCRATIC MEETING SPLITS AFTER ROW

SACRAMENTO, July 17, 1854 — The Democratic state convention met here today and split up into two conventions after the meeting broke up in a near-riot between the Broderick and anti-Broderick supporters. David Broderick, prominent San Francisco politician, is chairman of the party's state central committee.

Tension was high from the start of the session over the question of election of a president of the convention. Shouting members jumped from their seats in the course of the dispute and knives and pistols were drawn by many. The accidental discharge of a pistol in the chamber sent most of those in attendance to hasty exit by both doors and windows.

In the end, one convention group supporting the Broderick faction named Judge Edward McGowan as president. A second group selected ex-Governor James McDougal as its president.

Trustees of the Baptist Church, where the meeting was held, notified the delegates they would have to find another meeting place.

———o———

120 Chinese Die On Voyage

SAN FRANCISCO, July 21, 1854 — Nearly 120 passengers, Chinese bound for the gold coast of California, died as a result of the voyage of the barque **Libertad** from Hong Kong to San Francisco. Their unfortunate deaths are attributed to "ship fever."

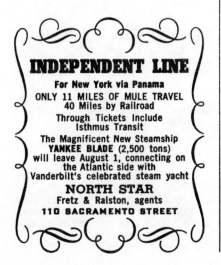
Havoc Caused by Fire Through California

SAN FRANCISCO, July 14, 1854 — Fires have caused tremendous damage in various parts of California during the past two weeks.

The latest reported was a blaze that broke out in Sacramento, in the block bounded by Third, Fourth, J and K streets, early yesterday morning. It spread rapidly and

ASPHALTUM PROMISES TO OPEN UP NEW FIELD

SANTA BARBARA, July 29, 1854 — It is reported that asphaltum, large quantities of which can be gathered in Los Angeles and Santa Barbara, and in fact through the whole southerly portion of the state, can be used to manufacture gas.

Gas produced from asphaltum is said to be less costly than that manufactured from coal. If experiments now in progress are successful, it probably will be used not only to reduce bills for light but also to open up a whole new field for labor, industry and capital in California.

———o———

Indians Steal Horses In Southern Country

LOS ANGELES, July 20, 1854 — A party of Pah-Utah Indians has been reported active in stealing large numbers of horses between San Gabriel and the San Jose rancho.

Don Ygnacio Alvarado lost 43 horses and Mr. Dalton a large number also. A posse took off in pursuit of the tribe. It overtook the Indian raiders near the Cajon Pass. There, the Indians killed some of the horses, but still managed to get away with all the rest, except for about 40 mares which were recovered.

———o———

Chinese in Battle

WEAVERVILLE, July 15, 1854 — An extensive battle was held between two large parties of Chinese miners near here today. The death list totaled 15, including one American who joined in the fray.

ranged for five hours, destroying six entire blocks of the city. The total loss is estimated at approximately $400,000.

Three days ago, the town of Columbia in Tuolumne County, in the heart of a rich mining district, was almost completely burned down with losses estimated at $500,000.

The town of Minnesota in Nevada County was razed by flames on July 8, excepting for three houses. As Minnesota is a small town, the total loss is only $52,000. Twelve buildings in Sonora were burned on the night of July 3, and 1,400 acres of ripening wheat were destroyed by fire in the Suisun and Vaca valleys on July 7.

In San Francisco, a blaze that began in the square lying within Washington, Jackson, Front and Davis streets destroyed the whole block, 65 houses in all, at a loss of $225,000. The devastated tract was built of wood on piles. The tide was out at the time, so that the fact the water was 12 feet below street level and very shallow, was a severe hindrance to the firemen.

———o———

SAN FRANCISCO MAN HANGED LEGALLY

SAN FRANCISCO, July 28, 1854 — William B. Sheppard, 27-year-old mate on coastal vessels, was hanged today from a gallows erected near the Presidio. It was a legal execution.

The crowd which attended the ceremonies was estimated at 10,000 people. Companies of the National Lancers and City Guards were on hand to preserve order and to prevent any possible attempts at escape.

———o———

Man Killed at Bear Fight

GRASS VALLEY, July 4, 1854 — A man named Swurblow, of Nevada City, was accidentally shot and killed by the owner of a grizzly bear during the Fourth of July festivities here today.

The bear's owner was using the pistol, to try to scare the bear out of his cage to fight for the amusement of a crowd, when a wild shot hit Swurblow.

Plan For Developing Gadsden Territory

SAN FRANCISCO, Aug. 20, 1854—Several companies are understood to be forming here for the purpose of developing resources of the Gila Territory, recently purchased from Mexico under the Gadsden treaty. Among the active parties are several prominent San Francisco businessmen.

The territory is reported to possess immense mineral resources, including the celebrated copper mines near the border. These are said to contain considerable gold as well as 75 to 80 per cent copper.

One group, the Colorado Company, is promoting the new city of Colorado to be erected near Fort Yuma. Its members also propose to open steam navigation on the upper Colorado to the nearest point for an approach to the Mormon settlement at Salt Lake to establish a new avenue of trade.

———o———

MISSION GAMBLING THREAT AVERTED

SAN RAFAEL, Aug. 5, 1854 — Hearing a report that an attempt was being made to desecrate the church of the Mission of San Rafael by converting it into a gambling house, a party of nearly 100 men came here from San Francisco by the steamer Rainbow yesterday.

The sheriff of Marin county, fearing there might be some trouble, procured a guard of 18 men and a field piece for armament. No difficulties occurred, however, and most of the San Francisco men returned home on the steamer last night. It is believed that the affair rose out of an attempt by several parties to squat on certain areas of mission lands.

———o———

400 Wagons For Oregon

PORTLAND, Ore. Ter., Aug. 3, 1854—J. B. Morgan of Eddysville, Iowa, has arrived in this city overland. He reports there are about 400 wagons on the way besides many droves of cattle.

SHORTER ROUTE FOR RAILROAD IS FOUND

SACRAMENTO, Aug. 4, 1854—Lieut. Beckwith and his overland surveying party arrived here today from Salt Lake City via the Humboldt and Fort Reading. They left Salt Lake on May 6.

Beckwith declares that he found a route over which he could lay out a road from Salt Lake City 150 miles shorter than any hitherto traveled. In the Sierra Nevada he explored several passes and found two that he considers eminently practical as a route for the Pacific railroad. The greatest difficulties for railroad construction, according to the lieutenant, are encountered in the "foot hills" of the Sierra.

A railroad linking California to the Atlantic States has long been needed, though Congress has so far refused to pass a bill. This, and other surveys, prove the practicability of a Central route.

———o———

CASKET OF A PIONEER FOUND BY WORKMEN

SAN FRANCISCO, Aug. 26, 1854—Workmen excavating for a sewer on Commercial street between Montgomery and Kearney streets today discovered a large box about six feet underground.

On breaking the box open it was found to contain a coffin. Through a piece of glass in the lid were visible the features of a man.

Investigation disclosed that it was the body of W. C. Rae, who was agent of the Hudson Bay Company here in the 1840's This identification was confirmed by Thomas O. Larkin, who was United States consul to California at the time, and knew Rae well.

Mr. Larkin said that Rae, who lived in the first two-story house to be built in what is now San Francisco, committed suicide in January, 1845.

———o———

SAN JOSE, Aug. 18, 1854—While boring an artesian well on his lot, Mr. Dabney of this city had gone down only a few feet when a powerful stream of water burst forth, shooting up 10 or 12 feet into the air.

Lynch Party Hangs Two Cattle Thieves

OAKLAND, Aug. 23, 1854—Two men were hung by a lynch party at nearby San Antonio today for cattle stealing. Their names were Amedee Canu and Pierre Archambault.

Alameda county has long been suffering from the depredations of cattle thieves. Yesterday, George Carpenter and a group of men out looking for stolen cattle found an enclosure holding several head, some of the animals had already been slaughtered.

The searchers arrested Canu, Archambault and several other suspects. Tremendous excitement ensued as the word spread and many ranchers assembled at the scene. There were many arguments pro and con a Judge Lynch sentence. At first, by a majority of one, it was decided to turn all the suspects over to the legal authorities.

Early this morning, however, a party took these two men, considered to be the ringleaders, and hung them each on a tree at the rear of the Mansion House, well known Contra Costa resort.

———o———

Unusual Rain at L. A.

LOS ANGELES, Aug. 21, 1854—An unusual, severe rainstorm lashed southern California today.

The amount of rain falling here in the past 24 hours almost exceeds belief. The ground was wet from 12 to 18 inches deep, and one man who had a tub sitting in his yard estimates the quantity as high as 10 inches.

———o———

Fugitive Law Invoked

SONORA, Aug. 19, 1854—Stephen J. Hill, a Negro, was arrested here today under the Fugitive Law of this state. He was brought to California by his master in 1849. Hill is worth about $4,000 and is a man of industrious habits.

———o———

PARTY CLIMBS MOUNT HOOD

PORTLAND, Ore. Ter., Aug. 12, 1854 — A party of men led by General Palmer has succeeded in reaching the summit of Mount Hood, which has been hitherto unexplored. They met with many difficulties on the way.

Paving Is Started On Montgomery Street

SAN FRANCISCO, Sept. 19, 1854 —Laying of cubical blocks of granite for pavement was begun today on Montgomery street at California street.

It speaks well for San Francisco enterprise, and gives positive assurance at home and abroad of the permanence of this great emporium of the Pacific American Coast.

Travel on Montgomery is greater than on any other street in the city, and a durable pavement is highly necessary. At present wood cannot be dispensed with for paving, because of the expense of more durable materials. For some time to come wood will be preferable in many instances. The adoption of stone for our street pavements, however, will no doubt be very general when all grading is finished.

———o———

BATTLE OF CHINESE

SACRAMENTO, Sept. 9, 1854 — Between 500 and 600 Chinese engaged in a battle here for an hour late last evening on I street between Fifth and Sixth streets.

Armed with tin hats, bamboo shields, tin and iron swords and pick handles, the Chinese fought until separated by the police. Of the wounded only one is reported in serious condition. Twenty of the most riotous were arrested and jailed.

———o———

Apaches on Rampage

SAN DIEGO, Sept. 16, 1854 — Henry Livingston arrived here today from the Colorado river crossing with the report that a company of 50 emigrants, all Texans, had been murdered recently by Apaches near the Pimos Valley.

Several women and children were in the party, and 600 cattle were driven off.

———o———

OAKLAND FIRE PROTECTION

OAKLAND, Sept. 14, 1854—Three large cisterns are being built on Broadway. When completed, they will add materially to the efficiency of the fire department.

RACE OF STEAMERS AROUSES ANXIETY

SAN FRANCISCO, Sept. 30, 1854 — Considerable anxiety has been felt by parties going to the Atlantic States by the steamers today because of reports that heavy bets have been made between the Sonora and the Yankee Blade.

Advertising of the bets and the deposits of the stakes have increased fears for the ship's safety.

The practice of ocean steamship racing is extremely reprehensible, and should be disapproved by both the traveling public and the steamer operators.

In this case the Pacific Mail Steamship Co. has ordered Captain Whiting of the Sonora not to engage in racing on any account, and the engineer not to carry any more than the usual amount of steam.

To prevent pushing the steamer, the Sonora has only been coaled for nine days and will go into Acapulco for the balance of her coal. The passengers will not be hurried into eternity, instead of to Panama.

———o———

LUMBERING FIRMS PROSPER GREATLY AT HUMBOLDT BAY

HUMBOLDT BAY, Sept. 22, 1854 — An immense lumber business is being done in this area.

Biggest firm is the Eureka Mill owned by Ryan, Duff & Co. It has four gangs of saws, one circular, one edger, one crosscut saw, two double lath machines, one shingle machine and two turning lathes. It can turn out in a day 60,000 board feet and 40,000 laths. Thirty-five men are employed, and the investment amounts to $100,000.

Other prominent mills are:

Ridgeway and Flander's mill, which employs 31 men and can cut 50,000 feet and 32,000 laths.

Pine & Bean, 8 men, 20,000 feet; Mula Mill, 3 men, 10,000 feet of framing stuff; Pioneer Mill, 10 men, 10,000 feet; Bay Mill, 10 men, 15,000 feet and 6000 laths; May & Brothers, 18 men, 20,000 feet and 10,000 laths.

The Union Mill and Modena Mill at Bucksport are also active. Aside from the mills, there are 200 men employed in getting out logs, with capital invested of over $400,000.

Emigrant Massacre Near Fort Boise

PORTLAND, Sept. 1, 1854—Stewart's Express Messenger has arrived from The Dalles with word of the massacre of an emigrant train some 15 miles east of Fort Boise.

The train, made up of four wagons, was attacked at daybreak by about 60 Indians. The party was so surprised that all eight men in it were killed. A boy was wounded and left for dead, while the Indians seized the four women in the party and some children, whose number is unknown. They made good their retreat with the wagons.

John F. Noble, well known Oregonian, found the boy when he came up in the train behind. A messenger was sent on to The Dalles for troops, and Major Haller has set out with 30 men. A volunteer party is also forming. Rumors are that the attacking Indians were of the Blackfoot and Snake tribes.

On his quick ride from Fort Boise the messenger passed 400 emigrant wagons.

———o———

'FRENCH LEGION' AT GUAYMAS REVOLTS

SAN FRANCISCO, Sept. 12, 1854 — News was brought here today by Captain Johnson, U.S.A., of a battle at Guaymas, Sonora, between French troops on one side and Mexicans, Germans and Irish on the other. All were members of the Mexican army in Sonora.

Count de Raousset Boulbon, who is well known here, landed at Guaymas and excited the French troops, who had been recruited in California, to revolt with him as leader. The Germans and Irish remained loyal to the Sonorans, and a battle ensued in the streets of the town.

The French forces charged a battery of two cannons and a howitzer but were mowed down, according to Captain Johnson. Estimates are that as many as 120 were killed in affair. Boulbon himself was said to have been wounded and captured, and may be executed.

Captain Johnson got the news from a party of Germans and Americans who arrived at Fort Yuma from Guaymas early this month.

Steamer Is Total Loss After Striking Reef

SAN FRANCISCO, Oct. 9, 1854— News arrived here today via the coastal steamer Goliah of the total loss of the Panama steamer Yankee Blade near Point Conception on October 1. The Goliah also brought up some of the rescued passengers.

It is uncertain how many people lost their lives in the wreck, but it is known that one boat with 21 persons, mostly women, overturned and all except three or four drowned. Many bodies were washed ashore near the wreck.

The Yankee Blade, with Capt. Henry Randall commanding, sailed from here September 30 with at leat 800 passengers and $153,000 in specie. She hit a reef not far from Point Conception in a dense fog the following afternoon.

Some boats were able to get ashore from the grounded vessel. Towards dark gangs of desperadoes from among the passengers were ranging and pillaging the ship, and it is reported one man was murdered on deck. By nightfall the promenade deck and the houses aft the shaft had washed away. There were scenes of wild confusion among those still left aboard.

At 8 o'clock the following morning, Capt. J. Haley's Goliah appeared and took 600 Yankee Blade passengers on board. Most of them were crowded near the bow as the stem was sunk in the water. Capt. Haley sent boats back and forth to make the rescue. He left most of those saved at San Diego.

———o———

Judge Rules Warrant By Telegraph Legal

SAN FRANCISCO, Oct. 18, 1854— Judge Freelon today decided that it is legal to arrest a man on information received by telegraph.

His ruling was made despite the objection by counsel for Rolla Powers, held here on the accusation of fatally shooting David Hoover at Georgetown on a warrant transmitted by telegraph. Powers had left California on the steamer Yankee Blade, but returned after the wreck and was arrested before he could take another steamer.

HENRY MEIGGS FLEES AFTER HUGE FRAUD

SAN FRANCISCO, Oct. 8, 1854— Henry Meiggs, one of the city's most prominent citizens is in flight, and stands accused of frauds totaling nearly $1,500,000.

Specifically Meiggs, who has often been called "Honest Henry," is accused of forging City Comptroller's warrants up to a million dollars and over-issue of the stock of his California Lumber Company by $300,000. It is also figured that the extent of his liabilities may amount to $800,000 additional.

———————————

OAKLAND GROWING BIG IN IMPORTANCE

OAKLAND, Oct. 11, 1854 — This handsome little city of oaks is fast growing in importance. The whole encinal, forming a beautiful grove, has been laid in streets 80 feet in width.

It is understood a pier is to be built at the termination of Eighth street, which will bring San Francisco and Oakland within 15 or 20 minutes of each other. This point would prove a lucrative location for a hotel, with salt water bathing, fishing, sailing, etc., available in addition to drives through the evergreens.

It seems very probable that, if the great Pacific Railroad stretches through Noble's Pass, the shrill whistle of the locomotive will be heard through the town.

———o———

Fine Oregon Apples

PORTLAND, Ore. Ter., Oct. 23, 1854 — Thomas Pritchard, Esq., of this city has been displaying the finest specimens of apples ever seen in any country. Many of them measured 15 to 16 inches in circumference and weighed 28 or 29 ounces. 15 or 16 of the apples were enough to fill a half bushel basket.

———o———

NEW RECORD TRIP

SAN FRANCISCO, Oct. 12, 1854— The Nicaragua Company's steamship Uncle Sam arrived about 8 p.m. this evening bringing passengers through from New York in the quickest time ever made on this route, 23 days and 4 hours. The Uncle Sam had only 50 passengers.

Discovery of the frauds occurred yesterday when a check was made of some city warrants that Meiggs had posted as collateral for loans. It was discovered that the signatures on the warrants, which were in amounts of $1.000 and $500, had been forged. Loans had been made on them at 50 cents on the dollar.

A few days ago Meiggs purchased the barque America for $10,000. This vessel cleared the port yesterday for "ports of the Pacific," and it is presumed that Meiggs, his family and his brother John stole aboard her. A steamer was sent in pursuit, but ran into difficulties and was unable to reach her.

Meiggs has been a member of the City's Common Council and noted as one of the most successful and enterprising businessmen in the community. John Meiggs had been named head of the Comptroller's department of the city for the coming year.

———o———

L. A. HAS REPUTATION

LOS ANGELES, Oct. 14, 1854 — This city has gained a reputation as a terrible place for murders, and seems determined to live up to it.

Last night a young man, Pinkney Clifford, was foully murdered at a livery stable by David Brown. Clifford was sitting in the stable office when some trivial altercation took place. Brown became enraged, walked up to Clifford and plunged a knife into his heart.

About an hour later a man ran into the Bella Union horribly cut up and in an hysterical condition. He apparently was set on and robbed by two supposed friends.

———o———

ACCIDENT PROVES FATAL TO PIONEER LEADER

COLUSA, Oct. 25, 1854—Dr. Robert Semple, well known pioneer who came to California in 1846, died today at his home near here of wounds suffered in a fall from his horse.

Dr. Semple took a prominent part in the Bear Flag Revolution soon after his arrival.

Ropes Break, Double Hanging Is Repeated

COLOMA, Nov. 3, 1854 — Two executions by hanging, the first ever conducted officially by officers of the law in El Dorado County, took place here today before the largest crowd ever assembled in the county.

The streets of Coloma were thronged with a dense mass of people, and thousands more assembled on the hills around town.

The two men executed were James Logan, 47, for the murder of Mr. Fennel in a claim dispute at Coon Hollow, and William Lipsey, 25, for the murder of Powelson at Cold Springs. Logan made a lengthy speech at the scaffold in which he claimed that he shot in self-defense, while Lipsey was near collapse.

When the signal was given for the double drop, both the knots slipped and the men fell to the ground. The ropes were readjusted, and on the second try the hangings went off successfully.

———o———

IMMIGRANTS IN TROUBLE

SACRAMENTO, Nov. 10, 1854 — The immigrants now coming in report many hardships on the trail. Snow is already piling up in the Sierra, obliterating the road in many places and causing heavy loss of stock.

Further to the East there has been considerable trouble with Indians, and some cholera.

FLOUR • WHEAT BARLEY

THE SAN JOAQUIN FLOUR MILLS, Stockton, are now complete and ready to grind Wheat and Barley in any quantities.

The above mills are not surpassed by any in the Atlantic States, and are capable of turning out 250 barrels of Family Flour per day.

Liberal advances are made on consignments of Wheat. The location of the mills offers superior inducements to Wheat growers to ship their grain direct to Stockton for milling.

LOLA MONTEZ TRIES TO WHIP EDITOR

GRASS VALLEY, Nov. 21, 1854 — The famous Madame Lola Montez created a pleasant sensation here today when she tried to assault Mr. Shipley, editor of the Grass Valley Telegraph.

The noted dancer rushed in a rage from her residence, and marched through Mill street to Main street brandishing a riding whip in one hand and carrying a copy of the paper in the other. She met up with the editor at the Golden Gate Saloon and struck at him with her whip while giving him a shrill tongue-lashing. Mr. Shipley took the whip from her; Lola appealed to the miners for help, but all they did was to laugh.

Cause of Mme. Montez' wrath was an article the editor had copied from the New York Times about her.

———o———

BIG STEAMER LAUNCHED

SAN FRANCISCO, Nov. 16, 1854 — The steamer New Bragdon, which will be the largest, longest and widest boat engaged in bay and river navigation, was launched at the foot of Third street.

She is 235 feet long, 33 feet in beam, has an 8-foot hold and will draw 4 feet of water. Two high-pressure engines generating about 800 horsepower will draw their steam from six boilers. The paddle wheels are 35 feet in diameter.

The New Bragdon was built in New Albany, Indiana, and then taken to pieces. She was shipped down the Ohio and Mississippi rivers to New Orleans, and thence to San Francisco. Her total cost is estimated at $200,000.

———o———

WEEK'S SCORE IN L. A. ONLY FOUR MURDERS

LOS ANGELES, Nov. 11, 1854 — The week past here has been comparatively quiet. It is true that four persons have been killed, but it has been considered a poor week for killings.

A head or two has been split open, and an occasional cutting has occurred, but these are minor matters and create but little feeling.

Sunday passed off without much happening. The jail was filled up with drunken Indians.

STAGE LINE CROSSING COUNTRY IS PRACTICAL

SACRAMENTO, Nov. 2, 1854 — There is a great deal of agitation for a stage line across the plains and mountains from the eastern states and California. A veteran stage driver calculates that such a line, run on a daily basis, not only is practicable but also would be a financial success.

This expert assumes that the distance is about 1800 miles and each team would be able to cover 15 miles each day. The line would then take 240 teams, or 960 horses, plus 100 extra horses. The investment required would amount to $150,000 for horses, $19,200 for harnesses at $80 each and $42,000 for 60 coaches at $700 each — making a total investment of $220,000.

Monthly expenses, he declared, would total $66,000, on the basis of $2 per day per horse and $50 a month for drivers. Figuring 10 passengers each way daily at $150, he believes receipts would amount to $90,000 monthly from this source, plus $19,000 from express and mail.

Thus, monthly profits from such a line would be $42,000, which would be 14 per cent per month on a capital of $300,000.

———o———

FREE LUNCHES RETAINED

SAN FRANCISCO, Nov. 22, 1854 — Because of the heavy expense they entail, proprietors of saloons here have been considering abolishing the serving of free lunches.

Two large meetings were held, and almost all the proprietors were for such a move. Four or five saloon-keepers, however, pointed out it couldn't be enforced. So, free lunches are still on tap for the free-loaders.

———o———

Gold Seekers Return Luckless From Mexico

SAN DIEGO, Nov. 20, 1854 — Five men of a party which left here last July to hunt for gold in Mexico beyond the Colorado and Gila rivers have returned in good condition, but without any luck.

When they found traces of gold in any quantity, there was no water to wash it. Five others of the party went on to Tucson after their arduous prospecting journey.

PRISONERS MAKE BREAK FROM STATE PRISON

SAN QUENTIN, Dec. 28, 1854 — A large number of prisoners made a break at the state prison today, seizing a schooner and fleeing across the bay to Contra Costa.

It is presumed that there were about 30 convicts on board, according to a count made from a sloop which passed close by the schooner.

Fighting and gunfire marked the escape. Several prisoners were wounded, and at least one, John Thompson, is known to have been killed. Another prisoner, Cherokee Bob, who was serving a ten-year term, was retaken after he suffered wounds which may be fatal.

In Contra Costa the desperadoes were reported to be robbing every ranch they came to. Capt. Pullum of the guards, who led the pursuit, was wounded in the hands and arms.

It is expected many of the prisoners will try to reach San Francisco, and the police there have been alerted. Most of the convicts have had half their heads shaved recently, according to J. M. Estell, prison director, who believes they will try to procure wigs to disguise themselves.

OFFICER KILLS THIEF

SACRAMENTO, Dec. 24, 1854 — While on his rounds last night, Policeman Walton discovered two men near the corner of Carpenter's Brick Building on Front street. One of them had a package under his arms, and the other a bag of potatoes on his shoulder.

The officer tried to detain the later, but he ran in the direction of the river. Policeman Walton fired, and dropped his man, who died half an hour later at the station house. He proved to be an old culprit who had frequently been confined to the prison brig. The second man escaped.

Weather Fine in South

LOS ANGELES, Dec. 21, 1854 — The beautiful weather of the past three weeks still continues here. The eye is greeted on every hand with the delightful characteristics of spring. Vegetation is growing, and the hills and plains are beginning to afford ample food for the countless herds of stock.

'DEPRESSION' IS NO BAR TO CITY'S PROGRESS

SAN FRANCISCO, Dec. 28, 1854 — Despite the unprecedented depression in general business and the almost universal cry of "hard times," the city is making steady progress in building.

Among the most important street improvements now going ahead, which will enhance the value of suburban property, are Brannan street from Rincon Point to Mission Creek, the planking across the marshes being nearly complete; the grading of Howard street, running between and parallel to Folsom and Mission streets; and the planking of Bush street, which is nearly finished as far as Larkin street.

———o———

ANOTHER CITY OFFICIAL ROBS TREASURY OF LARGE SUM

OAKLAND, Dec. 18, 1854 — Citizens of Oakland were thrown into great consternation today when it was learned that John Hogan, the City Marshal, had absconded with $20,000 in cash belonging to the city. The public had placed great confidence in him.

Hogan owned livery stables, and considerable property, which he quietly sold out. When he left San Francisco on the steamer John L. Stephens a few days ago, he is supposed to have had $50,000 in his possession.

This sort of thing is becoming only too common in California.

———o———

Bishop Leads Service

SAN FRANCISCO, Dec. 25, 1854 — Bishop Kip of the Episcopal Church, who recently arrived in California, celebrated the Christmas festival at Grace Church at 10 a.m. today, and also officiated at Christmas Eve services. The choir was greatly enlarged for the occasion, to present selections from Handel's Messiah.

———o———

60,000 Animals Imported

SACRAMENTO, Dec. 20, 1854 — It is estimated there has been a total importation of some 60,000 beef cattle, oxen and cows to California this year.

Christmas Day Race Draws Huge Crowd

SAN FRANCISCO, Dec. 25, 1854 — An unusual attendance was attracted to the Pioneer Course today by a contest between the roadsters of several well known gentlemen for a purse and sweepstakes of $800. Many of the city's most prominent citizens and business men were at the track.

There were many friendly bets, and before the start of the race the game began to be playd high and without a limit. The betting was even on Mr. Crooks' sorrel gelding Highland Chief against the field, and some bets were made on Mr. Ferguson's grey gelding Glencoe Chief against the field at $60, $75 and $80 to $100.

The "knowing ones," however, generally posted their spare change on anything against the bay Big Boy of Mr. Eyclesheimer, whose backers must have "realized" handsomely as they had great odds.

The race was scheduled to be for three out of five mile heats. Big Boy won the first, third and fourth heats with perfect ease — much to the astonishment of all and more particularly to the "knowing ones" who had witnessed the private performances of his competitors.

In a pacing race, Daniel Webster, owned by Mr. Crooks, beat Lady Mac and Fred Johnson.

One thousand persons attended the Christmas ball at the Turnverein Hall on Bush street, which lasted through the night.

THE GOLDEN GAZETTE 1855

Killings for the Year Total at Least 560

SAN FRANCISCO, Jan. 1, 1855—A homicide calendar kept by Editor Frank Soule of the California Chronicle lists the total number of killings in the state during the past year as 560.

March was the record month with 108 violent deaths recorded, but this figure included 87 Indians. Among the noteworthy items listed were four fatal duels, 20 convictions for murder and 33 hangings, of which 25 were by Lynch Law and eight legally conducted by sheriffs.

Editor Soule expresses the opinion that his score is without doubt defective and on the short side.

———o———

Storm Greets New Year

SAN FRANCISCO, Jan. 1, 1855—The New Year began with one of the most severe storms in the memory of the oldest inhabitants.

Vallejo, Benicia and Corte Madera were among other bay area towns which were also hit by the storm.

———o———

Coastal Steamer Lost

ASTORIA, Ore. Ter., Jan. 3, 1855—The well known coastal steamer Southerner has been lost as result of damage suffered in a heavy gale, but all on board are reported to have been saved.

———o———

Gold Exports Drop

SAN FRANCISCO, Jan. 1, 1855 — Gold exported from San Francisco in 1854 amounted to $50,840,009. This is lower than the $56,390,812 manifested for 1853 but higher than the 1852 total.

THREE THIEVES HANGED UNDER LYNCH LAW

LIVERMORE'S RANCH, Jan. 22, 1855 — Three cattle thieves were hanged by lynch law today at Turner's Ferry on the San Joaquin River.

Three days ago A. J. Neal, a resident at this place, was informed three men were seen on the mountains driving off a number of cattle. He got ten men and started in pursuit. After a chase of 50 miles Neal and one of his vaqueros came up with the thieves and found them with 25 head of cattle. They were Salvador Valdez, a Californian, and Jose Stode and Juan Gonzales, Chilenos.

Twenty-seven men were called as a jury to try the parties, and 24 voted for hanging, which was carried out today. Valdez confessed a number of crimes, and is acknowledged to have murdered seven persons in his time.

———o———

STREAM OF WATER USED IN MINING

IOWA HILL, Jan. 30, 1855 — The Jamison Company, engaged in mining, is using a novel method to extract its gold deposits.

The company has purchased in San Francisco about 350 feet of four-inch fire hose for $13,000. The hose will carry water from a reservoir 200 feet above the mining claim, this head giving a tremendous power of water through a nozzle two and a half inches in diameter.

A pipeman standing 30 feet from the bank plays the powerful stream at the foot of the bank, which crumbles away under the water. The hose is wrapped with strong cord to prevent its bursting.

A stream of water used in this manner will do more digging than 20 men.

60 PERSONS LOSE LIVES IN STEAMER DISASTER

SACRAMENTO, Jan. 27, 1855 — Sixty or more persons were killed this afternoon when the river steamer Pearl, running from Marysville to Sacramento, exploded while nearing her wharf here.

She had been racing the Enterprise, of a rival shipping line. Both steamers had left Marysville about 8 o'clock this morning.

At the time of the blast most of the Pearl's passengers were gathered near the bow, just over the boilers. They were either instantly killed when the boilers let go, or thrown into the water. The whole bow of the craft was shattered in fragments, which covered the river for a distance of a quarter of a mile.

The accident was witnessed by many people on the levee. Many boats were quickly put out to hunt through the wreckage for survivors. One section of the steamer remained afloat after the wreck. Late today, the river was being dragged for bodies.

It is probable that the true death toll may never be known exactly. The clerk's register of the Pearl contained the names of 93 passengers, but it is believed there were actually as many as 110 or 120 aboard.

———o———

CRESCENT CITY WAGES WAR ON INDIANS

CRESCENT CITY, Jan. 31, 1855—A war of extermination has been commenced against the Indians in this region.

An encounter took place a few days ago between a party of Klamath Rangers and some 35 Indians at the Lagoon four miles from here, and 30 Indians were killed.

The troubles have arisen to ruin the former good feeling that existed because of the deeds of both bad Indians and unscrupulous white men.

NORTHERN STEAMER DRIVEN ON ROCKS

SEATTLE, Wash. Ter., Feb. 12, 1855—The steamer Major Tompkins was wrecked near Esquimalt in a storm two days ago, but the passengers and crew were able to escape safely, according to information brought here today.

The steamer was en route from Port Townsend to Victoria when heavy squalls arose. Capt. Hunt tried to find a safe anchorage, but the anchors would not hold. Near midnight the ship was driven onto rocks.

Those aboard were able to jump from the ship to a large rock. Soon after striking all the top works of the steamer were washed away by huge breakers. At first it was not known whether the rock was on the main land or not, but a party located a sheltering cabin a few hours later.

———o———

California State University is Proposed

SACRAMENTO, Feb. 15, 1855—A bill has been introduced in the state legislature to establish a California State University.

It would have a "Collegiate Department" pertaining to languages, mathematics and material sciences, also for an agriculture department and a department of law and medicine.

Banks Closing; Panic Strikes California

SAN FRANCISCO, Feb. 28, 1855—The state has gone through a shattering financial collapse in the past few days.

———

TREATY MADE FOR OREGON INDIANS

PORTLAND, Ore. Ter., Feb. 10, 1855—General Palmer, Superintendent of Indian affairs for Oregon, has concluded an important treaty with all bands of Indians in the Willamette Valley.

The country covered by the treaty is over 7,500,000 acres, and the cost to the government will probably be about 3 cents per acre. A small advance is being made to the Indians in clothing, etc.

Under the treaty the Indians are given the right to occupy tracts in the valley as designated by the superintendent until a permanent home is selected for them.

Portions of the annuity payments to the Indians, extending over a period of 20 years, may be made in goods and services.

———o———

Big Sales of Coffee

SAN FRANCISCO, Feb. 10, 1855—Large quantities of coffee changed hands in the market today, in the most important sales of the season.

Some of the principal jobbers entered the market and bought the largest lots offered. The cargoes of the Mackson, amounting to 580,000 pounds of Rio coffee, and the Raven, 500,000 pounds of Rio, were sold, as well as some lots from the Osborne Howes and Lewis. The price is understood to have been about 13 cents.

———o———

Lynching at New Peak

SACRAMENTO, Feb. 9, 1855—Lynch Law is prevailing to an extent hitherto unknown in this state. As many as 20 men have been hung by mobs since January 1.

The most recent instances are: the hanging of Sheldon at Oakland on a charge of horse-stealing; a young man at Red Bluffs, suspected of stealing a mule, but subsequently ascertained to be innocent; James Moran, for murder, at Sawyer's Bar, Salmon River.

The leading banks of Page, Bacon & Co. and Adams & Co. have been forced to close, and it still is uncertain as to whether they will be able to reopen their doors in the future. The latter firm has several branches in the interior.

Other banks which have shut down are Robinson & Co.'s "Savings Bank" and Dr. Wright's Miners Bank in San Francisco, George W. Plume of Marysville and Hamlet Davis at Nevada City. In Jamestown, John H. Richardson, doing a banking business, closed his doors and departed for parts unknown. His depositors lose about $30,000. When broken open, his safe was found to contain only $20.

The panic was set off when the steamer mail brought news of the failure of the firm of Page & Bacon of St. Louis. A run began immediately on Page, Bacon & Co. here, and quickly extended to Adams and other banks. The total amount withdrawn in the run over a period of several days amounted to $2,434,000.

Banking establishments now open include Wells, Fargo & Co.; Palmer, Cook & Co.; Lucas, Turner & Co.; Tallant and Wilde, Drexel, Sather & Church; B. Davidson and Sanders and Brenham.

———o———

MINING ONLY FAIR NEAR NEVADA CITY

NEVADA CITY, Feb. 4, 1855—Perseverance is being rewarded at some of the mines in this area.

Duncan Robertson reports that the U. S. Company, on Bourbon Hill, have at last struck a lead that promises to repay them for the 16 months of labor and $28,000 that has been put into the project. The company is now getting prospects running from $1 to $6 to the pan, and the lead is extensive.

Miners at Red Dog are doing a fair business. The Chalk Bluff Ditch is delivering a considerable quantity of water to the miners' sluices and Long Toms. King and Co. on Red Dog Hill took out $400 in a week, with four men working.

Rains are badly needed to supply water to the dry diggings.

FREMONT'S MARIPOSA CLAIM CONFIRMED

SAN FRANCISCO, March 29, 1855—Private advices, received via the steamer Golden Age arriving yesterday, report that the U. S. Supreme Court has confirmed Col. J. C. Fremont's claim to the rich Mariposa grant.

This is probably the most important decision affecting California that has ever been made by the court. Col. Fremont retains a heavy interest in the claim, although one-half is said to be owned by a San Francisco banking house.

Value of the claim is immense. A standing offer for it of one million pounds sterling is reported to exist for a half as soon as it was confirmed.

———o———

Two Monterey Men Kill Each Other

MONTEREY, March 15, 1855—An affray here today resulted in the deaths of two prominent men, Dr. Sanford, formerly of New York, and Jeremiah McMahon, formerly of Philadelphia.

McMahon was the brother-in-law of Sheriff William Roach, who has absconded and is accused of having cheated Sanchez estate of some $50,000. Dr. Sandford was the husband of the widow of Jose Maria Sanchez.

A dispute had arisen between the two men out of a law suit relating to the estate. They met today at the United States Hotel. After some high words, they each drew revolvers and fired. The shots took effect in vital parts, and both combatants fell dead.

———o———

Attorney Flees

SAN FRANCISCO, March 15, 1855—G. J. Hubert Sanders, prominent attorney, failed to appear for a hearing today on a charge of forgery, and it is believed he has fled town.

Sanders was arrested a few days ago on an accusation of forgery in a mortgage for $8,000. He was freed on $10,000 bail posted by his law partner and a friend.

Superb Oranges Are Received from L. A.

SAN FRANCISCO, March 11, 1855—A package of oranges was received here today via the steamer America from the vineyards of Benjamin D. Wilson at Los Angeles. They are a truly fine sample.

The vineyards of Los Angeles are famous for the grape, pear, peach, apricot, apple and fig, and supply the northern part of the state with the first three fruits. In season the steamers come up loaded with grapes, pears and peaches which are shipped from here to Sacramento, Stockton and all the mining towns.

The orange has not been very extensively cultivated as yet. There are a few orange gardens in Los Angeles, and a very flourishing one at Mission San Gabriel. Its cultivation can be made as profitable as any other orchard, and we do not doubt that two or three years hence Los Angeles oranges will be found on every fruit stand in the state.

Mr. Wilson's experiment of making a first class champagne wine promises success, and we believe the time is not far distant when California will be an exporter of wine.

———o———

Citizens Open Vault Of Closed Bank

SONORA, March 4, 1855—A citizens' committee, headed by B. F. Moore, broke open the vault of the Sonora branch of the closed Adams & Co. bank here in fear that the deposits would be withdrawn to San Francisco.

Over the protests of Sheriff Solamon, the committee distributed $44,992.50 to depositors presenting certificates, according to the secretary's minutes.

———o———

BANK REOPENS

SAN FRANCISCO, March 29, 1855—Page, Bacon & Co., one of the leading banks that closed in last month's panic, reopened today in new offices at Clay and Battery streets.

The amount deposited exceeded that drawn out by more than $100,-000, so the bank may now be said to be in successful operation.

Miners Striking for Lower Water Rate

COLUMBIA, March 13, 1855—Three thousand miners of this region have "struck" for a reduction in the water rates of the Tuolumne County Water Co., which is presently charging $6 a day.

The miners demand that the company cut "the price of water to $4 per day for a full sluice stream." The company so far has refused on the ground that the amount received for their water has paid only about 2 per cent per month on the actual cost of the work.

Miners are proposing to keep a "black book" list of any miner found using company water. At a mass meeting one of the resolutions passed was "that we place upon our claims in large figures—$4 for water and no more—as a tombstone denoting that our claim is buried for a season."

———o———

TWO KILLED WHEN MOB STORMS JAIL

YREKA, March 7, 1855—At least two men have died, and several others are in bad condition from wounds as a result of a mob storming the jail here.

The difficulty arose out of the arrest of two men for contempt of court for breaking the Middle Green Horn Ditch.

NEW FREIGHT ROUTE TO SALT LAKE CITY

LOS ANGELES, April 21, 1855—There is a new feature to business in Los Angeles: trade to Salt Lake has commenced through the energy and enterprise of local citizens.

It has been demonstrated that merchandise can be taken from Los Angeles to Salt Lake quicker than from Missouri. Now that the hostility of Indians along the plains and mountain route has raised obstacles to the delivery of merchandise, attention has been turned to the Pacific.

As there is no difficulty in obtaining every variety of goods here, there is no reason why the entire trade of the Great Basin should not be through Los Angeles. Thousands of dollars of goods have left here within the last few weeks. Messrs. Hopkins and Rollins of San Bernardino started last week with several wagon loads. Messrs. Alexander and Banning, and W. T. B. Sandford will soon send of an invoice of over $20,000.

The road to Salt Lake is in such good condition there is no difficulty in taking loaded wagons through in about 20 days.

——o——

Legislature Passes Anti-gambling Bill

SACRAMENTO, April 13, 1855—Despite powerful combinations against it, a bill to supress gambling in California passed the state legislature today.

It provides fines of $100 to $500 for operating any game of chance, and for the owner of any property used for gambling.

——o——

VINEYARD PROPERTY SOLD

LOS ANGELES, April 8, 1955—The magnificent property of Don Luis Vigne, of this city, has been sold to Don Pedro Sansevain for $50,000, a small sum in comparison to the intrinsic value.

Don Luis has put back his entire income into improvements until he has made his vineyards and orangeries famous throughout the State. His white wines have become celebrated and known even in the East.

BUSINESS IS VERY DULL

SAN FRANCISCO, April 16, 1855—Business is dull here, and money is tight.

Some failures of mercantile houses and real estate owners have been noted, two of them persons who have recently ranked with the wealthiest in the State.

An overstocked market contributes to a depreciation of all kinds of merchandise. During the past week 17 clipper ships have arrived, all heavily loaded with goods, As a result, a large loss will result to the shippers. Because of the glut, prices for most articles, including the necessities, are as cheap as in any of the eastern markets.

——o——

Forgery Is Disclosed In Honolulu Firm

HONOLULU, April 14, 1855—Considerable excitement has been caused here by the discovery that a large amount of forged whalers' bills had been disposed of by L. Swan of the ship chandlery firm of Swan and Clifford.

The disclosure was made when one bill was returned as protested. As a result, all who bought bills from Swan and Clifford have held a meeting. There it came out that at least $44,000 of forged paper had been sold by Swan. The holders have offered a 20 per cent reward for the recovery of any amounts.

Both partners in the firm had previously left the islands, Clifford on a trading voyage to Japan, and Swan on the barque George, ostensibly on a whaling voyage.

——o——

Fort Construction Slow

SAN FRANCISCO, April 8, 1855—The works of defense under construction at Fort Point are proceeding slowly.

Masons are still employed on the platform, laying the foundation for the walls of the Fort with square massive granite blocks, cement and granulated rock. Granite continues to come in from the Monterey quarries and is absorbed in the deep foundation gulf.

Work on the ten-gun battery on the hill is completed, and the brick traverses are ready for placing and mounting the guns.

"Flying Cloud" Wins Yacht Race in Bay

SAN FRANCISCO, April 30, 1855 The yacht Flying Cloud won a race here today from her rival sloops, Eclipse and Mischief. Considerable amounts of money are understood to have been wagered on the race.

The day was gusty for safe sport, with a heavy, choppy sea throughout the bay. The route was from the foot of Broadway to a flag boat anchored off Fort point, and back around Goat Island to the point of departure.

Soon after the start, the Eclipse took the lead, but Flying Cloud passed her near Meiggs Wharf, with Mischief far astern. Flying Cloud completed the course in two and three-quarters hours. Eclipse was half and hour behind at the flag boat, but capsized while rounding it. Her six crewmen were rescued by one of the score of boats which followed the racers.

——o——

Oregon Plans Telegraph Line

PORTLAND, April 20, 1855—Agents of the Portland and Corvallis Line of Telegraph are "blazing out the line" preparatory to letting contracts for setting the poles.

Oregon City, Lafayette, Dayton and Salem are to be points on the route, provided sufficient encouragement is given to the work by interested citizens. The wires to Corvallis will probably be in operation in a few months.

The gap to Yreka, California, will be filled soon afterwards, providing within two years a continuous line from Portland to the States, bearing upon its vibrating wires news of mighty events.

——o——

Weber Grant Confirmed

SAN FRANCISCO, April 17, 1855—The Mexican land grant claim of C. M. Weber to 11 square leagues of land called Campo Francis, which include the site of the present city of Stockton, were confirmed here today by the U. S. Land Commission. Citizens of that city hold their titles from Mr. Weber.

Stockton Hoaxed By "Flying Man"

STOCKTON, May 12, 1855—This city was taken in by a huge hoax here today.

All during the past week posters were distributed, declaring that Mr. John White would fly from the top of the St. Charles Hotel at 4 p.m. today at the firing of the cannon.

By three o'clock, this afternoon a crowd began gathering in the streets, and by four there was an immense concourse of men, women and children. At about 4:15 a man appeared on the hotel roof, dressed in something that looked like a sheet.

While all eyes followed him, he walked back and forth, bowing occasionally to the crowd below. At last he stooped down as if to adjust his wings. Then he rose again while the multitude cheered.

Suddenly he made a swinging, surging motion of his body as if to take off. But instead of launching himself into the air, he drew a white goose from under the sheet and threw it from the roof. The goose flapped its way down to the street below, while the man on the roof disappeared from view.

There was a moment's hush; then the crowd broke into laughter at having been "sold" so thoroughly. Some people seized a man in a bar room, thinking he was the perpetrator of the hoax, and ducked him in the slough. But he was not the man.

———o———

Rich New Gold Finds

COLUMBIA, May 12, 1855—Reports have been received of some interesting, rich new gold discoveries.

At Stewart's Hill on the Calaveras, there have been some fabulous new finds in the hill diggings. Martin's company took out the total of $8000 in one day, and another company is said to be taking out $5300 daily.

A new lead has been found at Carson's which has prospected as much as $3 to the pan.

Walker Party Starts Nicaragua Venture

SAN FRANCISCO, May 4, 1855—The Walker Expedition to Nicaragua has sailed at last, surmounting financial and legal difficulties.

———————

LYNCHINGS AT L. A.

LOS ANGELES, May 14, 1855—Two men were shot in a tragic, messy lynching affair last night at the village of Lexington, or Monte, 12 miles from here.

A few days ago a man named William Paine swore in an affidavit that one Brown, a brother of the David Brown who was lynched several months ago, had organized a band of killers and robbers, and that part of the gang was at Turner's Pass.

Five men were arrested there and brought to Lexington: William Watson, William Hand, A. E. Moore, Pole Wilkerson and a man named Garretson. A lynch trial was held, and it was voted to hang all except Garretson, who was voted innocent. The convicted four were led out and ropes placed around their necks. Then a second vote was taken, with the result that it was decided to turn them over to the civil authorities.

They were placed in custody in a building. But the next night six or eight men entered and told them they would hang. Hand and Wilkerson were taken out first, but managed to loosen their bonds and flee in the darkness. However, Moore was shot in bed, and Watson was also shot, although there is some evidence an attempt was made first to hang him.

———o———

In Old Mining Areas

Much improvement has taken place in the district lying along the Forks of the Mokelumne river. A quartz vein has been located in the vicinity of Angel's Camp. At Carson's Hill, which has been in litigation for a long time, quartz operations will soon be commenced.

The Experimental Quartz Co. pounded out six pounds of gold last week. The expense of working, for the week, was about $300, leaving a clear profit of about $1000.

The brig Vesta left the harbor by subterfuge at 1 a.m. today. She had been lying for several days under attachment at the Stewart Street Wharf. After raising the attachment, she was still detained by the county sheriff for a matter of $350 in fees.

Deputy Sheriff Purdy was on board to hold the brig in custody, but never dreamed of the sailing plans. At about midnight Col. William Walker, the well known filibuster leader, asked the deputy to step below to examine some papers. There in the cabin Walker cooly told him that the vessel would get underway at once, and no violence would be offered if Purdy remained quiet as a prisoner. He did so.

By pre-arrangement, the steam tug Resolute pulled the Vesta out from her berth, and towed her until the Heads were cleared. The deputy, unharmed, was put on the tug then to return to port, while the Vesta spread sail to a spanking breeze.

Great hopes are held as the expedition sails at the express invitation of the present government of Nicaragua. Walker and his men are promised 75,000 acres when they succeed in quieting the Chamorro party and restore Nicaragua to peace.

———o———

FAMED GAMBLING HOUSE SUSPENDS BUSINESS

SAN FRANCISCO, May 11, 1855—The El Dorado, located at Washington and Kearny streets, has closed shop. The doors are closed and locked, and the words "To Let" posted outside.

El Dorado was the oldest, most frequented and most respectable of all the gambling houses in San Francisco. Probably more money has been made or gained in this building than in any other in California. To the last it had the appearance of doing as much business as any gambling house in town.

The proprietors have yielded to the law, and suspended their business before the new anti-gambling regulations recently passed by the state legislature take effect.

Well Known Pugilists In Savage Brawl

SAN FRANCISCO, June 17, 1855 — A desperate pugilistic encounter took place at 1 a.m. today in Lilly's cock-fighting pit on Commercial street between Yankee Sullivan and William Mulligan, who are both well known in sporting and political circles.

After an exhibition of cock-fighting, words passed between the two men. Mulligan assailed Sullivan as a "Sydney thief," etc., and Sullivan replied with a blow from his cudgel and an attempt to draw his knife.

After a short set-to, which was somewhat hampered by their friends, the two men adjourned to Tyson's Exchange, Mulligan having challenged Sullivan to fight alone in a room. A large crowd followed them, and the affair was about to begin when police officers arrived and put a stop to it.

Sullivan then went to another room, where he was followed by Mulligan. The latter struck Sullivan a heavy blow with his fist, knocking him down. Mulligan then drew a pistol and pummeled Sullivan with its butt, inflicting severe injuries.

Sullivan is said by his friends to be much emaciated and enfeebled, and not prepared for a fight; while others asert the difficulty was of his own seeking. Neither party has been arrested.

———o———

HEAT WAVE STRIKES INTERIOR OF STATE

SACRAMENTO, June 29, 1855 — Excessive heat has been experienced through the interior of California during the past week.

The mercury has reached unusual heights here. At Stockton, temperatures have ranged from 95 to 105 degrees. Sonora and Columbia reported records of 108, while Mokelumne Hill had 102 degrees.

In most places the heat has been so great that work has been halted in the mines except in the early morning and evening hours.

Board Confirms Land Grant Dispute in S.F.

SAN FRANCISCO, June 5, 1855 — The Board of U.S. Land Commissioners today handed down an opinion confirming the famous, controversial "Bolton and Barron" claim to three square leagues of land, much of it lying within or adjacent to the city limits of San Francisco.

The present value of the land included in the grant is reckoned in the millions of dollars. The original grant is claimed to have been made by Pio Pico, last Mexican governor of California, in 1846 to Padre Pedro Santillan. It is now held one-half by the firm of Palmer, Cook & Co. of this city, and the other half by a company of Philadelphia capitalists.

It is hoped that they will follow a policy of liberality to settlers on the land.

The claim was bitterly contested before the commissioners, and a tremendous mass of testimony was taken. The board's opinion was delivered by Commissioner Farwell. It is expected that the confirmation will be appealed to the federal courts.

———o———

Rail Equipment Arrives

SACRAMENTO, June 16, 1855 — The cargo of the clipper ship Winged Racer, which recently arrived from the East, consisted almost entirely of locomotives, baggage cars and machinery for the Sacramento Valley Railroad. The work should be completed and the cars in motion in a short time.

Joint Treaties Signed With Indian Tribes

PORTLAND, June 20, 1855 — Gen. Palmer has arrived here direct from the Indian country where, with Gov. Stevens of Washington Territory, joint treaties have been concluded with the Nez Perces, Walla Wallas, Cayuses and Umatillas.

The Nez Perces are reported to be very well off, possessing about 25,000 head of horses and cattle; and the Cayuses and Walla Wallas, 15,000.

After making treaties with these tribes, Gov. Stevens, with 35 men and 94 horses, started to the St. Mary's Valley to treat with the Blackfeet Indians.

On Gen. Palmer's return trip he succeeded in making treaties with Indians at The Dalles and other tribes along the Columbia river.

———o———

Grasshopper Plague Threatens Interior

MARYSVILLE, June 4, 1855 — The whole country for miles around has been invaded by myriads of grasshoppers.

Judge Cushing reported a column of the insects took his farm en route and stripped it of every green thing—leaf of grass, twig or plant. The grasshoppers also have attacked General Sutter's Hock Farm.

Fortunately for the farmers, the hay harvest is over, and most of the wheat and barley are too ripe to tempt the appetites of the 'hoppers. Most of the crop loss is in the fruit trees, and oats.

The invasion, however, provides a rich harvest for the Indians, who fancy the insects as food. They have caught and stacked tons of them.

———o———

ANGEL'S CAMP, June 25, 1855 — Fire this afternoon destroyed every building in this town, a total loss estimated at $50,000.

The flames broke out in a Chinese house, and in 20 minutes had spread throughout the town. The building occupied by Wells, Fargo & Co. was among those destroyed, but the company's safe, books, papers and treasure were saved.

DESPERADO GANG USES CHLOROFORM

SONORA, July 1, 1855 — One of the most barbarous deeds in the history of the county occurred at Yorktown early this morning.

Three or four masked desperadoes broke into the home of Judge Brunton, who was asleep with his wife and three children. Because of the heat, all of the family were sleeping close by open windows. The robbers reached through the windows to administer chloroform to all. Then they took the key to the judges safe, opened it and made off with $13,000 in gold dust, and coin and other valuables.

As they were leaving, Judge Brunton awoke from the drugging, grabbed a revolver and attempted to fire. A struggle ensued, in which the judge was disarmed and wounded. The robbers then gave him some more chloroform, saying, "Judge, we only want to keep you quiet till we get out of the way. We don't want to kill you."

The other members of the family did not awake until late in the morning, and found the judge prostrate and unconscious by the door. Medical aid has been given him.

Judge Brunton is public administrator of Tuolumne county. It was the second time in two years that he has been robbed.

———o———

HEAVY EARTHQUAKE IS FELT IN LOS ANGELES

LOS ANGELES, July 9, 1855 — The heaviest earthquake ever known in this country cracked large numbers of the town's one-story buildings from top to bottom.

Nearly every merchant suffered losses from goods being thrown from their shelves and windows being broken. Hardly a building escaped damage to the walls or contents. Walls up to 2½ and 3 feet thick were rent asunder.

Residents fled their homes as the shock lasted for several seconds. The quake appeared to lift the ground up and twist it about, and it was accompanied by a roaring noise like the approach of a hurricane.

30 DIE AS CHOLERA ENGULFS STEAMER

SAN FRANCISCO, July 14, 1855 — The dread disease cholera broke out on the steamer Sierra Nevada, which arrived here today, and 30 people in all died on her voyage north from San Juan del Sud.

The disease appeared a few days after the trip began. In one instance, a whole family—man, wife and child—died on three successive days, and in one four-hour watch there were seven deaths. The steamer's chief mate and two crewmen were among those who died.

Two Runners Shot By Skipper in Port

SAN FRANCISCO, July 11, 1855 — Two sailor boarding house runners were shot and wounded tonight by Capt. Doran of the ship Nazarine.

The ship, from Liverpool, had not let her anchor go when several boats appeared and attempted to board her. Capt. Doran, who had lost his crew when in this port before, was determined that the runners should not board his ship until the sails were furled and decks cleared up.

He warned the boats away with no effect. Then the men attempted to climb over the side of the ship, and the captain fired. The captain has been freed on $4000 bail, and the case will be brought before the Court of Sessions.

———o———

Whaling at Monterey

MONTEREY, July 21, 1855 — Six whales have been killed in Monterey Bay in the last week. There are only two boat crews working, and they do good business despite limited means. When they see a shoal of whales, they launch boats and often return towing a good-sized whale which they cut up and process on the beach.

Noted Pioneer Dies

MISSION SAN JOSE, July 19, 1855 — Capt. Joseph L. Folsom, 39, California pioneer and one of the wealthiest men in the state, died here today after an extended illness at the home of E. L. Beard.

———o———

Committee Boosts California Travel

SAN FRANCISCO, July 24, 1855 — Plans to promote California's agriculture, industry and immigration were discussed at a well attended, enthusiastic meeting of the preliminary committee of the Immigration Society here tonight at Musical hall on Bush street

George Gordon, secretary of the committee, proposed three methods of attaining the objects:

1. To disseminate continually and systematically information on California's soil, climate, agricultural products, the yield of crops, etc.

2. By business negotiations to reduce the price of passage to California and multiply the means of transport.

3. To procure employment for immigrants immediately on their arrival at some rate, however low, so they may not go idling about and become disgusted while they are still on the threshhold.

Gordon also drew cheers when he proposed the consideration of inducing the establishment of a line of vessels exclusively for the transportation of female passengers to California.

Bloody Battles Mark Primary Elections

SAN FRANCISCO, Aug. 21, 1855 —Bloodshed marked the Democratic primary election here today for candidates for the legislative and county conventions.

Two men were wounded, perhaps fatally, in an affray at the Sixth Ward polls on Kearny street. A dispute between James P. Casey and J. W. Bagley led to an exchange of shots, in which Bagley was dangerously wounded in the side.

A general tumult then ensued in which perhaps 20 shots in all were fired by other men. Knives were drawn, and wounds were given and received. A Mr. Cushing was stabbed critically in the left side.

John Ricketts was arrested for stabbing John Farley in an altercation which arose near the Second Ward polls.

After two previous fist fights at the First Ward polls, Martin Gallagher was jailed for a third battle at Net Gallagher's Saloon with a man named Banty. Connoiseurs who were present stated it was one of the hardest fought battles ever conducted in San Francisco. Both men, giants in physique, were covered with blood when it closed.

———o———

New "Steamer Day" Dates

SAN FRANCISCO, Aug. 20, 1855 —The city's time-honored "Steamer Day" is to be changed from the first and 16th of the month to the 5th and the 20th. This change will be very desirable to the community and the state generally.

Heretofore the arrival and departure of the mail steamers have often occurred on the same day. The result is that the city's business men have had only an hour or two to answer heavy mail from the Atlantic States, and sometimes no time at all. This new arrangement will also provide other cities an opportunity to reply by return steamer.

———o———

Hit-Run Driving

SAN FRANCISCO, Aug. 22, 1855 —A pedestrian was knocked down last night on Folsom street near Kearny by a buggy containing two men. They drove on at a rapid rate without stopping to see the extent of the pedestrian's injury.

First Train Operates Here in California

SACRAMENTO, Aug. 18, 1855 — Today marked a significant new first in California history, operation of the first train in the state.

The contractors for building the Sacramento Valley Railroad, Robinson, Seymour & Co., staged a short excursion behind a locomotive from the Levee to 17th street, the present eastern terminus of the tracks.

The train consisted of tender and three platform cars, which were densely crowded with about 20 people. Great cheers arose as the first train started from the Levee.

Transit over the tracks was accomplished smoothly and pleasantly to the manifest pleasure of the participants. They cheered frequently as the train proceeded, especially when they passed groups of spectators.

———o———

BETTER FUTURE IS SEEN FOR L.A.

LOS ANGELES, Aug. 12, 1855 — Another year will find this city in far better circumstances than at present.

Several flour mills are now in operation which will enable the community not only to make its bread but also to export.

In the manufacture of wine this area is destined to find a rich reward. Only a short time will elapse before the vintages of Los Angeles will become as celebrated as the sparkling wines of France and Spain. The Salt Works 15 miles from town are prospering as well.

Messrs. Alexander and Banning have made many improvements at San Pedro. Their buildings are in fine order, and they have provided good accommodations for travelers.

Now, instead of the need for laboriously dragging merchandise up the steep ascent from the beach, new and easy roads have been dug through the bank. Alexander & Banning have recently constructed a substantial pier.

The firm has on the road from 35 to 40 monster wagons drawn by 10 and 12 mules each, an ample supply of stages, lighters and boats.

Horror and Blood at Mining Town, 9 Die

JACKSON, Aug. 9, 1855 — Six murders, followed by the lynching of three men, occurred yesterday afternoon and last night at Rancheria.

The hours of horror began when a robber gang of Mexicans and Chilenos, which is said to include a few Americans, raided the town. In all, they killed four Americans, one woman and an Indian.

The robbers first entered a tavern, the Rancheria House, and there killed two men and a woman. At the store of Mr. French they took $7000 from a safe after killing French and his clerk.

When the news became known, a mob of over 1000 citizens from Rancheria and nearby mining communities gathered. They rounded up 36 Mexicans and took them to an oak tree near town.

A motion was made to hang all 36, but through the efforts of several calmer individuals a jury of 12 was picked from the crowd. The jurors found three of the Mexicans, who gave their names as Pertervine, Trancolino and Jose, guilty of murder.

The three men were then hung on the tree, under whose shade the trial was held. While the trial was underway, the community turned out en masse and burned the Spanish dance house and every Spanish house in town.

———o———

ICE PRICE IS BROKEN BY ARRIVAL OF SHIP

SAN FRANCISCO, Aug. 7, 1855— The arrival of a new shipload of ice, that very needful luxury, has broken the exorbitant prices which have been maintained during the recent scarcity.

The price of ice was run up to 42 cents a pound by speculators who bought it at the uniform price of 6 cents from the Sitka Ice Co. The price was broken with the arrival of the ship Zenobia from the island of Kodiak with a cargo of 580 tons of beautiful ice, as good as the best Sitka grade, for the Russian American Commercial Co.

FIRST DIRECT CARGO HERE FROM JAPAN

SAN FRANCISCO, Sept. 19, 1855 —The schooner Caroline E. Foote has arrived here from Japan, the first vessel ever to import a cargo directly from that country to the United States.

She brought in Japanese rice, said to be of superior quality, and over 140 cases of Japanese goods, including fine silks, lacquered ware, cabinets, porcelain, screens, colored glass and toys.

The little Yankee schooner is the forerunner of fleets which may hereafter make princely fortunes for our adventurous merchants.

---o---

DEVASTATING FIRES HIT MINING TOWNS

WEAVERVILLE, Sept. 8, 1855— A fire originating in a building used by the Society of the Sons of Temperance for its meetings burned down 50 buildings here last night.

Because of the highly combustible nature of the structure, the blaze rapidly swept down both sides of the town's street. The loss in buildings and property is estimated at $200,000 or more.

The office of the Trinity Times was destroyed, but the newspaper's press was saved with only slight damage. Its regular issue was printed today from a shop set up in the open air.

GRASS VALLEY, Sept. 14, 1855 — Fire which broke out in the French Hotel today nearly destroyed the whole town. Between 25 and 30 acres were burned over, and 350 houses were destroyed.

Estimates of loss run up to $400,-000. This figure is so high because merchants of the town had just laid in heavy stocks of fall goods.

---o---

Murieta's Head Sold

SAN FRANCISCO, Sept. 24, 1855 — The hand of "Three-Fingered Jack" and the head of the celebrated Joaquin Murieta were sold by the sheriff today for the sum of $36 to satisfy a judgment. Judge Lyons and J. V. Plume were the high bidders on this occasion.

TUOLUMNE SERVED BY 135 MILE DITCHES

SONORA, Sept. 30, 1855 — There are in operation and construction in Tuolumne County 135 miles of water ditches to serve the gold diggings. Of these only 35 miles remain to be completed.

The total original cost of these works is estimated to run $1,800,-000.

Tuolumne County Water Co.'s ditch, which runs for 50 miles, is assessed at $275,000. First cost of the Tuolumne Hydraulic ditch which is nearly 50 miles long, including branches, was $300,000, and it is now assessed at only $30,000.

When finished, Street's ditch will run for 50 to 60 miles and cost $175,-000. The Calaveras and Stanislaus River Water Co. has a capital of $300,000, of which $80,000 has been spent so far. Its ditch will be 50 miles in length.

Other ditches in the county are: the Jamestown and Chinese ditch, cost $12,000 Chile Camp, $3000, 4 miles; Seco ditch, $3000, 3 miles; Pine ditch, $2000, 5 miles; Yorktown ditch, $6000, 5 miles; Republican ditch, $3000, 4 miles; Jamestown ditch, $1000, 2 miles; Wood's Diggings ditch, $8000, 10 miles.

---o---

INDIAN CHIEF DIES

COLUMBIA, Sept. 3, 1855—After an illness of several weeks, Captain Charley, chief of the Walla Walla tribe of Indians in this section of the state, has died in his wigwam near the banks of the Stanislaus river.

Captain Charley was attended by many of his kin and tribesmen in his final illness. His body has been cut up and divided among various groups so that funeral rites can be held at various rancherias. Charley was one of the most respected Indian chiefs in California and had many friends among the whites.

---o---

Hold Agricultural Fair

SACRAMENTO, Sept. 26, 1855 — The grand exhibition of agricultural products of California was opened last evening with ceremonies in the Assembly Chamber of the Capitol that were heavily attnded. Exhibits displayed the miraculous productivity of the state.

'QUAKE DAMAGE IS UNLIKELY FOR S.F.
FEARS UNWARRANTED

SAN FRANCISCO, Sept. 1, 1855 —Fears are sometimes expressed that a ruinous earthquake is in store for California, and that the brick edifices of San Francisco are liable at any moment to be annihilated.

There is nothing in the history of the country to warrant such fears. The oldest inhabitant, it is true, often tells of earthquakes which visited this country years and years ago, and which, if renewed, would shake our brick walls to pieces.

But the old adobe churches scattered along the western coast of California—frail structures, many of them incapable of resisting the agitation of a violent earthquake —tell a different story. The church of San Juan Capistrano, 50 miles south of Los Angeles, is the only one which bears the marks of a severe concussion.

Within a few months past the city of Los Angeles was visited with the most severe earthquake in the state since its settlement by Americans. But Los Angeles is several hundred miles distant from San Francisco, and might be swallowed up without any risk to this city.

TRAVEL IS HEAVY IN CALIFORNIA

SACRAMENTO, Oct. 10, 1855—Traveling is proving popular in California these days. An unusual number of people are taking advantage of the low rates of fare on stages and steamboats.

The other day, the California Stage Co. coach brought 34 passengers from Marysville to Sacramento, and the opposition coach 29. The California Stage Co. on the same day was compelled to refuse passage to 20 persons from Sacramento to Nevada City. In the past few days upwards of 100 people have been unable to obtain seats to where they wanted to go.

The steamboats to and from San Francisco take unprecedented crowds of passengers. The Surprise and Defender each daily load and carry 400 to 600 passengers from Sacramento, while the other steamboats also convey large numbers.

Cholera Kills 48

SAN FRANCISCO, Oct. 9, 1855—The steamer Sierra Nevada arrived here tonight after a tragic voyage from San Juan del Sud in which 45 persons, 38 adults and seven children, died of cholera.

The sickness prevailed on the first few days of the trip, and it is reported that another 18 or 20 prospective passengers had died at San Juan before the steamer's departure. The Sierra Nevada brought up a total of 862 passngers, including 205 females.

New Lighthouse Lit

SAN DIEGO, Oct. 21, 1855 — The new lighthouse on Point Loma at the harbor entrance was lighted up for the first time last night. It stands in an elevated position, and the light can be seen in any direction by vessels approaching the harbor.

THE EVENING BULLETIN, NEW PAPER STARTED

SAN FRANCISCO, Oct. 8, 1855—The first number of a new newspaper, called the Evening Bulletin, made its appearance today. It is published by C. O. Geberding & Co., and edited by James King of William, former banker. It is a very neatly printed sheet and exhibits decided ability.

At present there are ten dailies in San Francisco and four tri-weeklies — a year and a half ago there were 14 dailies. In California there is now a total of 15 dailies, six tri-weeklies and 35 weekly newspapers.

FIRST BIG FIRE BREAKS OUT IN LOS ANGELES

LOS ANGELES, Oct. 23, 1855 — The first fire of any consequence in Los Angeles broke out last night in the bowling alley attached to the Montgomery Saloon. As the alley was built of wood and canvas, the flames spread rapidly to the two-story wooden building next to the saloon and quickly destroyed it.

The saloon itself, built of adobe, was saved although it was badly damaged, with the billiard tables, furniture, pictures and stock of liquor being destroyed. Heat from the fire melted the brea, or tar, on the flat roof and caused it to flow down into the building.

It is truly fortunate for our city that adobes form almost the only building material, or, because of the lack of water, we might have seen the entire destruction of the town.

Murderers Arrested

MARYSVILLE, Oct. 12, 1855 — Three of the Mexicans suspected of being concerned with the murder of the Chinese on State Creek, Sierra County, near St. Louis, on Sunday morning have been arrested here.

There were seven Chinese in the camp when the attack was made. Five were killed instantly; one has since died of his wounds, and it is believed that the other cannot survive.

It is now evident that the murderous attack was made upon the sleeping Chinese by seven Mexicans, each singling out his victim.

INDIAN UPRISINGS PROVE SERIOUS

PORTLAND, Ore. Ter., Oct. 25, 1855 — People of both Oregon and Washington territories are seriously alarmed at the Indian risings, which are also occurring as far south as Crescent City, and elsewhere in the northern part of California.

Governor Curry of Oregon has taken to the field with a thousand volunteers, all well armed and mounted, and 300 regulars are expected to operate with him. Gov. Mason of Washington has also called for volunteers.

Major Haller and a party of 100 men were attacked by about 1500 Indians near The Dalles. He lost five men killed and 16 wounded.

Various reports have been received which indicate there have been some 60 murders of whites by Indians, and a reliable correspondent says 70 Chinese have also been massacred. When bodies of whites and Indians have met in the Rogue River valley, large numbers of Indians have been killed.

It is probable that somewhat exaggerated accounts have been received, but what is actually known is sufficient to produce the liveliest alarm for the safety of whites throughout our frontiers.

Los Angeles Assessments Low

LOS ANGELES, Oct. 6, 1855 — According to the assessor's list, there has been a great falling off from the assessed valuation of real and personal property in Los Angeles county from last year.

The total valuation is $2,561,350. The state tax is 60 cents per $100 and amounts to $15,367.35. The county tax is 90 cents, and amounts to $23,050.99.

The assessments of many of our wealthy citizens are from 50 to 75 per cent less than in 1854. This reduction is probably owing to the great depreciation in the value of cattle.

Folsom Estate Valued

SAN FRANCISCO, Oct. 1, 1855—Appraisers of the estate of the late Capt. Joseph L. Folsom have completed their work and find that his real estate is worth $2,005,000 at present values.

STATE'S GOLD MINES NOW DOING WELL

SACRAMENTO, Nov. 29, 1855 — The gold mines at this time are yielding immensely, and almost every day there are reports of new discoveries and rich strikes.

Table Mountain, in Tuolumne County, still continues to be a marvel for its richness, and vast sums of the precious metal are being extracted every day. The whole mountain is being pierced with tunnels, and will soon become like a honeycomb for miles in succession.

To purchase a claim to 100 feet of this mountain or the adjacent flats would take a fortune. Thousands of miners who have recorded claims by right of discovery and possession feel sure of making the "pile" for which they came to California.

Copious rains have also set the miners at work in all parts of the state. Large piles of earth, which it has taken many months' labor to accumulate, are now yielding their treasure to their owners. Even from the Kern River come cheering accounts of the discovery of rich leads.

Many wonderful fossil remains have been brought to light by mining operations. At a depth of 159 feet decomposed oyster shells have been found in Table Mountain.

———o———

INDIAN WAR CONTINUES IN NORTHERN AREAS

PORTLAND, Ore. Ter., Nov. 17, 1855—The Indian War now raging in Washington and Oregon territories, still continues. At the latest accounts numerous families have been wiped out and many lives lost.

U. S. Marshal Is Shot By Noted Gambler

SAN FRANCISCO, Nov. 17, 1855 — Gen. William H. Richardson, 33, U.S. Marshal for the northern district of California, was killed tonight by the desperado and gambler Charles Cora.

Except for a trifling difficulty in a bar-room the night before, there was no known misunderstanding between the two. After a conversation at the "Blue Wing" on Montgomery street, Cora and Richardson walked down Clay street together. Near the corner of Leidesdorff street, they stopped. Witnesses saw Cora suddenly place a pistol against Richardson's left chest and fire. The marshal instantly fell dead on the sidewalk.

Excitement was widespread through the city. The Monumental bell was tapped, and many members of the old Vigilance Committee responded to its call.

Although there was some talk of lynching, it was conceded the murderer was safe in custody of officers of the law. Fifty men were selected from the Vigilance Committee to guard the county jail where Cora is confined.

It is believed the affair began when Gen. Richardson objected to the fact that the notorious Belle Cora, paramour of the gambler, was seated next to his wife at the theatre a few evenings ago. Richardson had been quartermaster general of the California militia and a delegate to the Democratic National Convention in 1852.

———o———

3 LIVES LOST WHEN DISTILLERY BURNS

SAN FRANCISCO, Nov. 2, 1855 — The Novelty Distillery Works, reputed to be the second largest such plant in the United States, was entirely destroyed by fire today following the explosion of a still.

Two men in the plant were fatally injured, and several others were badly hurt. One fireman was also killed, and four others wounded, when a center wall collapsed and fell on them.

The distillery was built at a cost of $300,000 and had a capacity of 2400 gallons of pure spirits per day. It was located half way from the city to Mission Dolores, but the fire engines rolled out the entire distance on the dead run.

———o———

CLIPPER SHIP TAKING CHINESE HOMEWARD

SAN FRANCISCO, Nov. 2, 1855 —The splendid clipper ship Challenger, Capt. William H. Burgess, will depart for Hong Kong on Monday.

Besides a considerable amount of gold, she will carry over 400 Chinese returning to the Flowery Kingdom. Many Chinese are now leaving California because of the foreign miners tax and the hostility displayed toward them by other miners.

The Challenger is a superior vessel of 1354 tons.

———o———

Famous Hotel Rented

SAN FRANCISCO, Nov. 17, 1855 —The Union Hotel, opposite Portsmouth Square, which once rented for $8000 a month and was at that time the rendezvous of fashion and political manners, has been rented for $1000 a month.

2 Prominent Men Are Slain While Traveling

MONTEREY, Nov. 11, 1855 — The Hon. Isaac B. Wall, collector of the port of Monterey, and T. S. Williamson, a county official, were murdered yesterday on the road to San Luis Obispo.

They were both shot through the head, from behind, about 25 miles from here. The wounds were apparently made by rifles.

Wall had over $1000 in a money belt on his person, and Williamson $150. None of the money was taken, which may indicate revenge, rather than robbery, was the motive. However, it may be that the killers were frightened away before they could complete a robbery. Wall's saddlebags were opened and his papers strewn about. His pistol was missing, and a ring taken from his finger.

A party of outlaws, presumed to be connected with the murders, was pursued to the Salinas River, where they made a stand. Reports are that two members of the posse were killed in the fight that ensued, and two others wounded.

PLENTY OF GAME FOR HOLIDAYS

SAN FRANCISCO, Dec. 15, 1855— There will be plenty of game available for Christmas holiday feasts.

The return of the game season has members of the sporting community extremely busy. At any hour of the day, parties may be seen with their hunting paraphernalia preparing for a trip on the bay, or landing from boats at the wharves.

Game is now in fine condition. Geese, brant, quail, grouse, snipe, curlew, rail, teal and duck in numerous varieties may be found at the market stalls. All of them are the result of but little trouble among the marshes and low meadow lands bordering the bay and its inlets.

Elk, antelope and deer are now cheap and plentiful, to say nothing of hare and small animals, and an occasional grizzly bear.

———o———

Gold Shipments Decline

SAN FRANCISCO, Dec. 31, 1855 — Shipments of gold from San Francisco to eastern and foreign ports totaled $44,640,090 for 1855, a decline of over $6½-million from the year before.

Total shipments of gold for the past five years have been:

1851	$34,492,000
1852	45,587,803
1853	54,905,000
1854	51,429,101
1855	44,640,090
Total	$231,053,994

———o———

Christmas Shooting

SACRAMENTO, Dec. 28, 1855— The Sacramento paper Spirit of the Age has received a report of a difficulty that occurred in Berryessa Valley Christmas night.

A slight altercation had occurred previously between some members of the Dollerhide and Berryessa families, but had been amicably settled. On Christmas night all happened to meet at a social party in their neighborhood.

During the evening a fight ensued in which one of the Dollerhides was so badly stamped that his recovery is doubtful. One of the Berryessas was fatally shot while riding his horse away from the scene.

OREGON VOLUNTEERS BATTLE INDIANS

PORTLAND, Ore. Ter., Dec. 15, 1855—A dispatch has been received from Lt. Col. James K. Kelly, commanding Oregon volunteers, telling of a fierce battle with the Indians on the Walla Walla river near Whitman's Station that began on December 7.

His column was attacked by about 400 Indians, and engaged in a running battle all day for a distance of ten miles along the river. The fighting was renewed on the 8th and continued until nightfall when the Indians again withdrew although their numbers had increased to 600 warriors. Col. Kelly said he expected further fighting.

Five of Kelly's command were dead, and several others badly wounded, but he reported at least 50 Indians killed. One was the chief of the Walla Walla valley, who had been captured but was shot while trying to escape.

Col. Kelly reported that his horses have become so worn that they cannot make a successful charge against the Indians, so that he is compelled in a measure to act on the defense.

———o———

Trotting Match Popular

SAN FRANCISCO, Dec. 25, 1855 —A large number of people attended the Christmas Day trotting match at the Union Course, and considerable money changed hands.

After trailing Barney Williams and Trade Wind in the first and second heats, Rhode Island won three heats straight. His best time was 2:43.

WEATHER IS CRISP, COLD FOR CHRISTMAS

SAN FRANCISCO Dec. 24, 1855 — It was cold weather today, such weather in which people show an affection for the sunny side of the street—regular Christmas weather, clear, cold and snappish.

Yet, in spite of the wintry coldness of the air, a profusion of flowers bloom in the open air — roses, pinks, fuchsias, heliotropes, geraniums and verbenas, which in the Atlantic States at this season must be carefully kept in heated rooms.

And where else in this latitude at Christmas time are fresh grapes and strawberries served up at Christmas feasts?

———o———

Columbia Editor Takes Holiday

COLUMBIA, Dec. 20, 1855 — The editor of the Columbia Clipper plans to "take it easy" during the holidays, but announced he will issue an extra for murders.

"Our issue appears this week in advance of its regular day," he announced, "in order to give the boys in the office an opportunity to go to the balls, eat fat turkeys, accept the invitation to 'nog' at the different saloons—besides many minor affairs that must be attended to during Christmas week.

"We will not issue again until Thursday, the 10th of January. Should anything of importance occur during the holidays, such as murders, etc., we will issue an extra."

———o———

Mission Land Confirmed

SAN FRANCISCO, Dec. 20, 1855 —The U.S. Land Commission today confirmed the claim of the Catholic Church to the Mission Church buildings, graveyards, orchards and vineyards attached to the 21 old Missions of California.

———o———

Many Attend Mass

SAN FRANCISCO, Dec. 25, 1855 — Between 1200 and 1500 people were present at midnight at St. Mary's Church at Dupont and California streets for the Grand High Mass to celebrate the anniversary of Christmas.

THE GOLDEN GAZETTE 1856

JANUARY 1856

JURY DISAGREEMENT IN CORA TRIAL

SAN FRANCISCO, Jan. 17, 1856 --The jury hearing the trial of Charles Cora for the murder of Gen. William Richardson was discharged at noon today when its members reported they could not agree on a verdict after nearly two days of deliberation.

One report was that the jurors stood six for a verdict of murder and six for manslaughter, but there also rumors of other counts. A new trial will probably take place soon.

The trial was one of the most exciting ever seen in San Francisco. Starting on January 8, it took five days to complete a jury, and a venire of 250 men was exhausted. The ablest lawyers in the state were engaged on both sides.

It was freely reported that efforts had been made to bribe jurors, and that some witnesses had been taken to the house of Belle Cora in an attempt to get them to alter their testimony.

Two Grizzlies Found Killed by One Shot

STOCKTON, Jan. 15, 1856 — G. Perkins, who lives at Round Valley near Marsh's Landing, a couple of days ago found two grizzly bears killed by a single shot under unusual circumstances.

The day before, hearing a hog squealing, he and another man went to the spot and found the hog dead from a grizzly's attack. Supposing the bear would return to eat the pig, Perkins that evening fixed a gun with a string attached to the hog.

During the night the gun went off. On returning in the morning, Perkins found, not just one, but two grizzlies dead. The grizzlies happened to be close together when the gun was dischargd, and one ball passed through both of them. Each bear weighed about 300 pounds.

GREAT SIERRA LAKE NEVER FREEZES

PLACERVILLE, Jan. 20, 1856 — The great lake of the snowy Sierra, at an elevation of 6000 feet, never freezes though it is surrounded by everlasting snows.

The reason undoubtedly is its great depth and the constant motion of its waters. It is only at the mouths of small stream that ice forms in any quantity.

A portion of the lake shore consists of marshes, and the numbers of trout up to 2 or 2½ feet in length are almost incredible. Kelly and Rogers, residing in the valley through the winter, are building a 20-ton yacht to be finished by May. Next summer the valley will be visited by hundreds of people.

---o---

FOLSOM ESTATE SELLS AT PROFIT

SAN FRANCISCO, Jan. 12, 1856— In two days of selling the executors of the estate of the late Joseph L. Folsom have realized a total of $605,000 from the sale of property in San Francisco.

The property has all brought very satisfactory prices. The sale was conducted by Selover, Sinton & Co. On January 16 will begin the sale of the town of Folsom on the American River, at present the terminus of the Sacramento Valley Railroad.

In the local sale the southwest corner of Montgomery and California streets brought the handsome total figure of $49,275. The 50-vara property was broken up into several lots.

---o---

FIRST PAPER MILL

CORTE MADERA, Jan. 15, 1856— Messrs. Taylor and Post have commenced building a paper mill, the first in California, at a Marin county location on Daniel's Creek ten miles from here.

Limantour's Land Claim Confirmed

SAN FRANCISCO, Jan. 24, 1856— The claim of Jose Y. Limantour to the land on which one-third of the city of San Francisco is located was confirmed today in an opinion of the Federal Board of Land Commissioners.

Preparations are already being made to take the case to a higher court, as it is in general believed that the case is a fraudulent one. The whole claim is assessed at $5,-000,000. Sales of some titles have been made by the claimant to existing owners who are anxious to clear title, at 7 to 10 per cent on the value placed on lots by the assessors.

Confirmation of the claim, however, is good only against the U.S. Government, and the same land has been confirmed in the same manner to the city under the Pueblo claim and to the assignees of Bolton and Barron under the Santillan claim.

Limantour is French by birth, but now is a citizen of Mexico. He claims the land was granted to him in 1843 under the Mexican laws. But it was not until nine years later, after the barren hills had been transformed into a well-built city, that he put forward his claim to the title in San Francisco.

---o---

Incendiary Destroys Oregon's Capital

PORTLAND, Ore. Ter., Jan. 12, 1856—The capitol building at Salem has been entirely destroyed by fire, supposed to be the work of an incendiary.

The Territorial Library, valued at $6000-$8000, was lost. Total damage to the building and library is estimated to run as high as $40,000. Among items destroyed were the papers and journals of the present session.

Violent Earthquake Hits San Francisco

SAN FRANCISCO, Feb. 15, 1856 — A violent earthquake was felt here at 5:23 a.m. today.

The vibrations appeared to run from northeast to southwest. The first movement was very sudden, accompanied by what sounded like a loud explosion, and was followed by rapid vibrations.

Buildings swung to and fro heavily. Occupants of the large brick hotels and boarding houses were terrified by the quake, and many rushed wildly into the streets for safety.

Considerable damage was suffered by numerous buildings and houses throughout the city. The fire wall on top of the Goodwin & Co. store on Front street was thrown into Oregon street. Two buildings at Battery and Washington streets were separated by three inches. Plaster was cracked and torn off many walls.

STAGE ROBBED OF $2000 BY UNUSUAL RUSE

SONORA, Feb. 5, 1856 — Dillon & Co.'s stage for Stockton was robbed of a trunk containing $2000 about 4 o'clock this morning while only about a half mile out of Sonora.

The trunk was loaded in the boot. The straps of the boot were cut, and the trunk removed while the stage was ascending a little hill. The owner of the trunk was sitting in the back seat with his hand on the trunk, so that he immediately felt it being slipped out.

He tried to give the alarm to the driver, but the stage moved on some fifty yards before he could make himself understood. When he ran back to the spot, he found the trunk on the side of the road, broken open.

Nursery Imports Plants

SAN FRANCISCO, Feb. 17, 1856 — The nursery operated by William Martin and John Valentine on Market street opposite the bridge has successfully imported 1000 choice plants and cuttings from Dundee, Scotland, via New York and Panama.

STEAMER EXPLODES; MANY LIVES LOST

SACRAMENTO, Feb. 5, 1856 — One of the worst riverboat disasters in California history occurred today when the steamboat Belle, bound for Red Bluff, exploded opposite the Russian Ford, 11 miles from here.

It is estimated that as many as 30 passengers and crew members were lost in the accident. The entire boat, with the exception of some 40 feet of the aft portion, sank immediately. The steamer General Reddington, on the downward trip, reached the scene shortly after the blast and took care of the survivors.

Capt. Charles H. Houston of the Belle is among those known to have been killed. Among the injured is the well known Major John Bidwell of Chico.

---o---

Sacramento Valley Railroad Inaugurated

FOLSOM, Feb. 22, 1856 — The Sacramento Valley Railroad, running a distance of 22 miles from Sacramento to this town, was formally inaugurated with elaborate ceremonies today.

Two thousand guests were brought here and entertained by the railroad, which had 18 waiters distributing 55 baskets of champagne, 11 boxes of claret, two casks of ale and porter and an eighth cask of brandy. There was much hilarity and some quarrels, but these resulted in few injuries because only fists — and no weapons — were used by participants.

Return of part of the crowd to Sacramento was delayed by the fact that one of the railroad's engines burnt out a flue.

Trans-Bay Railway and Road Sought

SACRAMENTO, Feb. 13, 1856 — A bill was introduced into the State Senate today by Senator McCoun to grant the North Pacific Railway Co. a right-of-way for a railway and wagon road across San Francisco Bay.

Heading the company are William M Lent, James Eldridge, P. C. Hyman, T. J. A. Chambers and Joseph R. Beard. It is proposed to build the road across the bay from a point near Rincon Point in San Francisco to a point in or just southerly of Oakland in Alameda county.

Under provisions of the bill the company would be authorized to make rail charges no higher than for other railways in the state. Maximum charges for use of the wagon road, per mile, were established in the following schedule: one horse and rider, 20 cents; one horse and buggy, 25 cents; one horse with wagon or cart, 22 cents; two horses and carriage, 40 cents; each added horse over two to a wagon, 12½ cents; loose horses, 10 cents per head; loose cattle, 10 cents per head; loose animals, 5 cents per head; foot man, 5 cents.

---o---

TREASURE SALVAGE OF SHIP PLANNED

SANTA BARBARA, Feb. 5, 1856 — The schooner Ada, under command of Captain Randall, arrived here today to attempt to recover lost treasure from the wreck of the steamer Yankee Blade.

The exact position of the boxes of specie and gold dust in the sunken ship is known, and Captain Randall is confident he can recover them. On board the schooner is a sub-marine apparatus under the charge of Captain Matthews, who is an expert in the business of diving.

---o---

WHALE STRANDED

SAN LUIS REY, Feb. 10, 1856 — A large white whale has floated ashore at the mouth of the valley. George B. Tebbetts and John Curry, who reside at the Mission, have secured it and expect to get 600 gallons of oil from the carcass.

EXPRESS IS ROBBED BY DISGUISED MEN

MARYSVILLE, March 13, 1856—Rhodes & Whitney's Express was robbed of $16,000 on Trinity Mountain near Shasta yesterday by 12 disguised men.

Five men were in the company with the expressmen, and they were robbed individually of enough to run the total to $25,000.

The robbers jumped out of the bushes while the company was going up the mountain and had them all secure before their victims could offer any resistance. They told Brastow, the messenger, they had been on the watch for him through rain and snow, for over two months.

As soon as the news arrived in Shasta, forty men, led by the messenger, took off on the trail of the robbers, and 100 more start today.

---o---

ICE HARVESTED ON AMERICAN RIVER

SACRAMENTO, March 20, 1856—Two thousand tons of ice have been cut on the head waters of the American River this winter by B. Tallman.

This should be enough to supply the interior markets as well as Sacramento. Tallman has contracted to deliver ice for 7 cents a pound, which is 5 cents less than the prevailing prices for this commodity last summer.

Tallman has built nine ice houses in various mining communities in the northern part of the state to serve the market. A project for cutting ice from Lake Bigler in the Sierra was started last year, but the enterprise seems to have died out.

From all accounts it is evident that many portions of California will not have to depend on Sitka, Alaska, for ice in the future.

---o---

TRADE WITH RUSSIA

SAN FRANCISCO, March 26, 1856—Quite a trade is springing up between San Francisco and the Russian possessions. The Cyane sailed this morning with a large cargo of assorted merchandise suited to the wants of the residents of those ice-bound regions.

SAN QUENTIN PRISON IS LEASED OUT BY STATE

SACRAMENTO, March 28, 1856—The State Prison Commissioners have made a contract with Gen. William Estell to lease the state prison at Point San Quentin for five years at $10,000 a month.

The prison was formerly leased to Estell, but the state had taken over direct operation several months ago. However, it was found that costs of operation ran high.

Under the new contract Estell takes charge of all prisoners, provides guards and overseers, food and clothes for the prisoners and guarantees to erect additional buildings as needed. He is also to exercise due diligence for the capture of escaped prisoners and pay reasonable awards as assessed by the commissioners.

There are now at San Quentin 420 prisoners, including one woman. At the prison itself are 344, and 74 men at work on Marin Island quarrying stone. A large proportion of the prisoners are under three to five-year sentences.

The veteran inmate is James Burns, alias Jimmy - from - Town, committed August 1, 1851, for ten years for grand larceny. The prisoner with the longest sentence ever given in the state is Thomas Rogers, recently convicted of rape in Calaveras county and sentenced to 21 years.

Among other well known prisoners are William Morris, alias Tipperary Bill, ten years for grand larceny; Coyote Charlie, alias William Mickle, ten years for highway robbery; and Cherokee Bob, ten years for grand larceny.

Mt. Expressman Arrives From Carson Valley

SACRAMENTO, March 28, 1856—John A. Thompson, the mountain expressman, arrived today from Carson Valley.

He came by the surveyed route and ran into only about twelve miles of snow, none of it over four feet deep. Thompson traveled on the crust in the mornings and evenings and thus was able to discard the snow shoes he has worn on previous trips over the mountains. He will return tomorrow.

There has been no rain in the Carson Valley, and the miners have literally "dried up."

RECORD SET BY CLIPPER FROM LONDON TO S. F.

SAN FRANCISCO, March 29, 1856—The new English clipper ship Florence Nightingale, under the command of Capt. J. Rossiter, set a new record for its passage from London to San Francisco on her arrival today. She made the voyage in 121 days.

With the exception of one gale in which she lost her main topmast and jib boom, the clipper had good weather in the Atlantic But she ran into severe storms after rounding Cape Horn.

The Nightingale was on her first voyage. She measures 165 feet long, with beam of 27 feet. She registers at 465 tons but carried an assorted cargo of 920 tons. Her hull is built in a peculiar manner—the outside timbers running diagonally fore and aft and her inside timbers in a contrary direction. The standing rigging is made of wire.

---o---

INDIANS ATTACK CASCADE TOWN

PORTLAND, Ore. Ter., March 29, 1856 — Indians have attacked the settlement at the Cascades, destroying the town and killing some twenty persons. They are reported also to have captured and destroyed the steamer Mary. Altogether, Indian affairs in Oregon look very gloomy.

---o---

DROUGHT BROKEN IN L.A.

LOS ANGELES, March 29, 1856—Some rain has fallen to break the drought in this area, which has been suffering severely from the lack of seasonal rain.

A sizeable number of herds of stock, both cattle and horses, have been moved north because of the resulting scarcity of feed. Grass is said to be good in the Tulare Valley. As there are relatively few cattle in that section, thousands of stock could be preserved by driving them there. Otherwise, they will perish here.

The low distress prices of cattle have attracted a number of stock dealers from northern California. It is estimated over $100,000 is on deposit here for that purpose.

FATAL FIGHT OVER CLAIM DISPUTE

SPANISH FLAT, April 22, 1856— One man was killed and two wounded in an affray here today. There has been a dispute over a ditch and some mining claims between a company known as "John Irish's Boys" and the firm of Brown and Burris.

Today some of Irish's group set sluice boxes on property claimed by Brown and Burris. The boxes were removed, and then Jackson, one of the "boys," took a revolver and set out to replace them.

Brown and Burris told him to stop. Burris is supposed to have fired the first shot with a double-barreled gun, killing Jackson instantly. One of the Irish party wounded Brown, whereupon Burris fired and wounded the assailant.

At the conclusion of the fight, Burris gave himself up, but Brown fled. He was overtaken by a mob and was about to be hanged when Mrs. Burris, thinking he was her husband, arrived and cut the rope. This gave the sheriff time to arrive and take Brown in charge.

HYDRAULICS USED

COLUMBIA, April 20, 1856—Hydraulic washing has been commenced in this gold mining district with great success.

Heavy streams of water are doing their work in places that have been worked on by the old, slow process of pick, shovel and sluiceway. The abundant water available from the flumes of both the Old Company and the New Company have enabled miners to turn to this labor-saving method.

Big piles of dirt and hill sides are disappearing, and heavy clay deposits reduced to a consistency that enables collection of the gold they bear. On the Broadway road a head of water has been elevated about 30 feet, and from that height is played by hose and pipe on dirt ordinary washing wouldn't affect.

Pioneer Resident Dies

SAUCELITO, April 20, 1856 — Capt. William A. Richardson, one of the oldest foreign residents of California, died today of asthma.

Isthmus Riot; Natives Kill Scores of People

PANAMA, April 15, 1856 — From forty to fifty passengers awaiting to board the steamer John L. Stephens for San Francisco are missing — and it is feared most of them have been killed — in a riot that broke out with natives here today.

Fifteen are known to be dead, and numerous others are badly wounded. The passengers had arrived from New York on the steamer Aspinwall and had just crossed the Isthmus.

The riot started after a dispute over payment between a steerage passenger and a native vendor.

---o---

Record Coinage By S.F. Branch Mint

SAN FRANCISCO, April 21, 1856 —Operations of the United States branch mint here set a new record during the past week.

Over $1,200,000 in gold, numbering 600,000 pieces, went through all the operations of coinage and were prepared for issue. This immense amount was all adjusted and passed through the hands of 13 women employes.

Almost 500 deposits were received during the week, amounting in total to 43,000 ounces of gold valued at $750,000. The week's assays numbered 1600, and silver ingots to a total value of $22,000 were also made.

TWO LEGISLATORS QUARREL, 1 SHOT

SACRAMENTO, April 8, 1856— Col. Williams of Placer and Mr. Borland of El Dorado, both members of the state Assembly, had an altercation in the Orleans bar room last night in which Borland was shot in the breast. The quarrel grew out of the removal of the El Dorado county seat.

Williams first struck at Borland with a cane, and the latter drew his revolver. After a struggle, Mr. Quirk, assembly door-keeper, wrenched the pistol from the grasp of both combatants.

The two men then went out the Orleans door still fighting, and a pistol was discharged. After they were separated, Borland felt faint, and it was discovered he had been shot. Borland claimed that Williams shot him, but the latter denied this, and there were many reports as to what happened.

During the day there were several other difficulties in town, growing out of the Sacramento municipal election, but none was serious.

---o---

$100,000 SUIT FILED

SAN FRANCISCO, April 28, 1856 —A suit for $100,000 for a lynching attempt was filed today by Stephen Comstock against William Gerrard and 21 other defendants.

Comstock claims that he was held prisoner for 24 hours on the night of last December 15 at San Ramon Valley in Contra Costa County. During that period, he says, attempts were made to make him accuse other persons he did not know.

Angered, the defendants tried to hang him, according to the complaint, but were prevented. While he was held, he was beaten and and bruised for the space of 20 hours, Comstock declares.

---o---

Cattle Driver North

SANTA BARBARA, April 17, 1856 — Ten droves of cattle, each numbering from 200 to 1000 head, have passed through this city during the past week on their way to the northern market. The recent abundant rains have caused grass to spring up luxuriantly, and there will be no scarcity of pasturage this season.

CRUSADING EDITOR SHOT ON STREET

GREAT EXCITEMENT

SAN FRANCISCO, May 14, 1856 — James King of William, editor of the Evening Bulletin, was shot through the left breast and seriously wounded late today by James Casey, a supervisor and publisher of the Sunday Times.

The shooting took place at 5 p.m. near the corner of Washington and Montgomery streets. Witnesses reported that as King approached along the street Casey drew a pistol and fired at relatively close range. The affair was prompted by the fact that King, who has crusaded against corruption in the city's civic affairs and elections, printed the record that Casey had once been an inmate of Sing Sing prison.

An immense excitement was created throughout the city. The wounded editor was carried into the Montgomery Block, where he is being treated by several physicians. Casey was taken to the Station House, where a great crowd gathered and shouted for a quick hanging, but was balked by the guards there.

Later in the evening Casey was removed to the county jail, where another large crowd was assembled. Thomas King, brother of the editor, addressed the people and called for a general assault on the jail to get Casey and hang him. But no overt action was taken by the throng.

VIGILANTES HANG CASEY AND CORA

SAN FRANCISCO, May 22. 1856— Today was a day never to be forgotten in the history of San Francisco!

While several thousand people watched and followed the burial procession of the martyred editor, James King of William, 20,000 more gathered around the Vigilance Committee rooms on Sacramento street and watched the hanging of James Casey, King's murderer, and Charles Cora, the gambler who shot Gen. Richardson several months ago.

The funeral services for King began at noon at the Unitarian Church on Stockton street. The church was jammed, and there was a huge crowd outside. A great procession, which took 35 minutes to pass a single point, followed the body to Lone Mountain Cemetery.

While the funeral was going on, the Vigilance Committee prepared efficiently to carry out the execution of Casey and Cora. It deployed its full force, numbering 3000 men armed with rifles, muskets and bayonets, around its building. Two cannons were placed to command Davis street and Front street.

At about 1 p.m. workmen prepared the gallows, and the prisoners were brought through windows from the committee rooms to stand on the platform. Casey made a wild talk protesting his innocence of murder, but Cora remained silent. At 1:20 both men were hung.

Terrible Calamity On Panama Railway

PANAMA, May 7, 1856 — One of the worst disasters in railroad history occurred late yesterday afternoon when over 40 persons were killed and at least 100 were injured on the Isthmus railroad near Aspinwall.

Nine passenger cars leaped the track when the lead car became separated from the engine. They were badly splintered, and toppled into a marshy, water-filled ditch alongside the tracks. The surviving passengers had to stand knee deep in water in order to assist the sufferers. All survivors could not be taken to Aspinwall until today.

———o———

Chronology of the Fateful Days

May 14, 5 p.m.—Editor James King of William accosted and shot on street by James Casey.

May 15—The Vigilance Committee of 1851 reorganized, meeting at Sacramento street, and began signing up many new members to meet the crisis.

May 19 — Vigilance Committee members assembled at headquarters, 2000 men in all, under Chief Marshal Charles Doane. The army marched to the county jail. With the artillery unit's cannon aimed directly at the jail door, Sheriff Scannell offered no resistance and turned Casey over to the Committee. Later the Committee took Gambler Cora from the jail. Both men were lodged under guard at the Committee rooms.

May 20 — Although hopes had been held at one time for King's recovery from his wound, he took a turn for the worse early in the morning and died at 1:30 p.m.

May 22—King's funeral held. Vigilance Committee hanged Casey and Cora before crowd estimated at 20,000 persons, with scene guarded by 3000 armed men.

May 30—Great excitement has continued in the city. The committee devoted several days trying to find and arrest Edward McGowan, indicted as an accessory of Casey in King's murder. The committee has also arrested several other men who have had to do with the management of elections

Vigilantes Arrest Justice Terry

SAN FRANCISCO, June 22, 1856 —David S. Terry, associate justice of the state supreme court, was arrested yesterday by the Vigilance Committee for the stabbing of Sterling A. Hopkins, a committee policeman who was head of a group seeking to arrest James R. "Rube" Maloney, a San Francisco politician.

The affray took place on Jackson street between Dupont and Kearny streets, close by one of the main armories of the "law and order" party. Judge Terry, who claimed he acted in self-defense, knifed Hopkins in the neck, and the latter is in a serious condition.

Terry and four men who were with him fled to the armory at the corner of Jackson and Dupont. The buildings there were soon surrounded by armed Vigilantes. A surrender was agreed upon, and Terry and Maloney were later taken to the Committee headquarters as prisoners.

Three hundred stand of arms in the armory were also seized. Vigilante forces also moved on other "law and order" armories, seized more arms and took 89 men prisoners. Today all but six of the prisoners of war were released after being marched in groups of four past a file of Vigilantes.

FEWER FLOATING BODIES FOUND HERE

SAN FRANCISCO, June 26, 1856 —It has been a most remarkable fact that since the organization and operations of the Vigilance Committee the city has been free from many occurrences of a lamentable character, that were daily witnessed before.

One of the most striking instances is the fact that few, if any, bodies have been found in the bay, while before the excitement the coroner was called upon almost daily to pick up some unfortunate man who was supposed to be accidentally drowned.

We know of only two such deaths for the last five weeks. Consequently we are forced to the conviction that these were not all accidental deaths, but that there have been a set of men in this city who have made a regular business of waylaying men and, after robbing them, throwing them off the dock.

This was but the latest event in the tense period which followed the murder of Editor James King of William last month. On June 4 Governor J. Neely Johnson issued a proclamation declaring San Francisco in a state of insurrection. This was received with general indignation throughout the state, and efforts to enroll militia to put down the Vigilance Committee have met with little success. General Wool has also refused to turn over to the governor any U. S. arms.

A score of notorious individuals arrested by the committee have been banished from California and put aboard outgoing vessels. Eleven were shipped out on the steamer Sierra Nevada two days ago after 2000 armed Vigilantes had massed to prevent a possible attack and rescue attempt.

One of the most noted prisoners, Pugilist Yankee Sullivan, committed suicide in the committee rooms.

---o---

VIGILANTE QUARTERS FORTIFIED

SAN FRANCISCO, June 20, 1856 —The Vigilance Committee has strongly fortified its headquarters on Sacramento street to ward off any possible attacks by "law and order" men or any forces that Governor Johnson may yet be able to assemble to try to enforce his insurrection proclamation.

The committee rooms proper front on Sacramento street in the block bounded by Front, Davis and California streets. Breastworks of sandbags have been built in front and back of the rooms. Several pieces of cannon have been mounted on the rooftops to command all the streets leading to Fort Vigilance.

Also on the roof is suspended a large bell to give the alarm in cases of emergency.

---o---

TWO EXECUTED

SACRAMENTO, June 27, 1856— Two men were hanged by the authorities here today.

One was Samuel L. Garrett, executed for the murder of Amiel Brickell last August; the other was William S. Kelly, condemned for the murder of Daniel C. How of El Dorado. Both men briefly addressed the assembled crowd before the hangings and denied their guilt.

INDIANS BEATEN IN SO. OREGON BATTLE

CRESCENT CITY, June 25, 1856 —Sergeant Nolan of Capt. Bletzo's Company of Volunteers, serving against the Indians in Southern Oregon, has brought word of a battle earlier this month on the Rogue River, about four miles below the mouth of the Illinois River.

The volunteers, numbering 41 in all, and Company K of the regular troops, numbering about 60, met 250 Indians of the Shasta Costa', Macinootoonys, Tututnees, Joshua and Uqua tribes. The regulars were on the north side and the volunteers on the south side of the river.

The regulars commenced the fight about noon, killing six Indians, and driving the rest across the river. There the volunteers killed 24 Indians, took six prisoners and routed the rest of the force. It is believed another 50 Indians were drowned.

The Indians had fortified themselves lower down the river, but had moved to what they thought was a stronger position. The volunteers suffered one man killed and two wounded.

The day following, four principal chiefs sought to make a treaty. As a result 200 Indian men, women and children surrendered and were sent to the reservation at the mouth of the Rogue River.

---o---

Romeo and Juliet Tragedy Presented

SAN FRANCISCO, June 28, 1856 —Shakespeare's tragedy of Romeo and Juliet was presented tonight at the Metropolitan Theatre. The production, one of the most difficult to enact, was well received by the audience.

Mrs. Julia Hayne, who recently arrived from New York, starred as Juliet and was greatly applauded. Charles Pope played Romeo with his accustomed ability. Although perhaps a little too "heavy" for the character, his elegant reading and neatness of style more than made up for this fault.

Vigilance Committee Executes Two Men

SAN FRANCISCO, July 29, 1856 —The Vigilance Committee today publicly executed two men, Joseph Hetherington and Philander Bruce.

The scaffold, with its platform ten feet above the ground, was erected in the center of Davis street, halfway between Sacramento and Commercial streets. It is estimated that 15,000 spectators, including 1000 women, witnessed the double execution, while the Vigilance Committee had 3000 men under arms as a guard.

Some building owners charged admission to see the hangings, and the roofs of two or three buildings collapsed from the load of people massed on them.

Each side of Davis street was occupied by Vigilante infantry. Brass cannon were stationed at the intersection of Davis and Sacramento, loaded and with fuses lighted. In the rear of the infantry were some cavalry, and large bodies of armed men occupied the streets.

---o---

EXCITEMENT AT L. A.

LOS ANGELES, July 25, 1856 — Los Angeles is fairly quiet after several days of great excitement that began when William Jenkins, a deputy constable, went to serve a writ of attachment on the property of Antonio Ruis.

Meeting some opposition, Jenkins drew his pistol and fatally shot Ruis. The deputy surrendered to the authorities, and was free on bail on a charge of manslaughter, but the Spanish population was offended that he was left at large and armed.

It was rumored that an attack on the town was planned, and suspicious crowds gathered. Some arms were seized by a party of banditti.

By Tuesday evening a mob of 200 or 300 men had assembled, and Marshal W. C. Getman, with a small party, rode out to scatter them. Some firing ensued, and Getman was wounded. The military company on guard at the jail marched to the Plaza, but by the time of arrival the mob moved off.

On Wednesday more military companies were formed by the citizens, several arrests made.

NED McGOWAN HUNTED IN SANTA BARBARA AREA

SANTA BARBARA, July 6, 1856 — A report circulated here today that Ned McGowan, the former San Francisco judge hunted by the Vigilantes there as an alleged accomplice of James Casey in the shooting of Editor James King of William, had been recognized at the City Hotel.

The sheriff was called to go and arrest McGowan. At first he demurred for lack of a bench warrant, but later he decided to go to the hotel with a group of six or eight men. By this time it was found that the man supposed to be McGowan left minutes earlier.

A search was then instigated by the sheriff, and it was noted that certain persons of considerable notoriety exhibited a great deal of concern. The Noriega (de la Guerra) garden was searched, and the tules around a lagoon at the rear of the garden were fired in an attempt to drive "the stranger" out.

There is little doubt that McGowan is concealed somewhere in town. He is reported to have been ill and in a weakened condition as a result of the long ride down from San Francisco.

---o---

Road to Yosemite Valley Completed

MARIPOSA, July 1, 1856 — The road to Yosemite Valley is now finished. It follows the old trail, with slight deviations to the South Fork of the Merced River, thence down the river, crossing it two miles above the mouth of Alder Creek and then to near its head, keeping on the high ridges to the head of the valley.

SEVERAL CITIES RAVAGED BY FIRES

PLACERVILLE, July 6, 1856 — Practically all the south part of this town, including the business section, was destroyed by a fire which broke out in the Union Hotel at 11 a.m. today. Total loss is estimated at about $1,000,000.

The flames spread rapidly, sweeping down Main street. The 10-year-old daughter of Walter J. Burwell and two men, names unknown, perished in the fire.

FAIR PLAY, July 12, 1856—Fire, supposed to have been of incendiary origin, today ravaged this mining town, located five miles from Indian Diggins, Eldorado county.

GEORGETOWN, July 7, 1856 — The town of Georgetown, with the exception of about 50 scattered houses and buildings, was razed by fire today. All were frame structures.

NEVADA CITY, July 20, 1856 — Flames broke out this afternoon in Hughes' blacksmith shop on Pine street and in the incredibly short space of two hours destroyed the entire town. A high wind from the west helped spread the fire.

It is estimated over 800 buildings were lost, including the recently completed $50,000 courthouse and all but six of the town's 26 fireproof brick buildings. At least eight men are fatally burned.

---o---

JOAQUIN AGAIN?

SONORA, July 1, 1856 — It is reported that the celebrated bandit Joaquin, who was reliably reported to have been killed by a posse three years ago, is again in this state and said to have a force of 200 men. A gentleman from Santa Cruz states he has seen five persons who know Joaquin is around.

---o---

Gold Being Mined At Discovery Site

COLOMA, July 8, 1856 — Gold is being mined within twenty yards of the spot where the first lump of gold in California was found in 1848, with every prospect of doing well by the five shareholders.

FIRST IMMIGRANTS OF YEAR AT L. A.

LOS ANGELES, Aug. 2, 1856—The first party of immigrants across the Plains has arrived here. It numbers 25 men, who report another company on the way.

They left San Antonio March 3, reached El Paso April 13 and Warner's Ranch on July 1. There was no trouble with the Indians.

The party started with the intention of prospecting the Gadsden Purchase for gold, which was found in sufficient quantities for working, but there was no supply of water. The men were well received by Mexican officers at the border.

The Tucson area was prospected for two weeks without discovering the color of gold. Tucson is a small place of about 300 people, mostly Indians. There are 30 to 40 Americans there, engaged in such occupations as keeping store and bar and in hunting the Indians, for which purpose there is an organized company of Rangers.

Four Americans started from Tucson for Douglas Ranch about 40 miles away, but were killed along the way. They were in search of a silver mine they had heard was in the vicinity.

The party of immigrants arriving here gave a most unfavorable report of the Purchase. It contains copper and silver, which require a large capital to work. There is no gold and no land capable of cultivation. The district is spoken of as destitute of everything necessary for the sustenance of human life, there being neither timber nor water, and the land is bare, sandy, parched and sterile.

---o---

Arrivals From Missouri Include Theatre Troupe

PLACERVILLE, Aug. 11, 1856—Twenty-four persons have arrived here from St. Joseph's, Missouri. Among them are Dr. Sager, his wife and four children, who form a theatrical troupe which has performed at all the various places on the route.

There was some difficulty with Indians. One man in the company was shot through the thigh by an arrow. They also found the bodies of a man and woman at Raft River who had apparently been killed by the Indians.

Their stock is in good condition.

WOMAN IS KILLED IN STAGE ROBBERY

MARYSVILLE, Aug. 12, 1856—An unprecedented and daring highway robbery attempt this afternoon resulted in the death of one woman and the wounding of three men.

Six mounted highwaymen tried to hold up the Comptonville stage as it neared Marysville, with the object of getting $100,000 in charge of Langston & Co.'s express messenger, Mr. Dobson.

Dobson fired the first shot, and unhorsed the leader of the robber band with one shot. At least fifty shots were fired on both sides.

During the battle Mrs. Tilghman, a stage passenger and wife of a Marysville barber, was shot in the head and killed, and two other passengers were wounded. John Gear, driver of the stage, was wounded in the arm. The stage itself was completely riddled with bullet holes.

---o---

DESPERADO HELPED IN ESCAPE FROM JAIL

SANTA BARBARA, Aug. 14, 1856—Juan Salazar escaped from jail last evening during the absence of the sheriff and his deputy. He was convicted of a brutal assault at the last term of the Court of Sessions and sentenced to ten years in State Prison.

Salazar was assisted in his escape by a group of 10 or 12 men. They first entered the building through the back door of the sheriff's office. After failing in their effort to break down the door into the jail, they punched in the window of the county clerk's office and cut a passage-way into the jail.

---o---

ATTEMPT TO FIRE CITY

SAN FRANCISCO, Aug. 6, 1856—A daring apparent attempt to fire the city was made between 1 and 2 o'clock this morning by John McGunnell and Thomas Murray.

The two men rolled a 44-gallon barrel of camphene from the store of Tubbs & Co. on Front street to the boarding house of Hans Miller on Jackson street between Davis and Drum streets. There they knocked in the barrel head, but the noise attracted Officer Lang.

VIGILANTES HOLD GIGANTIC PARADE

SAN FRANCISCO, Aug 18, 1856—In one of the largest demonstrations ever held i the West, the Vigilance Committee today held a general review and parade in preparation for suspending its military operations with the exception of a guard to be maintained at its Sacramento street buildings.

Nearly all the stores in the city were closed for the event, and every available window along the line of march was occupied by ladies. Many banners were stretched across the streets, and numerous buildings were handsomely decorated. About 10,000 is a fair estimate of the number of spectators who gathered to see the parade.

About 1 p.m. all the Vigilante companies of cavalry and artillery and the four regiments of infantry marched out on Third street to be reviewed by the Executive Committee. In all the Committee mustered between 3000 and 4000 men.

After the review, the Vigilante army marched down Market street to Montgomery street and then followed to the committee rooms.

---o---

VIGILANTES RELEASE JUDGE DAVID TERRY

SAN FRANCISCO, Aug. 7, 1856—Justice David S. Terry of the state supreme court, who had been held a prisoner by the Vigilance Committee for the knifing of Vigilante Policeman Hopkins, was suddenly released at 3 o'clock this morning.

Several members of the Executive Committee escorted him to a hotel where he remained until daylight. Then, on the pleading of his friends, Judge Terry went on board the U.S. sloop-of-war John Adams, anchored in the bay.

It is reported that the decision of the Executive Committee was viewed with dissatisfaction by many Vigilantes, and the citizens generally expressed great indignation that he was given his freedom.

Shortly after 4 o'clock this afternoon Judge Terry and his wife left for Sacramento on the steamer Helen Hensley. A cutter took Terry from the sloop and put him aboard the steamer shortly after she had left her wharf. A vast crowd gathered at the waterfront.

FEDERAL JURY FREES TWO VIGILANTES IN 5 MINUTES

SAN FRANCISCO, Sept. 11, 1856 —It took only five minutes for a jury in federal circuit court today to acquit John L. Durkee and Charles E. Rand, Vigilante members, of a charge of piracy.

The charge grew out of the seizure by a Vigilance Committee posse last June of six boxes of muskets from the schooner Julia. The arms were being sent down from Benicia on the order of Governor Johnson during the late troubles in San Francisco.

The acquittal brought cheers from the crowded courtroom, and the two men were carried out on the shoulders of the triumphant crowd. A procession numbering at least 1000 men then escorted Durkee and Rand to the Vigilance Committee rooms.

———o———

JOHN MARSH, NOTED PIONEER, MURDERED

MARTINEZ, Sept. 25, 1856 — Dr. John Marsh, well known citizen of Contra Costa who pioneered in California many years ago, has been brutally murdered near here.

His body was found yesterday near the ranch of Col. Gift, shockingly cut and mangled. Robbery seems to have been the motive as his watch and money were gone. Suspicion has fastened on three men, with one of whom he had a law suit a few weeks ago.

———o———

Artist Sails for East With California Sketches

SAN FRANCISCO, Sept. 5, 1856— Thomas A. Ayres, well known artist, left on the steamer Golden Age today for the eastern states.

Since 1849 he has been indulging his genius in visiting nearly every section of the state from San Diego to Mount Shasta sketching all the remarkable and beautiful scenes with which California is so abundant. Many citizens have seen his truthful sketches of the wonders of the Yosemite Valley.

Mr. Ayres is taking with him several hundred of his drawings and hopes to conclude an arrangement with Harper's for their publication.

7 Bandits Are Slain in Carson Valley

PLACERVILLE, Sept. 9, 1856— A party of immigrants arriving here brought a report of a fight in Carson Valley in which seven bandits were killed. The information received is crude, but the main points are vouched for.

A man disguised as an Indian was first shot dead when he was caught in the act of robbing an immigrant. Soon after, a group of his friends, seven in number, appeared, and a battle ensued in which six bandits were slain and the seventh escaped.

Pursuit was given by the immigrants, who ran onto three men whom they captured with about 160 head of stolen horses and mules.

———o———

TELEGRAPH TRAP

SAN FRANCISCO, Sept. 2, 1856— At 1 o'clock yesterday afternoon Police Chief James McElroy received a telegraphic dispatch from Marshall Nightingale of Marysville announcing that a man named Theall had gotten away after passing a number of forged checks there.

Within an hour Chief McElroy, assisted by Officer John Nugent, succeeded in finding and arresting the man on Commercial street. Theall was sent up to Marysville on the afternoon boat.

———o———

HUMBOLDT TAX ROLL RISES

EUREKA, Sept. 8, 1856—The total assessment for Humboldt County this year, as reported by D. D. Williams, deputy assessor, is $642,355 as compared with $468,861 a year ago.

There are nine steam saw-mills in the county capable of manufacturing 24,000,000 feet of lumber and 12,000,000 laths per year; also, three grist mills. Twenty thousand acres of land have been pre-empted; swamp and overflowed land, purchased from the state, 1833 acres; under cultivation, about 10,000 acres.

———o———

GRAPES FROM L. A.

SAN FRANCISCO, Sept. 9, 1856— The steamer Sea Bird today brought up 4200 boxes of grapes from Los Angeles. This deluge of the fruit, doubtless, will reduce the price considerably.

SEEK TO RELIEVE SAD LOT OF SAILORS IN S. F. PORT

SAN FRANCISCO, Sept. 2, 1856— Some ladies of San Francisco have formed The Ladies' Aid & Protective Society for relieving the condition of seamen in this port. Mrs. C. Thomas is directress.

The sailor here is not allowed to land before he is waylaid. The runner of sailor boarding houses—usually dens of more iniquity than the gambler's hell—boards the ship as soon as she enters the harbor, and plies poor Jack, thirsty from a long voyage and brackish water, with liquor that is fatal at 500 yards.

From that moment until the land-sharks have bagged his wages, the sailor is a flying-fish in fate, kept under the influence of liquor until his last dollar has been filched. Then, often without his knowledge, he is put on some outbound hulk with his month's advance appropriated for alleged charges to his bill.

Already the ladies have prepared a wardrobe for shipwrecked and destitute seamen, and they desire to be able to build a home for their comfort, protection and salvation.

———o———

Machine to Aid Miners

SAN FRANCISCO, Sept. 12, 1856 —Mr. Steen is taking to the mountains a stone-boring machine that should be a blessing to miners.

He has been experimenting with it on the hill side on Broadway, and gave it a final trial yesterday when it ran for nearly two hours and cut 25½ inches. The tunnel it cuts is six feet in diameter. Mr. Steen figures he can run it for 24 hours without stopping for more than an hour or two for oiling, etc.

INDIANS REPORTED ON RAMPAGE AGAIN

PORTLAND, Ore. Ter., Oct. 11, 1856—Reports have been received that the Indians have again become troublesome in the Walla Walla country. They had full possession of the region north and east of The Dalles except for a blockhouse or two. There were in the area about 3000 Indians, most of them armed.

Governor Stevens has been obliged to come to The Dalles, and Col. Steptoe was also on his way there. While the governor was at the council trying to obtain a treaty of peace, the chiefs of the Nez Perces sought to destroy him and his party. Col. Steptoe sent two companies of men to his relief, and they routed the Indians, killing and wounding 13 braves.

After the Indians burned the prairie about Walla Walla, Col. Steptoe was obliged to retire. He will try to relieve a blockhouse held by 50 men in the Walla Walla valley as soon as he can get forage for his horses.

It seems to be the unanimous opinion in the territory that there will be still further trouble with the Indians, and perhaps even a general war.

———o———

California's First Cotton On Display

SAN FRANCISCO, Oct. 9, 1856—A sample of California-grown cotton was displayed here today, part of the first such crop that has ever been produced in the state. It was raised as far north as Shasta and is equal in staple to anything in Georgia or Alabama.

In this wool-like flock we see new sources of production, new areas of wealth and opening to the industry and enterprise of the future.

———o———

GOOD PRICES RECEIVED FOR NEW TRACT LOTS

SAN FRANCISCO, Oct. 13, 1856—Prices ran well in the sale of 75 lots in the new Hayes Tract.

Among the prices realized by Auctioneer John Middleton were: a 50-vara lot on the southeast corner of Oak and Laguna Streets, $250; Northwest corner of Page and Franklin Streets, $600; southeast corner of Gough and Fell Streets, $460.

Noted Highwayman Arrested & Hung

STOCKTON, Oct. 7, 1856—Word has been received here that Tom Bell, the noted highwayman who has operated in various parts of the mining regions, has at last been arrested and summarily executed.

For some time it had been supposed that Bell was living in a camp between the Merced and Chowchilla Rivers. Captain Belt, with eight or nine men, has been searching the vicinity. Yesterday they found the camp where Bell was staying with a woman and her three daughters.

After some resistance, it is reported they managed to secure Bell and then took him to a point on the Merced River where they hanged him about 4 o'clock in the afternoon.

Bell wrote several letters before his death and made a statement of confession to his nefarious deeds.

———o———

LARGE SUSPENSION BRIDGE ERECTED

KNIGHT'S FERRY, Oct. 8, 1856—A large and magnificent suspension bridge now spans the Stanislaus River at Two-Mile Bar.

It was built by Messrs. Slocum, Ross and Bell, and offers good facilities for wagons and travelers going to Stockton. The bridge is 284 feet long, 14 feet wide and 40 feet high. Its arch spans 130 feet.

Buttresses for the bridge are of solid masonry and extend on either side far back into the hill. The main arch required 125,000 feet of lumber and 10 tons of iron. The bridge cost $25,000.

———o———

STATE FAIR OPENS

SAN JOSE, Oct. 7, 1856—The State Agricultural Fair opened here today with a brilliant display. Most of a large quantity and broad variety of horticultural and agricultural wonders were already in place, but more were due to arrive from Alviso. They had been delayed by the late arrival of the steamer from San Francisco.

Decorations of the City Hall and the yard at the rear were deemed more beautiful than last year's fair at Sacramento. Notable among the exhibits of fruit were the apples and pears.

NEW MINING ACTIVITY IN GADSDEN PURCHASE

SAN DIEGO, Oct. 4, 1856—N. P. Cook arrived here with news from the Gadsden Purchase.

Mr. Posten, who represents a large company of capitalists in Cincinnati and New York, has come to Tucson with a party of men who will commence working the silver mines at Tubac. These extensive mines are said to be very rich, and the company plans vigorous operations as it has very substantial backing.

Capt. James Douglass, who has spent many years in Mexico, has also begun operation of a rich silver mine in the Purchase.

At the Arizona Copper Mines, matters are going on briskly. They have about 100 tons of rich ore out, and part of it packed as far as the Gila River. Capt. Taylor, superintendent of the works, has had a small boat built and has sounded the Gila River for 80 miles from its junction with the Colorado.

He pronounces the river navigable for light-draft steamers even at the low water stage. If his observations are accurate, this should tend to greatly enhance the value of stock in the copper and silver mines in the Gila Valley area.

———o———

Anastacio Garcia, Noted Outlaw, Caught

LOS ANGELES, Oct. 25, 1856—Anastacio Garcia, accused of the murder of Messrs. Wall and Williamson en route from Monterey to San Luis Obispo last November, has been captured near here by Undersheriff W. H. Peterson.

After having received information Garcia was in the area, Peterson and three officers rode out to search for him. About 13 miles distant, they met three men on the road and recognized one of them as Garcia. When arrested, Garcia was carrying two revolvers and a long-bladed knife.

Garcia is said to have admitted other shootings. Since he escaped, though wounded, from a sheriff's posse, he has been lurking about various places in Los Angeles County. He will be taken up to Monterey on the steamer and turned over to the authorities there.

SHERIFF SHOT BY MISTAKE IN DARK

NEVADA CITY, Nov. 4, 1856— Sheriff Wright was killed at Gold Flat, near here, last night in a tragic mistake shooting while he was searching for three notorious robbers who had escaped from the county jail.

At about dark the sheriff received word that the robbers, Webster and the two Farnsworths, had concealed themselves in a cabin at Gold Flat. He started out with four other men. On the way he was informed that some horses were tied up in a ravine near the flat and went there with the intention of taking persons coming for horses.

Unfortunately, another party was hidden nearby and watching for the same purpose. Neither group knew of the other's nearness, and they fired at each other, thinking the robbers were at hand.

Sheriff Wright was killed instantly by a shotgun blast, and P. Johnson of his party was also wounded critically.

———o———

DARING ATTEMPT MADE TO SINK NEW STEAMER

SAN FRANCISCO, Nov. 9, 1856— An apparent attempt, daring but unsuccessful, was made last night to sink the new Nicaragua steamship Orizaba at the Washington street wharf.

The first indication of anything wrong came at 7 a.m. today when the ship's officers discovered she had listed heavily to port, and found between two and three feet of water in the hold. The crew was set to work at the pumps, and in a few hours the Orizaba was entirely free of water — and there was no sign of a leak.

It was discovered that coal passers had left the coal port open. The water could not have entered the hold in any way except through the "stops" in the engine rooms, and these were closed. It is presumed that some scoundrels entered the ship at low tide, opened the stops and let the water flow in until the steamer grounded, in anticipation that when the tide rose the coal, mostly to the port side, and the water would cause her to list below the open port and sink.

LOS ANGELES HIT BY DUST STORM

LOS ANGELES, Nov. 19, 1856— This area was hit by a severe tempest starting at 10 o'clock this morning.

Dust and sand were lifted from the earth in a great cloud that obscured every object from sight. At times it was not possible even to see across the street. All road travel had to be suspended, and from noon on the sun was blanked out. Within the city awnings were quickly blown away, and many houses were unroofed by the winds.

From the beach at San Pedro to the coast range nothing was visible but clouds of sand and dust. In pasture lands there were drifts of sand several feet deep. The amount of damage resulting from this storm — the first of its type since March, 1845, is almost incalculable.

———o———

Big Trees Discovered

STOCKTON, Nov. 13, 1856 — A grove of over 1000 trees, varying in size from 6 to 32 feet in diameter, has recently been discovered on a branch of King's river. Many of the trees are from 325 to 350 high. They are of the arbor vitae species.

———o———

GRASS VALLEY, Nov. 27, 1856— Messrs. Donahue, Colbert and Daniels, owners of the Allisson Ranch quartz lead, have produced $30,000 in gold lumps in three weeks.

This is the result of their mill running eight stamps twelve hours a day. Last week, in twelve hours' work, they crushed out the neat sum of $12,000.

———o———

TWO BUILDINGS FALL

SAN FRANCISCO, Nov. 17, 1856 —Two large frame buildings fell with a tremendous crash into the water below them about 8 o'clock last night when the piles supporting them gave way. The buildings were located in the block bounded by Clay, Commercial, Drumm and East streets.

The first intimation of disaster was a loud creaking noise and settling of one of the posts on Commercial street. Persons occupying the building tried to remove the grain and produce stored on the

Folsom Properties Draw Good Prices

SAN FRANCISCO, Nov. 14, 1856 — A grand total of $423,135 was realized from the two-day sale of the estate of the late Capt. Joseph L. Folsom, much more than the executors had expected to realize in the light of the general level of California business.

The sale covered only the San Francisco properties owned by Folsom, and was the biggest real estate sale ever held in California. It was conducted by the firm of Selover, Sinton & Co. at Memorial Hall, with H. A. Cobb as auctioneer. There was a large number of purchasers, and prices ruled high.

Among well known pieces of property sold were: City Market property, southwest corner of Battery and Sacramento streets, 124 by 90 feet, brick fireproof building, $46,-500; Custom House block property, southeast corner of Sacramento and Sansome streets, 185 by 124 feet, building covering whole lot, $47,500; lot on southwest corner of Sansome and Sacramento streets, with one-third interest in three-story brick building, $24,500; Union Theatre property on Commercial street, between Kearny and Dupont streets, 80 by 60 feet, $8600.

The French gardening firm of John Wieland & Co. paid $10,000 for Capt. Folsom's homestead lot, 147 by 275 feet, on the west side of Second street near Folsom street, together with his elegant cottage residence. It is planned to convert this into a public pleasure garden.

———o———

INTO WATERS OF BAY

first floor, and 300 to 400 bags of buckwheat were removed from the store on the Drumm street side. By this time the structures began to fall, and workmen barely had time to escape.

George Lencher of Engine Co. No. 5 and a drayman named Avery were hit by the falling timbers and knocked into the bay. Both were rescued alive, but were severely injured. On the upper floors of the buildings were a number of lodging rooms, but it is believed no one was trapped in them.

LIMANTOUR JAILED FOR LAND FRAUD

SAN FRANCISCO, Dec. 10, 1856 —Jose y Limantour was arrested today on the ground that his claim to ownership of a large part of the City of San Francisco under a Mexican land grant was a complete fraud. His bail was set at the sum of $30,000.

Limantour's arrest was made under an indictment for forgery by the grand jury of the United States Circuit Court. It is charged that the papers concerning the famous Limantour claim, purporting to have been executed in California in 1843, were in fact forged in Mexico City in 1852.

The U.S. Land Commission has confirmed Limantour's claim to much of the city and also to one of the islands in the bay. This decision threw present land titles into question, and caused much consternation among San Francisco property owners.

As a result, Limantour succeeded in inducing numbers of small property owners to clear their ownership by paying him or his agents for a title deed. It is said that he has realized a considerable amount of money in this way.

———o———

Big New Warehouse

SAN FRANCISCO, Dec. 3, 1856— One of the notable improvements in the city is the splendid warehouse now being completed by Daniel Gibb & Co. on the northwest corner of Front and Vallejo streets. The building is estimated to cost $40,000, and the lot on which it stands is valued at $20,000.

The structure is of two stories and a basement, and measures 130 by 47 feet. The basement walls are made of Angel Island stone, two feet thick. The walls and massive piers of granite from the Folsom quarries rest on heavy compactly driven piles.

———o———

SAN FRANCISCO, Dec. 8, 1856— A vermicelli and macaroni manufactory is currently being built here on a very extensive scale.

The proprietors, Brignardelli and Machiavelli, say they can make 50 boxes of 25 pounds each per day.

Christmas Observed In Variety of Ways

SAN FRANCISCO, Dec. 26, 1856 —Residents of this city by the Golden Gate observed the Christmas festival in accordance with their individual characters — and there was a variety of attractions.

Christmas Day was bright and clear, and the breeze was gentle, although the previous day had been very cloudy and foreboding. Although practically all the stores were closed, with the exception of the markets, the main streets were crowded with people.

Churches were well filled for their Christmas services, and the Sunday Schools of several churches held special programs. Christmas Eve the Pilgrim Sunday School held its annual festival at Musical Hall, with refreshments and gifts for both adults and children, as well as entertainment that included songs by the children's classes.

Social events attracted many of the citizens. Many open houses were held at private residences, and the First Light Dragoons held their third grand ball last evening at Assembly Hall. The spacious hall was appropriately decorated, and supper was furnished by a favorite caterer. In its Christmas night performance the American Theatre presented Macbeth, starring Mr. Fleming.

An added feature at the Christmas race meeting at the Pioneer Course was the attempt of the champion pedestrian, James Kennovan, for a $500 purse, to drag a sulkey six miles in 58 minutes. Kennovan, who recently walked for 106 consecutive hours, was unable to continue when he fell in the fifth mile. Today, the police court had 48 cases before it, mostly dealing with charges of being drunk and disorderly.

66 INDIANS MOVED TO RESERVATION

SACRAMENTO, Dec. 20, 1856— Sixty-six Indians, half of all that remain of the Yuba tribe which numbered 2000 individuals ten years ago, arrived here today on the steamer Cleopatra from Marysville.

The Indians are being removed to the Nome Lackee reservation near Tehama by Col. T. J. Henley, Indian agent. Of the 66, there are 20 women and 10 children, all of whom are under 8 years of age. Among the group was Chief Joseph.

The removal is being carried out because the Indians were in a badly demoralized state at their rancheria near Marysville, where many were diseased and deaths were occurring daily. Chief Joseph said the reason there were no older children was that all had died off.

However, the Indians were unwilling to leave their homes until forced to do so. It was found necessary for the police at Marysville to round up many of the tribe. The Indians managed to destroy their lodges by fire before leaving.

After landing at the levee, the Indians were provided with shelter for the night under the shed at the foot of I street.

———o———

Walking Dark Streets Can Be Dangerous

SAN FRANCISCO, Dec. 24, 1856 —In these dark nights, without any gas lights, it is really dangerous to walk through the streets of San Francisco.

The gas has been turned off as a result of a controversy over price between the gas company and the city. The company wants $15 per 1000 cubic feet, the same price as to individuals, and the city refuses to pay so much. It is hoped some sort of a compromise will be reached soon so that citizens will not be required to walk in darkness as they now must.

———o———

SACRAMENTO, Dec. 15, 1856— The state legislature will convene here on January 5, with the choice of a United States Senator among its major tasks. Prominent candidates are William M. Gwin, David C. Broderick, Milton S. Latham, John B. Weller, J. W. Denver, J. W. McCorkle and Stephen J. Field.

THE GOLDEN GAZETTE 1857

OAKLAND GROWS AS S. F. BROOKLYN

OAKLAND, Jan. 22, 1857—A beautiful little place is Oakland, embosomed as its name indicates among oak trees--the bright-leaved, gleaming evergreen oaks of California.

One of these days, when the facilities for communication between San Francisco and Oakland are improved and increased, Oakland will become a considerable place. Already a number of gentlemen who do business in San Francisco have their homes among the green trees of Oakland.

The citizens have recently raised a subscription and have let a contract for dredging the bar on which the boats so often strike, so that the distance will be somewhat shortened and the probability of delay avoided.

There is a good deal of pleasant, agreeable society in Oakland, and it bids fair to become to San Francisco what Brooklyn now is to New York. There are three churches in Oakland, and a very excellently regulated young ladies' school.

———o———

Railroad Reports Good Profit for Past Year

SACRAMENTO, Jan. 2, 1857— The Sacramento Valley Railroad Company has reported on its business for 1856 and shows net earnings of $76,800.

Total receipts from passenger and freight traffic over the 22-mile railroad during its 335 days of operation amounted to $162,200, and operating costs were $85,400.

Operating statistics for the year included: passengers, 82,000; freight, 17,000 tons; distance run by trains, 50,000 miles; wood consumed, 1200 cords; average daily movement of passengers in November, 250; average daily freight in November, 80 tons.

L. A. SHERIFF, POSSE SLAIN BY BANDITS

LOS ANGELES, Jan. 23, 1857 — Sheriff J. R. Barton and three other members of his small posse were killed today in a battle with bandits about 55 miles south of here. The other men slain were Constables William H. Little and Charles R. Baker and Charles Daly, a blacksmith.

News of the fatal fight was brought here by Frank C. Alexander, another member of the sheriff's party who rode the distance in six hours. After his arrival, Marshal W. H. Getman organized a band of 40 men to hunt for the robbers, who are believed to be led by Juan Flores. The bandits have their headquarters in the mountains near San Juan Capistrano, which they have robbed several times.

The fight came about after a young American named Hardy, who had gone to San Juan with a team of four fine horses for a load of hides, received information that the robbers planned to kill him. He sent a messenger to Los Angeles asking for help and Sheriff Barton organized a small posse that included only the men named above, a brother of Hardy and a guide.

En route, they heard the bandits, fifty strong, were on the road they were traveling, but Sheriff Barton persisted in pushing ahead. The members of the posse became separated by a ruse and were attacked by separate groups. It is believed two of the robbers were killed, one of them by Barton before he died.

Alexander and the younger Hardy were pursued by seven or eight robbers for several miles.

———o———

Broderick, Gwin Named Senators

SACRAMENTO, Jan. 12, 1857 — David C. Broderick, for the long term, and William M. Gwin, for the short term, have been named United States Senators by the state legislature.

This represents a great triumph for Broderick, as Gwin is reported to have surrendered his patronage rights in exchange for Broderick's support. Gwin was elected only after 14 ballots.

———o———

ROUGH AND READY, Jan. 7, 1857—It was discovered today that four men were killed on the night of the 4th by a snow avalanche which destroyed their cabin.

INCREASE IN EMIGRATION TO GADSDEN PURCHASE

SAN DIEGO, Jan. 22, 1857—Captain Catlett, who has just arrived here from the Colorado River, reports that a very large emigration has crossed the river at Fort Yuma for the Gadsden Purchase.

The discoverers of the new copper mine 25 miles above Fort Yuma on the Gila River are very much encouraged, according to Captain Catlett, as a vein of great extent and richness has been found.

Reports from the Arizona Mining Co. are also of the most flattering kind. Their vein of ore increases in size and value the further it is opened up.

———o———

QUAKE FELT WIDELY

SAN FRANCISCO, Jan. 20, 1857 —The earthquake felt here January 9 seems to have extended nearly the whole length of the state.

The shock was felt at Sacramento at 7:45 a.m.; San Francisco, 8:15 a.m.; San Diego and other southern coast points, 8:30 a.m. At San Diego it was the most severe quake in the memory of residents, the shock lasted several minutes.

Fort Tejon was severely hit, with adobe walls and chimneys shaken down. One woman was killed there. Many streams in the lower country were turned from their usual channels by the force of the earthquake.

Juan Flores Is Taken From Jail, Hanged

LOS ANGELES Feb. 14, 1857 — Juan Flores, leader of the band of robbers that killed Sheriff Barton, was taken from the jail here today and hanged at 2 p.m. on top of the hill which has been customarily used for such purposes.

Earlier in the day, a large throng assembled from this city and other nearby towns to determine what to do about Flores and the other prisoners in the jail. The vote was practically unanimous for hanging Flores. However, in the case of two horse thieves the canvass of the people was: for hanging, 257; against hanging, 395. As a result, the horse thieves were allowed to remain in the custody of the authorities.

Capt. Twist's company guarded Flores en route to the place of execution, with an escort also provided by Capt. Furgot's French company and a large group of mounted Californians and Americans.

Two priests were in attendance upon Flores, a young man of 22. He was dressed in white pants, light vest and black merino sack coat. The drop from the scaffold was so short that Flores struggled in agony for a considerable time.

Flores was first captured by a posse along with three other men. He was able to escape, then was recaptured later. In the weeks since the killing of Sheriff Barton and three other members of his posse many other alleged robbers have been rounded up, and twelve in all have been killed.

RAILS FOR MARKET ST.?

SAN FRANCISCO, Feb. 23, 1857 —It would be very desirable to see Market Street opened to the Mission, and a railroad track laid upon it.

The street is of sufficient width to permit even a double track without any interference with other modes of locomotion. The advantages of a line of cars running every few minutes through the day and evening would be very great.

The portion of the city through which Market Street runs is admirably adapted for residences. Were a railroad track laid there, the whole line would in a very short time be filled with dwelling houses. Rents would be comparatively cheap there, and the business part of the city would be easily accessible.

———o———

Party of Men Hangs Notorious Outlaw

MONTEREY, Feb. 16, 1857 — A party of men today broke into the Monterey jail and hanged the notorious outlaw, Anastacio Garcia, who was being held for trial for murder.

Garcia was arrested last fall on suspicion of having been involved in the murder of Messrs. Wall and Williamson, and there were also four other murder indictments against him. He was scheduled to be tried at the next session of the district court.

Garcia was a native Californian and a man of outstanding personal attraction—the very beau ideal of a brigand. He was 28 years of age, and leaves a wife and child. He seems to have inherited his blood thirst from his father, who was a murderer before him.

———o———

WHALE WASHED ASHORE AT HALF MOON BAY

HALF MOON BAY, Feb. 18, 1857 —The carcass of an immense whale was washed ashore on Dennison's Ranch here last night. This is the second whale which has come ashore on the same ranch this winter. The first yielded 743 gallons of oil and netted $500. The present whale is larger and should yield more.

RESERVOIR BREAKS, TOWN IS FLOODED

NEVADA CITY, Feb. 15, 1857—A 250-acre reservoir under construction on Deer Creek three miles above town gave way at 5 a.m. today as a result of the recent heavy rains, and flooded the town.

The waters carried destruction in their path. They swept away the Main Street, Broad Street and Old bridges, and wrecked the Spring Street bridge, which is some 30 to 40 feet above the low-water mark.

Miners' cabins and driftwood were carried along by the torrent. Several buildings in town were razed, and every mill of any type on the creek below here was entirely destroyed. Heavy castings from quartz mills, weighing several tons, were carried hundreds of yards down stream.

Several people narrowly escaped with their lives, but no lives were lost as far as can be determined. Property damage is estimated at $60-70,000.

———o———

Treasure Is Taken In Stage Robbery

STOCKTON, Feb. 18, 1857 — The stage from Murphy's to Stockton was held up and robbed early today of treasure valued at $15-$20,000, belonging to Wells, Fargo & Co. and the Pacific Express Co.

The stage left Murphy's at 1 a.m. with only one passenger. About an hour before daylight, in one of the most lonely parts of the road midway between Angel's Camp and Hawk-Eye, three men jumped out of the bushes and stopped the stage.

As it was dark, it was impossible to recognize the features of the robbers. One was a large man who spoke in a Scotch accent and was apparently a veteran highwayman. After getting the treasure box, the others ordered the driver, Mr. Dickinson, to proceed.

———o———

Men Frozen to Death

PORTLAND, Ore. Ter., Feb. 26, 1857 — During the recent cold weather two expressmen are reported to have been frozen to death between Walla Walla and The Dalles. One of the men is said to be Thomas Hughes, a printer, and the other a regular soldier.

MARE ISLAND AIDS STEAMER REPAIR

MARE ISLAND, March 23, 1857 —The dry dock of the Navy Yard here has enabled the damaged Panama steamer Golden Gate to be repaired with the least possible delay.

The steamer departed from San Francisco three days ago with 500 passengers and $1,645,358 in treasure. Near Fort Point she struck a sunken rock and had to return when water poured in through a hole in the hull.

After discharging her passengers, the Golden Gate headed for Mare Island. The clipper Keystone was then in the dock, but work was hurried through on her. At 5:30 a.m. yesterday the steamer was hauled into the dock. Work was completed by evening and the Golden Gate refloated. She will be able to sail from San Francisco tonight.

The Golden Gate, weighing about 3200 tons, including 600 tons of coal, was the heaviest ship ever handled by the dock. Damage to her was found not to be serious, and only three or four planks had to be replaced.

———o———

'NOTORIOUS' JACK POWERS ARRESTED

SAN FRANCISCO, March 28, 1857 — The "notorious" Jack Powers, as the newspaper Evening Bulletin terms him, was arrested in a house on California street between Powell and Stockton last night by Police Chief Curtis.

The arrest of Powers, well known in Los Angeles and Santa Barbara as a horseman and gambler, was made on a warrant from the south charging him with burglary. Colonel James, his attorney, said he would seek Powers' release on the ground the warrant is faulty.

The Bulletin lashed out at Powers with the statement, "The people of San Francisco know this Powers by reputation, many of them personally. He is the man who assised the infamous McGowan to escape pursuit . . . and kept him concealed. He . . . has been notorious for years as an unscrupulous and desperate character."

CLIPPER PASSAGE MISSES RECORD

SAN FRANCISCO, March 9, 1857 —The clipper ship Great Republic, under command of Captain Limeburner, arrived here today just 91 days from New York.

It was the fifth best California passage on record, and might have set a new mark except for the last 500 miles. This distance normally would have been only a two days' sail, but the Great Republic took five days because she met up with light airs, calms and fog.

The big clipper arrived off the Farallones yesterday, but had to heave to in the thick fog and wait for daylight today. She took her pilot aboard at 11:30 a.m. and was towed in to her anchorage by the steam tugs Martin White and Hercules. The ship left New York on December 7.

The Great Republic has made as high as 413 miles in 24 hours and on this trip ran a distance of 360 miles in the North Atlantic in 19 hours. She brought 5000 tons of assorted cargo here for her owners, Messrs. Lowe Bros. and others of New York.

This was the first trip to the Pacific Coast for the world-renowned ship, built by the famous Donald McKay. She is of large proportions, with an extreme length of 325 feet and beam of 53 feet. The Republic carries four masts, the fourth or spanker mast being schooner-rigged.

———o———

OREGON SHIP LINE

SAN FRANCISCO, March 6, 1857 — Messrs. Abernethy, Clark & Co., well-known ship owners, have established a line of first class packets from this port to Oregon.

One of the vessels is to be dispatched every 10 days, as near as winds permit. The line is composed of the J. B. Lunt, Ocean Bird, Charles Devans, Nahumkeag and Jane A. Falkinburg, all five craft known in the coasting trade.

———o———

SUGAR COMPANY FORMED

SAN JOSE, March 7, 1857 — The San Jose Pioneer Beet Sugar Mfg. Co. was organized here today, with capitalization of 500 shares at $1000 each. So far subscriptions have been taken for 160 shares.

McGOWAN REAPPEARS; TRIAL SCENE CHANGED

SACRAMENTO, March 20, 1857— Edward McGowan, San Francisco politician accused of being an accomplice of James Casey in the murder of Editor James King of William last year, is now to be tried in Napa district court instead of San Francisco.

This was brought about as a result of the legislature passing a special bill permitting McGowan to obtain a change of venue. As a result the trial, if held at all, will be at Napa in the month of May.

McGowan, who had been in hiding ever since the Vigilante excitement last year, suddenly appeared in Sacramento early this month and gave himself up to the authorities. It was at first supposed that the Vigilance Committee would seize him, but it determined to leave him with the constituted authorities. However, McGowan is not in custody although he is charged with a capital offense.

———o———

First River Steamer Reaches Oroville

OROVILLE, March 5, 1857 — Arrival here today of the steamer Gazelle, coupled with that of the barque Shoalwater two days ago, marks the beginning of a new era in the growth of this town.

The barque was brought up the Feather River by Captain Daniels, one of the pioneer navigators of the upper Sacramento who expressed the opinion that the Feather River is navigable this far at all seasons of the year. The Shoalwater was loaded with flour, vegetables and merchandise. She drew 19 inches and was propelled most of the way up from Marysville by poling.

Captain Whiting brought the Gazelle through in 10 hours from Marysville, being detained by ferries along the route as no provision had been made for dropping their ropes.

This was the first time a steamer has made her way directly to the mines, and the Gazelle was greeted by a large and cheering crowd.

HUNTER IS KILLED BY GRIZZLY BEAR

CLEAR LAKE, April 8, 1857 — A young man named Church, a school-teacher visiting with relatives, was killed yesterday by a grizzly bear in Round Valley, 18 miles from here.

A party had been made up to hunt deer, and while out started the bear. A few shots were fired, but they only wounded the grizzly just enough to make it furious. In the excitement of the chase, the hunters followed the bear into some chaparral, and were soon scattered.

Young Church went into the brush with a cousin and became separated from him. One of the party climbed a tree to see if he could locate the bear. While up in the branches, he heard growling and at the same time saw chaparral violently shaking. Still later, the bear drove several of the men into the trees.

After the party returned home, it was discovered that Church was missing. Several men returned to the scene and found his lifeless body badly mutilated at the point where the bear had been heard breaking down the chaparral.

About a year ago Church had most of his clothes torn off by a grizzly. Before starting out on yesterday's hunt, he remarked that he would be more prudent this time.

———o———

Steam Wagon Man Building Road Engine

SACRAMENTO, April 29, 1857 — J. P. Overton, the steam wagon man, is now here making preparations to construct a road-engine suitable for drawing a team of four carriages between Sacramento and Marysville.

The apparatus will have double cylinders of a power calculated to haul about 14 tons, either freight or passengers. The passenger cars will be about 26 feet long and 8 feet wide. It is figured that the "train will be able to make 10 miles an hour over California roads."

Mr. Overton has also sold to Ryan & Cole of San Francisco the right to run such a train to San Jose. Should the enterprise succeed, it will work a revolution in internal navigation in California without a doubt.

POWERS ACQUITTED

LOS ANGELES, April 27, 1858 — After coming south on the steamer Senator with his attorney, Col. James of San Francisco, Jack Powers was freed today of the charge of burglary. Although many witnesses were called in the court hearing, nothing was elicited to connect him with the offense charged.

Accused Of Attempt To Burn Nevada City

FOLSOM, April 14, 1857 — John Myers, accused of attempting to burn the town of Nevada City, was re-arrested here today by Marshal Plummer and John O'Brien as the result of astute detective work.

Myers was under bond for court appearance, but was endeavoring to make his escape.

After Myers was first released on bail, a man named Charles Whitehead sought his friendship and ostensibly tried to get Myers to join a robber gang. He won Myers' confidence to the point that Myers admitted not only to the attempt to set fire to Nevada City because of a grudge but also to an earlier robbery and murder.

———o———

GIFT FOR PRESIDENT

SAN FRANCISCO, April 12, 1857 — An old western hunter, Seth Kinman of Humboldt County, brought down on the steamer Goliah today a curiously wrought chair he is taking to Washington, D.C., to present to President Buchanan.

The chair is made entirely of the antlers of deer, with a high sloping back and convenient arms. A pair of antlers, with six points each, form the front legs and arms; another pair, with five points, form the rear legs and back. Small antlers, with two points each, join the chair together. The seat is made of dressed deer skin.

All told, there are just 31 antler points in the chair, corresponding with the number of states now in the union. The hunter has engraved his address on the left arm.

VIOLENCE IS FREQUENT THROUGHOUT STATE
Over 50 Casualties

SAN FRANCISCO, April 20, 1857 — Here is the record of crimes and casualties which have been reported in California within the past fortnight or so.

A man named Stephens shot and killed another man named Hobiler at Mariposa in a mining dispute.

Violent assaults and murders still continue frequent around Los Angeles.

Three men named Lake, Johnson and Ringold were hanged by citizens of Bangor on April 2 for having engaged in the commission of crimes in that vicinity.

The Chinese at Rancheria had a row, and three of their number were fatally wounded.

Twenty-eight persons were killed and ten badly maimed in mining accidents during March.

Jose Maria Egare was hanged on the San Joaquin about ten days ago for horse stealing.

A party of drunken Indians having entered the home of a lady on the Hay Fork of the Trinity River, a company of whites attacked the Indians and killed 15.

A. J. Golden shot and mortally wounded a man named Bartolo on the San Joaquin River.

———o———

CRABB'S ENTIRE FORCE IS SLAIN

SAN DIEGO, May 9, 1857—Word was received here today of the annihilation of the Sonora expedition led by Henry A. Crabb. The entire party of 84 was slain by the Mexicans.

Crabb's party entered the town of Cavorca on the Gulf of California on April 1. The Americans immediately met a Mexican force led by Roderiguez and killed him and several others. The filibusters took possession of several houses in the town, but soon after were hemmed in.

Guerilla fighting went on for eight days, with the Americans losing about 25 men and the Mexicans about 200. Finally, when they ran out of ammunition and the last building they occupied took fire, Crabb and his 58 surviving soldiers laid down their arms.

On the following day the entire party was taken out in squads and shot. Crabb was allowed to write his wife a farewell letter, and then he too was led out and tied with his back to his executioners. A hundred shots were fired into his body. He was decapitated and his head put on exhibition.

Among those killed were a number of well-known California political personages. Crabb himself was regarded as leader of the old Whig party in California and had served two years in the senate.

A few days after the massacre a detachment of 25 Mexicans crossed the border, seized four of Crabb's men who had been left there sick and executed them. About 20 recruits marching from Tucson to join Crabb were attacked by 200 Mexicans near Cavorca. After severe fighting they managed to reach the border.

Lovely Kites Stolen

SAN FRANCISCO, May 10, 1857 —The two kites resembling birds, which have been so much admired by all watchers, were stolen yesterday by a mean petty thief.

They had been up in the air about two hours, and the Chinese owner was drawing them in when they fell on top of a building on Commercial Street. The owner went after them, but they were gone. Someone had cut the cord and made off with them.

The kites cost about $25 apiece. They cannot be of any use to the thief, because they will be readily recognized if he flies them.

Copper Shipping Contract

LOS ANGELES, May 12, 1857 — J. J. Tomlinson of Red Bluff arrived today with seven six-mule teams and 25 men on his way to the Gadsden Purchase to commence a 15 months' contract to haul copper ore for a wealthy San Francisco company.

SUTTER'S FARM SHERIFF SALE

MARYSVILLE, May 23, 1857 — Hock Farm, the home of General John A. Sutter, on the banks of the Feather River near here was sold by the sheriff today for $14,000. The purchasers were Messrs. Packard and Woodruff.

Hock Farm, his favorite dwelling place, was the last of the great domain that Sutter once held in California. It is a pity that those who have enriched themselves through his means should not at least have seen that the General in his declining years had a home of his own.

Improvement Seen At Los Angeles

LOS ANGELES, May 23, 1857 — Despite the general cry of hard times, there are some people here actuated by the spirit of improvement.

On Main Street, where a fire occurred sometime ago, a brick building has been erected and neatly fitted up as a meat market.

Mr. Beaudry is preparing to put up a block of brick buildings at the corner of Los Angeles and Aliso Streets. This will be a very extensive work and will greatly improve the appearance of that section of the city. Several brick buildings are projected in other parts of town.

Grounds of the Mission church have been fenced following the building's renovation and decoration.

30,000 CATTLE SOLD IN SOUTH COUNTRY

LOS ANGELES, May 20, 1857 — It is estimated that so far this season 24,200 cattle have been sold from ranches in this area, and 6000 from San Diego county.

Prices ruling the market are: cows, calves and steers 3 years old and upwards, $16-18; dry cows, 3 years old and upwards, $15-18; cows and steers, 2 years old, $10-13; cows and steers, 1 year old, $7-9.

All the cattle are being purchased here by drovers and butchers and driven north for sale. It is a singular fact that not one ranchero is driving his own stock this year. Of the total sold there were not more than 3000 large steers, the greatest part being breeding cattle. There will probably be 5000 more leaving the southern country within a month.

FISHING IS GOOD AT HALF MOON BAY

HALF MOON BAY, May 12, 1857 —The California angler can find no spot better for display of his piscatorial skill than the brooks flowing into this bay south of San Francisco.

Parties of gentlemen from San Francisco recently have had extraordinary luck and have taken back wagon loads of beautiful speckled trout.

After two days of sport, four expert fishermen counted the number caught and found that they had captured 2000 trout. The roads here are fine, the scenery magnificent and the accommodations at the farm houses near the bay good.

BAD LUCK STRIKES NEW CLIPPER SHIP ON MAIDEN VOYAGE

SAN FRANCISCO, June 21, 1857 — On her first voyage from New York, the new and magnificent clipper ship Golden Fleece went aground early today on the east side of the North Shoal about four miles from Point Bonita.

Sail was quickly made, and the ship swung free. However, it was found that she was taking water fast, and by the time the Golden Fleece reached the Vallejo Street Wharf she had 17 feet of water in her hold. The steam tug Hercules came to her rescue, and towed her to the mud flats near the wharf and set to work to free her with powerful steam pumps.

No blame can be attached to either Captain Lunt or Pilot Van Ness, as the grounding occurred during an unusual low tide which had fallen nearly 12 feet. Oddly enough, the Golden Fleece was built by the same owners to replace a ship with the same name that was lost on the rocks near Fort Point three years ago.

The Golden Fleece was drawing 24 feet of water as she had a heavy cargo of 3000 tons of goods and coal. A new ship of 2000 tons, she was 125 days out of New York.

---o---

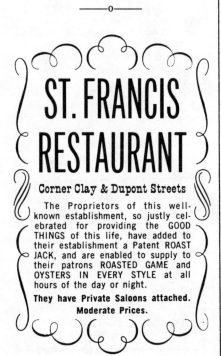
EDWARD McGOWAN IS ACQUITTED BY JURY

NAPA, June 2, 1857 — Edward McGowan, "The Ubiquitous Ned," was acquitted of being an accessory in the murder of Editor James King of William in a verdict that was returned by a jury at midnight last night. The jurors took only five minutes to reach their decision.

The shooting of King by James Casey, a politician, on a San Francisco street a year ago led to the great Vigilante uprising. McGowan, an associate of Casey who was hanged by the Vigilantes, was eagerly sought by the Committee but managed to hide out and escape. When he reappeared early this year at Sacramento, the legislature ordered his trial removed from San Francisco to Napa.

McGowan's defense introduced testimony that he was not present when Casey shot King, and also tried to prove that King's death was caused by the medical treatment given him and not by Casey's shot.

The trial here has attracted a great deal of attention throughout the state.

---o---

Five Grizzlies Killed Near Yosemite Valley

MARIPOSA, June 21, 1857—Within the past fifteen days five grizzly bears have been killed on and near the Mariposa and Yo Semite trail by visitors to the valley. Fortunately, in every instance there was no injury to the victors.

The snow on the ridge and at the meadows this side of the valley is about melted, and bear, deer and other game are attracted in large numbers.

---o---

Adventurous Citizens Seek Pirate Treasure

SAN FRANCISCO, June 12, 1857 —The schooner Henry, under the command of Amos Henry, sailed today for Cocos Island in search of the buried treasure that is supposed to be located there. The expedition was financed by the contributions of a few prominent citizens as an adventure.

The story is that the treasure is worth more than $15,000,000. It was shipped from Acapulco in 1823 for Spain via the Cape of Good Hope.

GOVERNMENT PARTY TO SURVEY BORDER

SAN FRANCISCO, June 15, 1857 --The U.S. survey party to locate the boundary line between the territory of Washington and the British possessions will sail for Puget Sound this week on the U.S. Steamer Active. Archibald Campbell is in charge of the expedition, which numbers more than 30 men.

At Puget Sound the party will meet the English government vessel Satellite. It appears that the only point in dispute is the island of San Juan, on which both governments now have officers stationed.

---o---

RECORD TRIP TO CATCH STEAMER

SAN FRANCISCO, June 5, 1857 —Thomas J. Fiske, a resident partner of the banking firm of Drexel, Sather and Church, made a record overland journey from Sacramento to San Francisco yesterday in order to get some vital papers off on the Atlantic steamer leaving today.

There was no other regular transportation that would do the trick after Fiske missed the regular Sacramento River steamer yesterday. First, he rented a light buggy and team from the stables of Covey & Co. on Second Street and made the 60 miles to Benicia in six hours.

There, it took Fiske a quarter of an hour to find a boatman and half an hour to row the three miles to Martinez. Another half hour was lost trying to locate a team, and Fiske then drove the 25 miles to Oakland in three hours. At Oakland he found an available boat within a half-hour and made the nine-mile row across the bay to San Francisco in one and a half hours.

Total time for the distance of 97 miles was 12¼ hours.

---o---

STRAWBERRY CROP IN DEMAND

SAN FRANCISCO, June 12, 1857 —The quantities of strawberries raised in the immediate vicinity of San Francisco are enormous and they are in great demand.

By far the greater number, if not the finest berries, are grown in Alameda County.

Launching of Large Sternwheeler Here

SAN FRANCISCO, July 16, 1857 —A sternwheel steamer for Capt. C. W. Gunnell, designed to run between Sacramento and Red Bluff, was launched at Steamboat Point this evening.

She measures 145 feet along her keel by a beam of 26 feet, and draws only 10¾ inches of water. The steamer has two high-pressure engines with 14-inch cylinder and five-foot stroke generating over 100 horsepower.

The owner, Capt. Gunnell, is the pioneer steamboat man of California, having built the first steamer in the state: the old Sutter which used to run to Stockton in 1849.

The vessel was built under the supervision of Capt. Cole and Capt. Galloway, who is to command her. She is made of the best material and her cabin accommodations are handsomely arranged. Her total cost, when finished, will be $38,000.

———o———

Democrats Nominate Weller for Governor

SACRAMENTO, July 15, 1857 — The Democratic State Convention adjourned tonight after nominating John B. Weller for governor in a boisterous session.

The anti-Broderick party was in the ascendant and bore down on all opposition. A strong effort was made to adopt harsh resolutions condemning the Vigilance Committee, but the majority was unwilling to renew the agitation on that exciting subject.

———o———

Escape in Buggy Crash

OAKLAND, July 20, 1857 — Col. Williams, mayor of Oakland, and his wife had a narrow escape in a buggy accident. They were on their way from Oakland to Martinez, and driving down a gorge in the hills when part of their horse's harness gave way.

Fortunately neither of the Williams was injured, but their narrow escape should be a warning to travelers to check their vehicle and harness carefully before venturing into the steep and rocky passes of our hills.

'HULA HULA' CONDEMNED

HONOLULU, July 1, 1857 — The Commercial Advertiser, newspaper which has just completed its first year here, has come out strongly in condemnation of toleration of the native dance known as the "hula-hula" as being productive of immorality.

The paper says that unless some measure is soon taken to check the evil, the consequences will be felt in every household, and on every farm and plantation because so infatuated do people become under it that it will be useless to urge them to industry or to make any efforts to uplift them.

MANY FIRES OCCUR IN MINING REGION

SACRAMENTO, July 26, 1857 — Several disastrous fires have occurred in the last few days in mining region towns, with considerable loss of property. It is reported, however, that no lives were lost in the conflagrations.

On July 19 the brewery of Goodwin & Co. at Mokelumne Hill burned down with a loss estimated at $5000. On the next day a brewery at Shasta, together with a stable and several other buildings, was destroyed. The loss was $10,400.

The flourishing mining village of Michigan Bluffs in Placer County was totally destroyed by flames on July 22. Here the loss amounted to $162,000. Yesterday not a house was left standing by a blaze which swept through St. Louis, an active mining town in Sierra County. The loss at St. Louis was estimated at $200,000.

The Winchester Saw Mills at Grass Valley, valued at $25,000, were also razed by fire yesterday.

———o———

NEW COASTAL BRIG

SAN FRANCISCO, July 15, 1857 —The brig Ellen H. Wood has just arrived here on her maiden voyage from the Umpqua River in Oregon, where she was built. She may be looked on as the first actual experiment in shipbuilding on our Pacific Coast as she is the largest seagoing craft ever built in California or Oregon.

OVERLAND STAGE CONTRACT AWARD

SAN FRANCISCO, July 31, 1857 —Postmaster Weller announces he has received an official copy of the Postmaster-General's order awarding the contract for transportation of the mails to California by the southern route.

The bid accepted was for $595,000 per annum for semi-weekly service as made by John Butterfield and James V. P. Gardner of Utica, N. Y., William B. Dinsmore and Alexander Holland of New York City, William G. Fargo of Buffalo, N. Y., and Marquis L. Kinvon of Rome, N. Y.

The Postmaster-General has selected the following route as combining more advantages and fewer disadvantages than any other:

From St. Louis, Mo., and from Memphis, Tenn., converging at Little Rock, Ark.; thence via Preston, Texas, or as near as may be found most advisable, to the best point of crossing the Rio Grande, above El Paso, and not far from Fort Fillmore; thence along the new road being opened and constructed under the direction of the Secretary of the Interior to Fort Yuma, Cal.; thence through the best passes and along the best valleys for safe and expeditious staging, to San Francisco.

———o———

Overland Immigrants Reported Attacked

PLACERVILLE, July 31, 1857 — Crandall's Coach arrived here this evening, having made the journey from Carson Valley with passengers, mail and Tracy's Express in 12 hours' traveling time.

The stage brought the news that friendly Indians have reported that the advance immigration had been attacked by the Snake Indians near the Sink of the Humboldt. They said 15 wagons had been taken and plundered and several whites killed.

Some fears are felt that the report is true although there is some room for doubt. As the advance immigration should have reached Carson Valley before this time, something must be wrong.

FIRST OVERLAND MAIL ARRIVES

SAN DIEGO, Aug. 31, 1857—The first Overland mail from the East arrived here today under the contract between the Government and James Birch.

The mails left San Antonio on July 9 and 24, with the second mail making the trip in 34 days.

J. E. Mason, in charge of the mails, left San Antonio with four men on July 9. The time for preparation was too short to send relays of mules on ahead, but at El Paso they took an ambulance. They had got as far as Cienga de Sang when they were overtaken by the second party in charge of Capt. James Skillman, who came in an ambulance for the entire distance.

The two parties then proceeded together as far as the Pino villages. There Mason took both mails, and with one companion pushed on with pack mules. They made the trip to San Diego in the unequalled time of nine days across the worst part of the route, including the Colorado desert.

Plenty of water was found along the entire route. On the 80-mile stretch of desert from Tucson to the Gila River water was found in three or four places in sufficient quantities to supply hundreds of animals.

---o---

Police 'Showoff' in Plaza Condemned

SAN FRANCISCO, Aug. 12, 1857—The board of supervisors has passed a resolution condemning the conduct of Chief of Police J. P. Curtis in parading sixteen young men before the public in the Plaza.

Chief Curtis had the sixteen—ranging in age from 18 to 25, and known to the police as thieves and pickpockets, several having been repeatedly arrested and convicted—picked up several days ago. They were kept in confinement at the station house for three days.

Then he had them handcuffed together in pairs and tied to a rope, and publicly paraded so that the citizens would know them, in the hope that they might be enduced to leave the city. There was a great deal of excitement on the part of many residents, and considerable resentment was expressed.

---o---

New Territory Sought

CARSON VALLEY, Aug. 8, 1857—People of this and adjacent valleys held a public meeting today and voted to petition Congress to separate the area from the territory of Utah and establish a new territory.

The petitioners would take in an area as large as California. They estimate the number of white inhabitants in the whole area at 7000. There are 1300 in Carson and the nearby valleys. James M. Crane, formerly of San Francisco, was chosen as delegate to go to Washington and present the petition to Congress.

FAMOUS THEATRE RAZED BY FIRE

SAN FRANCISCO, Aug. 15, 1857—The noted Metropolitan Theatre, located on Montgomery street between Washington and Jackson, was destroyed by fire last night. The flames are believed to have been set by an incendiary.

Only the night before the Metropolitan had been used for a benefit performance for Billy Birch of the San Francisco Minstrels. Last evening the theatre was not in use. About 8 p.m. smoke was seen issuing through the dome and windows. Before the firemen could enter the building, the interior was in flames.

The building was erected in 1853 by Joseph Trench at a cost of nearly $200,000. It was opened on Christmas Eve under the management of Mrs. Catharine Sinclair, who held control until January, 1855. Under her direction receipts were over $400,000.

SEASON'S OVERLAND TRAINS ARRIVING

PLACERVILLE, Aug. 20, 1857—The vanguard of the season's overland immigration has at last crossed the Sierra Nevada. For the past week trains have been pouring into the State through the various mountain passes.

The great mass of immigrants, so far, have come in via the Carson Valley and this place, and over the road now being rapidly completed between these two points. All reports agree as to the great numbers on the way, more than in any other season since 1852. There is also much stock en route, and considerable quantities have been driven into Carson Valley in good condition.

The immigrants bring startling accounts of depredations by the Indians beyond the Sink of the Humboldt and in the Goose Creek Mountains. Many lives are reported to have been lost, but most of these stories are probably exaggerated as little authentic evidence has been produced. However, it is undeniable that the Indians have killed and driven off an unusual number of stock. Nearly every train has suffered on that score.

---o---

HUGE FIRE IN MINING TOWN DESTROYS MANY BUILDINGS

COLUMBIA, Aug. 25, 1857—This flourishing mining town was almost swept out of existence today by a conflagration that broke out in the Chinese section.

Within an hour the whole business part of the village was in flames. Little was spared except the Masonic Hall, Courier office, two or three thoroughly fireproof buildings and the dwellings in the suburbs. A fearful explosion of gunpowder in the brick store of H. A. Brown blew down the walls and killed five men who were standing about the building.

---o---

SACRAMENTO, Aug. 10, 1857—Yesterday will be long known in California as "the hot Sunday."

In some areas of the state the mercury ran up as high as 120 degrees in the shade. In only a few places, except in such seacoast towns as San Francisco, did it fall below 100 degrees.

INDIAN TRIBES IN DESERT BATTLE

SAN DIEGO, Sept. 19, 1857—News has reached here from the Pimo Villages of a serious engagement between the Pimo Indians on the one hand and the Yuma and other Colorado River Indians aided by a number of Apaches.

Some time ago the Pimo chief informed Colonel Burton, in command of Fort Yuma, that the Yuma Indians were becoming insolent and that he might have to chastise them. Then only recently, some Yumas and others entered the Pimo country and killed some women and children.

The Pimos were called to arms and pursued the intruders. They fought a battle seldom equalled in western Indian warfare. It is reported 150 of the allied Indians, nearly all of the raiding party, were killed, while the Pimos lost some 25 men.

The Pimo Indians, for more than half a century, have been a peaceable and friendly tribe and have cultivate the soil. They have never been the aggressors but have always fought whenever there was provocation against them.

———o———

MARIPOSA PROGRESSES IN MILLS, FARMING

MARIPOSA, Sept. 26, 1857—The Gazette here provides some interesting statistics that show the progress being made in Mariposa County:

100 miles of toll road, costing $38,000.

8 steam quartz mills worth $75,000, with 75 stamps producing 2,200 tons per month.

10 water mills, $30,000, with 60 stamps capable of crushing 60 tons per day.

8 steam sawmills, $60,000, sawing 400,000 feet of lumber per month.

1 steam grist mill, 1 tannery, 2 breweries.

4,500 acres of land enclosed, and 2,500 acres under cultivation.

5,000 cattle and 4,000 hogs slaughtered last year.

1,500 pounds of butter and 4,500 pounds of cheese produced by dairies.

HIT-RUN ACCIDENT

SAN FRANCISCO, Sept. 21, 1857—The little son of ex-Gov. John McDougal was run over and injured by a horse and buggy yesterday afternoon on Clay Street near Kearny. The former official has lodged a bitter complaint with the police that an officer refused to arrest the driver, who proceeded on his way.

The accident occurred when McDougal, his wife, son and daughter were walking from the St. Francis Hotel to a nearby restaurant. The buggy, traveling at a furious pace, knocked the boy down and nearly hit the others. The man drove off when Mr. and Mrs. McDougal went to the aid of their son. The ex-governor asserted that a policeman saw the entire affair but took no steps to arrest the driver.

———o———

Drytown Robbers Persecute Chinese

DRYTOWN, Sept. 22, 1857—Robberies are becoming so frequent in this vicinity that they attract little notice. Announcement of an outrage of this character no longer startles the community. Men roam about and plunder with impunity, and Chinese are almost universally the victims.

Last Saturday night six Chinese cabins were entered on Dry Creek, below Whittle's store, and the inmates robbed. This week four companies were robbed on the Cosumnes.

One evening, about twilight, a mile below here, two ruffians attacked Ah Coon, a Chinese butcher, and took his money at pistol point. Although they are known to the Chinese, the men who did the outrage feel secure because they are legally protected by the exclusion of Chinese testimony.

———o———

WELLER NAMED GOVERNOR

SACRAMENTO, Sept. 15, 1857—Fairly complete returns throughout the state show that John B. Weller, Democrat, has been elected governor over Edward Stanly, Republican, and Bowie of the American party. The legislature also will be overwhelmingly Democratic. Total vote in the state fell much below the last election.

WAGES AND PRICES ARE LOWER THAN BEFORE

SAN FRANCISCO, Sept. 18, 1857—The current rates for wages and prices in San Francisco now are lower than they were at the height of the Gold Rush boom.

Weekly wages for workmen today are: blacksmiths, $24-30 per week; on a per day basis, carpenters $4-5, stone masons $5, bricklayers $4-5 and laborers $2-3. Where board is provided, pay for some common classes of labor is as follows: men cooks, $6-20 per week; teamsters and farm laborers, $7-10 per week; gardeners, $450-800 per year; thorough servants $40-80, housemaids $25-40, women cooks $25-50, nurse maids $15-20 and needle women $25-30 per month.

Sirloin Steak is now priced at 20-25 cents per pound, and porterhouse steak goes for 25 cents. Turkey is 50 cents a pound and crabs 75 cents a dozen. Water costs from 50 cents to $1 a hogshead.

———o———

Police Involved In Row at Belle Cora's

SAN FRANCISCO, Sept. 16, 1857—A disgraceful scene occurred last night at Belle Cora's house on Pike Street.

A police officer, holding a warrant, went into the house in the belief that the man he was seeking was inside. Belle ordered him out. When he told her what he wanted, she called to the policeman on the beat, who came up and put the first officer out by main force.

The persistent officer with the warrant broke away and came back to Belle's place. When he entered a second time, a crowd of the women who reside there surrounded him, and one of them broke a champagne bottle over his head. After that he was again put out by the policeman on the beat.

———o———

Brig Brings Finest Timber from Washington

SAN FRANCISCO, Sept. 8, 1857—The brig Merchantman has arrived from Washington Territory with a full cargo of the finest red fir timber. The planks are 55 feet long and straight as an arrow. They are intended for the steamers now being built at Steamboat Point.

Turtles Are Caught For Shipment to S.F.

WEIGH 10-200 POUNDS

SAN DIEGO, Oct. 20, 1857—Off Lower California and in the vicinity of Cedros Island turtles in sizes ranging from ten to 200 pounds are being found in considerable numbers.

R. E. Raimond of San Francisco and J. C. Bogert have started a business gathering them and shipping them to market in San Francisco. They have a vessel operating from here and then ship their catch north.

The animals are caught in a strong seine and then deposited in a "corral" until they are brought into San Diego. Here they have another "corral" to preserve the turtles in excellent condition.

A fair cargo for the vessel is 125 turtles, which are easily caught and offer little resistance. The largest specimen captured so far weighed 212 pounds, and the average runs from 40 to 80 pounds.

FISHING IS GOOD IN SACRAMENTO

SACRAMENTO, Oct. 20, 1857—Fishing for the last two months in the Sacramento River has been very productive. At least 3000 barrels of salmon have been salted since August 20, and about 40,000 fish have been sold fresh in the same period.

It is expected that 1500 barrels have been or will have been shipped to New York, Australia and other markets within the next 30 days. Exports are increasing yearly, owing to improvements made in curing the fish.

It is much to be regretted that mining on the upper waters of the Sacramento has roiled and thickened the water so much as to nearly cover up all the spawning beds in the river.

Some idea of the quantity of the run may be gained from the fact that at Cache Creek in late September two men with one gill net took 221 salmon in one night averaging 18 pounds each. In two cases nets have been sunk and lost from the weight of salmon in them.

Train of Immigrants Massacred in Utah

LOS ANGELES, Oct. 9, 1857—News has reached here of the massacre of a train of immigrants at Mountain Meadows at the rim of the Great Basin in southern Utah.

The train was made up of from 130 to 135 men, women and children from Arkansas and Missouri, all bound for California. The only known survivors are reported to be 10 or 12 small children.

The train had passed through Salt Lake City. Circumstances of the massacre are not known exactly. Surviving children were brought in to the settlement of Cedar City.

Constitution Voted

PORTLAND, Ore. Ter., Oct. 1857—The convention drawing up a proposed constitution as a preliminary to seeking entry of Oregon to the Union as a state has passed the document 35 to 10, with 15 absent. Almost every newspaper in the territory has taken a stand against its adoption by the people, on the ground that it contains clauses at variance with provisions of the United States constitution.

Famed Couple to Depart

SAN FRANCISCO, Oct. 20, 1857—Mr. and Mrs. James Stark, pioneer theatrical artists in California, announce they will leave by steamer next month to tour the Atlantic States and Europe.

The Starks came to California early in 1850 and may be considered as sponsors of the drama in the state.

CALIFORNIANS LOST IN SEA TRAGEDY

SAN FRANCISCO, Oct. 22, 1857—San Francisco was thrown into mourning today when the steamer Panama arrived from Panama today with the news that the Atlantic steamer Central America had sunk with a loss of more than 400 lives.

The Central America, formerly known as the George Law, went down off Cape Hatteras on September 12 with the California mails of August 20 and over $1,500,000 in gold. The passengers and cargo of the ill-fated vessel had left San Francisco on the steamer Sonora.

En route from the Isthmus to New York, the Central America foundered in a tremendous hurricane. The steamer ran into difficulties early on the 12th when her fires went out. The women and children aboard were taken off in small boats and put aboard the sailing barque Marine of Boston, but the latter had trouble with her gear and so had to leave and run before the wind.

The steamer sank soon after. About 50 men were able to cling to wreckage and were picked up, some of them after 12 hours in the water, by the Norwegian barque Helen. It is estimated that 419 persons, including a number of prominent Californians, have been lost in the disaster.

SHAFT BREAK FORCES STEAMER TO RETURN

SAN FRANCISCO, Oct. 10, 1857—The mail steamship Golden Gate, which left here October 5 for Panama with 638 passengers, returned here today as a result of breaking her shaft.

Four nights ago, when the ship was 350 miles below San Francisco, the center shaft broke, disabling the starboard engine and wheel. The next afternoon emergency repairs were completed, and the Golden Gate was able to return with the aid of one wheel and her sails.

The skilful management of the officers and their attention to their duties won the favorable consideration of the passengers, who held a meeting and passed complimentary resolutions. Among those on board were Senator D. C. Broderick and the Hon. J. C. Fremont.

3 CONVICTS KILLED BY CANNON SHOT

SAN QUENTIN, Nov. 6, 1857—Three prisoners were killed and five seriously wounded today when a prison guard, James Curtin, fired on a work party unloading a wood scow at the prison wharf.

Curtin has charge of a 12-pounder field piece, loaded with grape shot, that is mounted on a hill overlooking the wharf. About noon a scow came in, and the usual work party was sent on board to unload. When the wharf close by became filled with wood, the order was given to move the scow along to a clear space.

A strong breeze was blowing at the time, and the barge drifted a short distance beyond the assigned spot. Curtin became afraid that an escape was about to be attempted, and fired the cannon into the boat at almost point blank range.

———o———

RAIL BUSINESS GROWS

FOLSOM, Nov. 16, 1857—Gratifying evidence of the rapidly increasing business of the Sacramento Valley Railroad is to be seen in the long, fully freighted trains which daily run between here and Sacramento.

Over 100 tons of assorted merchandise and more than 50 passengers were deposited here yesterday, and the returning cars were loaded with cobbles and granite destined for the government works at Fort Point, San Francisco.

———o———

NEW QUARTZ MILL AT BIG OAK FLAT

SONORA, Nov. 1, 1857—The new gold quartz mill recently built at Big Oak Flat by the San Francisco and Big Oak Flat Quartz Co. is operating successfully and is a good example of the energy of our mining men.

The company was organized last June under the management of Col. Roderick McKee of San Francisco, with a capital stock of $150,000. The mill and its facilities were erected in the astounding time of two months and 25 days. During the same period a large corps of miners has opened up several veins, sinking shafts and running tunnels.

Camel Train Reaches Southern California

LOS ANGELES, Nov. 20, 1857—Lieut. Edward F. Beale and his party arrived here today with a train of camels after exploring a southern wagon route under orders from the government.

The camels, imported to test their value in wilderness and desert travel in the United States, performed the journey from San Antonio, Texas, in a highly satisfactory manner. Beale left San Antonio on June 25. To help handle the 23 camels and three dromedaries were two Greeks and a Turk. The camels were packed with a large portion of the grain for ten teams of mules.

The train reached Albuquerque, a distance of about 1000 miles, August 10, with the camels keeping easy pace with the mule teams. At Albuquerque some of the wagons were left behind. On reaching the Colorado River October 19, Beale had the camels swim across the river, while the baggage was ferried over on an India rubber boat brought for the purpose from New York.

Beale reports that the experiment with the camels and dromedaries was highly successful. They have shown themselves well adapted to traversing the wastes of western America. In some instances the camels went a week without water.

———o———

Mammoth Tree Grove Discovered

STOCKTON, Nov. 5, 1857—Another grove of mammoth trees has been discovered in Mariposa County.

The trees appear to average 300 feet in height and from 10 to 30 feet in diameter. There were no exact instruments for measuring, but it is thought that some of the trees are larger than the largest found previously.

This is the third mammoth grove in Mariposa. The first grove discovered has 427 trees; the second one, 30, and this latest one has 86 trees. These groves are near the road to the Yo-Semite Valley. The most celebrated grove in the state, however, is in Calaveras County.

———o———

CONSTITUTION FAVORED

PORTLAND, Ore. Ter., Nov. 10, 1857—Early returns from yesterday's election indicate that the people have voted in favor of the proposed state constitution. They rejected a proposal for slavery, and also voted to exclude free negroes.

LOTS OF WILD GAME FOUND IN MARKETS

SAN FRANCISCO, Nov. 29, 1857—Few markets are better supplied than this city with an abundance and variety of game at low prices.

Game stalls here are now filled with grizzly bear, elk, deer, antelope, hare, grey Canada, brant and white goose; canvas-back, mallard, sprig and spoonbill ducks; widgeon, teal, the English, black-breasted, sand and dowiches snipe; the common, and mountain quail, and grouse. In addition, there are many kinds of geese, duck and snipe for which hunters have no names.

It is estimated that 15,000 wild duck and geese are sold in the San Francisco market each week. Elk, deer and antelope were extremely abundant in California ten years ago, but they now are disappearing rapidly. They are still plentiful, however, in the San Joaquin and Russian Rivers, and in the more remote plains and mountains.

Their meat now retails for 25 cents a pound. Mallard duck weighing 2½-3 pounds bring 75 cents each, as will grey goose weighing 4-5 pounds. Quail cost $3 a dozen.

Grizzly bear is not hunted commercially, but is killed in the mountains to the north, south and east of the bay.

Steamer Sails After Damage Is Repaired

SAN FRANCISCO, Dec. 22, 1857 —The steamer Columbia, commanded by Captain Dall, left today for the Puget Sound after the damage she suffered on her last trip was repaired.

The steamer's rails and some of her upper works were swept away when she was crossing the bar of the Umpqua River on her last down voyage.

On this occasion, as she entered the heavy line of breakers at the Umpqua bar, a monster roller suddenly began sweeping down on the vessel. Some of those on deck sprang into the rigging, and others clung hard to whatever they could grasp. For a short time the whole hull was under water, and even the bridge was buried.

The force of the water wrenched open the steamer's hatchways, and there was four feet of water in the hold after she had crossed the bar. Cabins and saloons were completely flooded.

Captain Dall fortunately had ordered all his passengers to remain below before making the crossing.

———o———

Large Water Wheel Is Built

STEINER'S FLAT, Dec. 20, 1957 —The Red Bar Company on the Trinity River above here has just completed the largest water wheel ever built in Northern California.

The wheel is 55 feet, 4 inches, in diameter and has 40 paddles and buckets on each side capable of raising 18 gallons of water each. Making at present about two revolutions per minute, the wheel is supplying nearly 3,000,000 gallons of water every 24 hours.

Such water wheels supply many mining claims from streams nearby.

———o———

BOY HUNTS FOR FATHER

LOS ANGELES, Dec. 19, 1857— Thomas Jeremiah Loveall, a boy of 12, has arrived here from Salt Lake after having traveled much of the way alone and on foot.

He is searching for his father, Hiram Loveall, who left him at Salt Lake. The boy supposes his father to be in the Russian River valley.

S.F. Population 60,500

SAN FRANCISCO, Dec. 30, 1857 — Messrs. Henry G. Langley & Co., who are now completing the San Francisco Directory for 1858, estimate the total population of the city is 60,500.

The Langley company reaches its conclusions on the basis that the register contains 18,500 names. In addition, the compilers list 7000 foreigners, including Chinese who are not registered, 4000 floating population and persons employed on the rivers, and 15,000 females. They estimate there are 16,000 in the city under 21 years of age.

RAINS CLEAR AWAY FOR CHRISTMAS DAY

SAN FRANCISCO, Dec. 25, 1857 —This city, as well as the state at large, has been lashed by heavy rains of late, but Christmas Day dawned clear and beautiful.

The sunshine held throughout the day, so there was no interference with Christmas festivities. The streets were enlivened by crowds of people, all apparently seeking the most pleasant means of enjoying a Merry Christmas.

At 5 a.m. high mass was celebrated at St. Mary's Cathedral, with the city's finest musical talent performing Mozart's Mass No. 12. Imposing services were held at Trinity and Grace Churches.

165 WHALERS REPORTED AT SANDWICH ISLANDS

HONOLULU, Dec. 5, 1857—One hundred sixty-five whalers have arrived at the Sandwich Islands during the past season-—149 American, 9 French, 2 Hawaiian and 4 Bremen. Of the whalers, 151 have been right whalers and 14 sperm whalers and traders.

During the season the right whalers have taken 127,539 barrels of oil and 1,591,543 pounds of bone. The average of 845 barrels and 10,540 pounds per ship is better than that for 1856.

The Kodiak Sea is the favorite whaling ground, and about 60 ships cruised there. The Emerald took the season's largest whale, measuring 80 feet long and turning out 240 barrels of oil.

Four ships are known to have visited the Arctic Sea, but one of them, the Indian Chief, was lost. The others averaged 11,000 barrels, reporting that there was a great plenty of whales but that the weather was very rough.

———o———

New Yacht Imported

SAN FRANCISCO, Dec. 1, 1857— The most beautiful yacht ever brought to this country is offered for sale for $2000.

Captain Howland of the ship Susan Howland acquired the yacht George Steers after the death of her builder, the noted marine architect George Steers, and carried her as one of the cargo items on his most recent voyage here.

Last June the yacht won the golden cup in the New Rochelle Regatta from 15 other boats in her first racing trial. Built after the model of the Julia and the America, she is completely rigged and has a fine suit of sails. The George Steers measures 29½ feet in length and 11 feet in beam, and draws 3 feet of water without her centerboard which has a drop of 6½ feet.

———o———

L. A. Prosecutor Energetic

LOS ANGELES, Dec. 22, 1857-- Gen. E. Drown, the new district attorney, has been most energetic about cleaning up crime.

The pressure he is putting on has produced a stampede among the gamblers. Notwithstanding the law, there never had been previously a cessation of monte and other games in this city.

Index

Items about San Francisco, Sacramento, Stockton and Los Angeles are so numerous as to make indexing impractical.